Down we went, guns blazing. As we broke through eight hundred feet we started taking rounds through the metal floor. They banged real loud as they crashed through.

By the time we broke through four hundred feet, the rotor blades had so many holes in them they were whistling, and every once in a while a tracer flew in my door and out the other side. I was saying strings of Our Fathers and Hail Marys. Good Catholic upbringing!

By now it was late afternoon, and as it got darker the tracers got bigger and brighter. Rounds were smacking into the tail boom as we flared, then set down into the rice paddy, and my M-60 barrel was glowing because I still hadn't let up on the trigger.

Just as the chopper settled into the rice paddy, I saw Victor Charlies running out of the tree line. There were so many I couldn't even begin to count them. Some were firing, but most were just running for us as fast as they could.

It took me a moment to realize they were trying to overrun us and capture the chopper!

SEAWOLVES

First Choice

Daniel E. Kelly

IVY BOOKS • NEW YORK

An Ivy Book
Published by The Ballantine Publishing Group
Copyright © 1998 by Belle R. Kelly
Foreword copyright © 1998 by Barry W. Enoch

http://www.randomhouse.com

Library of Congress Catalog Card Number: 97-95283

ISBN 0-8041-1767-5

Manufactured in the United States of America

First Edition: July 1998

10 9 8 7 6 5 4 3 2 1

This book is dedicated to the forty-four
of our brothers who didn't return!

Special thanks to:

The late Sheriff Ken Bowden

Commander Bill Harker, USN (Ret.)

Rick Abbott, Seawolf Det 3 (autobody man)

Don Ashlock (Dallas County Constables Precinct 4)

Bud Barnes, Seawolf Det 1 (airline pilot)

Commander John F. Brennan Jr., USN (Ret.)

Terry Bryant, SEAL Team 1

Robert Christenson, Seawolf Det 1 (truck driver)

Dennis Cummings (author)

Joe Denomy (sergeant, Dallas Police Department,
Tactical Division)

George Hudak, SEAL Team 1

Captain Con Jaburg, USN (Ret.), first executive officer
of the Seawolves

Keith Jasmann, Seawolf Det 1 (builder)

Tim Kast (author)

Gary Linderer, Green Beret (author and publisher)

Owen Lock (editor, Random House)

Richard Marcinko, SEAL Team 2 (author and consultant)

Jim Mosser, Seawolf Det 3 (attorney)

Tom Olby, Seawolf Det 1 (police officer)

Rick Saddler, Seawolf Det 1 (police officer)

Frank Sparks, SEAL Team 1 (Hollywood stuntman)

Ron Spears (Director, Collin County Police Academy)

Captain Mack Thomas, Seawolf Det 1 (active-duty navy)

Mike Walker (Naval Operational Archives)

Mike Walsh, SEAL Team 1 (author and consultant)

John Ware, SEAL Team 1

Jim "Patches" Watson, SEAL Team 2 (author and consultant)

Mark Wertheimer (naval historian)

Jon Peter Zimmer (Department of the Treasury, Bureau
of Alcohol, Tobacco, and Firearms)

Mark of Aardvark Cycle in Lucas, Texas; without his help I
wouldn't be riding my Harley-Davidson motorcycle today.
My last dream come true.

Foreword

Scramble Seawolves!

Among the armed forces of the United States, U.S. Navy SEALs are frequently the "tip of the spear": the first to penetrate and the first to draw blood. However, the tip is also the most vulnerable part of the blade, the first part to be blunted. It must be inserted in the right place at the right time or be shattered. It is also the smallest part of the blade, and improperly applied, it can easily be broken against enemy armor.

Navy SEALs operated in Vietnam in commando units as small as four men and rarely more than fourteen. They penetrated deep into Viet Cong and NVA strongholds to capture or eliminate the Communist infrastructure. The SEALs soon became masters of camouflage and were able to move through the jungle without detection and under the cover of darkness. Upon reaching their objective, they were often met with overwhelming odds. Then the tip of the spear needed help from above, and radio silence had to be broken. The word went out: "Scramble Seawolves!"

In Vietnam, for maximum mobility and firepower over the jungles and rice paddies, the helicopter was the essential support vehicle for our riverine forces. The navy's answer to the problem of SEAL support in an operating environment of unbroken jungle, rice paddies, or open water was the UH-1B helicopter gunship, call sign Seawolves. Mounted on each side of the

Seawolves Hueys were 2.75-inch rocket launchers, and there were two M-60 flex-mounted machine guns per side. Unique to the Seawolf gunships were its two gunners, one seated on each side of the helicopter, with a freehand, shoulder-fired M-60 machine gun. These very special young gunners hung out of the helicopter with one foot on the rocket pod and fired to the side, under, and to the rear, as the gunship rolled in and out of an attack run.

Not only does many a SEAL owe his life to the Seawolves, but the units often operated together as a team. Very often, we were located at the same base of operations, and we developed friendships that are still alive today. Operating well outside standard operating procedures, the Seawolves have lifted SEALs out of enemy encirclements, and I have known them to land in a hot LZ to airlift out a cache too large for the SEALs to pack out. They also evacuated our wounded when medevac helicopters were not available. Most important, they were always there for us when we were down in the mud and darkness, the night illuminated with red and green tracers, the VC behind every shadow. Many times, after we were out of danger, they stayed with us until we were safely extracted, in the middle of the river, and out of range of enemy fire.

It is important for us to remember young men like Dan Kelly and his teammates. His story tells of their choices, good and bad, of what it's like to grow from a young man who should not yet be out of high school into a combat warrior with responsibility for others' lives. In a few short chapters, he takes you into the Seawolves' most intimate places. You witness their courage and their fears, learn of their successes, and experience their pain. Kelly's story is packed with the action and true-life experiences of young warriors in the air. This book brings to life the memories of the "Brown Water Navy." Turn the pages, and you can fly with them.

Barry W. Enoch
GMGC, U.S. Navy (Ret.)
SEAL Team 1

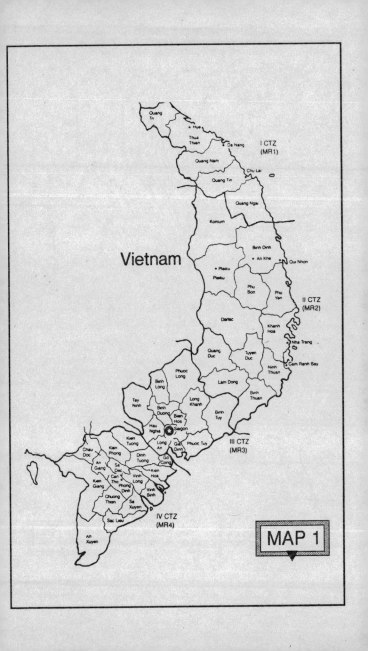

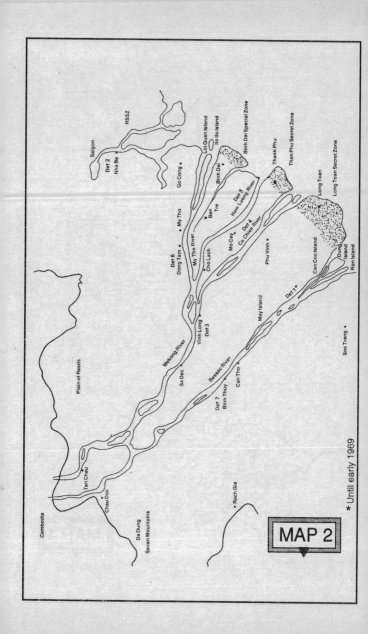

MAP 2

* Until early 1969

Cambodia

Plain of Reeds

Da Dung
Seven Mountains

Tan Chau
Chau Doc

Rach Gia

Mekong River

Sa Dec

Bassac River

Binh Thuy
Can Tho

Der 7

Vinh Long
Der 3

Soc Trang

May Island

Der 1 *

Dong Tam
Der 6

My Tho River

Cho Lach

Mo Cay

Co Chien River

Phu Vinh

Can Coc Island

Dung
Island

Ron Island

Saigon
Der 2
Nha Be

RSSZ

Go Cong

Loi Quan Island
Ilo Ilo Island

Binh Dai

Ben
Tre

Der 5

Ham Luong River

Der 4

Binh Dai Special Zone

Thanh Phu

Than Phu Secret Zone

Long Toan

Long Toan Secret Zone

My Tho

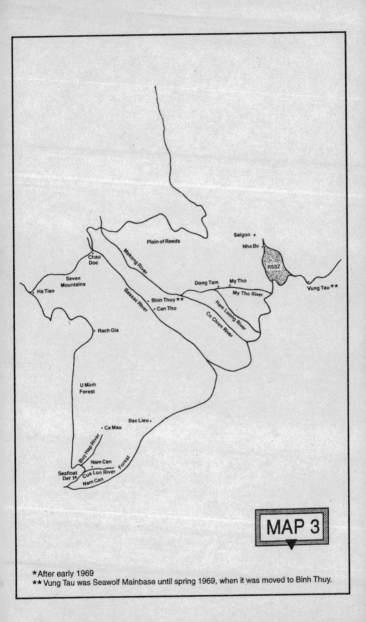

MAP 3

*After early 1969
**Vung Tau was Seawolf Mainbase until spring 1969, when it was moved to Binh Thuy.

Chapter 1

Life is full of choices. We choose to fight, we choose to run, or we choose to do nothing and just take whatever comes, wallowing in self-pity. All of these involve attitude, which in turn affects our actions.

Attitude is developed through upbringing, just like language. The parents you have and the social surroundings they raise you in, the children you play with, peer pressure, all affect your attitude, which in turn affects the choices you make on how to act when "shit happens." I've had experience with all three, and I don't mind telling you there's not much satisfaction in the third choice.

Do you remember seeing that all-too-famous bumper sticker SHIT HAPPENS? Well, I used to think of that as a very negative thing to have stuck on the back of your car. However, I've come to realize that there's a lot of wisdom in it.

Things do happen that we have no control over, and the sooner we realize that, the sooner a lot of stress disappears from our lives. We spend entirely too much time worrying about things before they happen. Problem is, you can do everything right and still have a bad result.

For example, my wife and I have a very good friend who had shit happen to her. This lady and mother, who shall remain nameless, married another good friend of ours. Both were very successful in their chosen professions. He was an architect, and she was a stewardess. They both seemed to be doing

everything correctly, making all the right choices in life, finan-
cially and emotionally.

They have two beautiful children. The daughter is extremely
sweet, outgoing, artistic. And she is a cheerleader. Their son
has taken part in all sports, loves golf, is involved in the Scouts.
He's a musician and very creative.

On the surface, all was well. What the mother didn't know
was that her husband was living another life. There was
another woman. When the truth finally came out, divorce
came into their lives. Another seemingly perfect pair of lives
destroyed.

Adjustments had to be made by all involved. Change always
seems to bring pain. She realized that there was only one
person she could count on and one to make decisions for. That
was herself! You can't control your partner, so why should you
worry about what they might or might not do while you're not
there? You make the choices for you, no one else. Our friend
chose to make the best of her situation and move on. Crying
about it wouldn't change things. Because of her good attitude,
she fought back and is moving on with her life because she
chooses to. She will be rewarded for choosing wisely.

Everyone I have ever known who has chosen to fight back
has been rewarded. Those who chose to run away, or to stay
the same in the face of changing circumstances, never made it.
Things just got worse. Sure, we do make choices in our lives
that can cause negative things to occur, but usually, we have no
way of knowing that until it happens. Remember, if you're not
making mistakes, you're not doing anything. So, shit happens
to all of us; the choice we all have is how we handle it.

One day when I was seven years old, halfway through the
second grade, I walked into class, and in front of everyone, the
teacher said, "Why are you here? You're supposed to be back
in the first-grade classroom. You've been put back a year.
Didn't your parents tell you?"

Taking me by the hand, the teacher walked me out, in front

of all the laughing children, and escorted me into the first-grade classroom.

Years later, I learned that happened because in those days in Iowa it was apparently against the law to be left-handed in school. You had to be taught to write right-handed; I was born left-handed. In the attempt to change me into a right-handed student, I developed a learning disability and did very poorly in school.

None of that had anything to do with *my* choices except how I handled it. As I had not been warned by my parents and was embarrassed, I *chose* to lower my self-image a few notches.

When I was halfway through the second grade a second time, we moved to Texas. When we were living in Austin, my dad would sit me down to help me with my reading. When I made a mistake, he would slap me out of my chair. I remember not being able to see the words through the tears in my eyes. I *chose* from that point on to hate reading, and I *chose* to drop my self-image a few more notches. We lived in a household that believed in negative motivation. We were never rewarded for positive performance, so I really never had a reason to *choose* to raise my self-image.

Fourth grade, I didn't want to go to school one day because I wasn't feeling well. My dad beat me because he was convinced I was faking. Mom protected me, so he beat her, too. I *chose* to blame myself for her beating, and of course, it follows that I *chose* to drop my self-image even further.

After a long series of such situations, my parents divorced. I *chose* to live with my mother because of the abusive nature of my father. My older brother, John, stayed with Dad because they had a better relationship than Dad and I had.

I joined a Little League team to play baseball, and just as my self-esteem was coming back up because I did the Little League thing on my own, my thumb was torn off in the gears of a cement mixer, which ended my baseball career. My thumb did get sewn back on. Never was quite the same, though. Shit happens.

To add insult to injury, trying to come back from that minor setback, I joined the school band and became a band geek. I couldn't even be a good geek, because I made bad grades in all my other classes.

Then my mom married a band geek who was smart. He got me to join the Civil Air Patrol because he knew that I liked "army stuff." That helped my self-image some, but not enough to overcome the damage that had been done. Older brother John did all he could to help me. He had great insight and could see what was going on. Unfortunately, being big brother just didn't give him enough clout to make things right. I owe him a lot. He was the best protector little me could have had!

My first childhood hero was Fred Jones. He was in the army while I was going to Pearce Junior High School in Austin. He was the older half brother to Bill Strawser, who also played a big role in my development. I looked up to both of them. They were smart, and they were natural athletes. Bill was two years ahead of me, a football hero and a basketball star at school. Fred, whom I'll never forget, came and picked me up from school in his uniform the day he got back from Vietnam. He made me feel important. Both of them always treated me like I was somebody special.

Looking back at it all today, I think it was a few special moments like that that kept a fire going in my dream machine. The fantasy that I lived in my head, one that shielded me from a lot of strife, was to someday be an Action-Adventure Hero!

However, this dumb geek was destined to drop out of school and join the navy. But all the *choices* had been made by me.

We all could cop out and say that the choices were made by circumstance, and we were forced to make those choices, but that's just not the truth. The one God-given thing we all have is freedom of *choice*. That's one thing nobody can take from us.

I eventually discovered that the older you get, the more

choices you have to alter your destiny. You have the God-given power to change directions and be whoever you want to be. If you're an underachiever, the way I was, because of negative reinforcement in your upbringing, then you have to work twice as hard as others to achieve the same thing. Obviously, to alter the direction in which I was headed was going to take a lot of work.

It's ten-thirty in the morning on a warm and clear fall day in a suburb of Austin, Texas, 1966. I'm lying under my car, a 1956 Pontiac two-door, disconnecting the muffler so I can hear what the engine really sounds like. When you're seventeen years old, things like that are important.

My longtime friend Bob Liarakos is with me. As the two of us lie on the cool concrete under the car, fighting the rusty bolts on the exhaust, we start reminiscing over the year's events. I concentrate on how I quit the band and sold my horn for car parts because my mom and stepdad never seemed to come to any of the halftime shows to watch me play. My *choice*.

Then we talked about how many classes we had skipped and what we were going to do in the future. We talked about running away from home and joining the Marines. But we weren't old enough; you had to be eighteen years old, and we were only seventeen. Plus, you had to have a high-school diploma or GED to get in. Our big dream was for the two of us to be able to ride out to California on our own Harley-Davidsons and ride all the way up the West Coast on Highway 1.

About then, the milkman drove up across the street. He got out of the truck, walked up to the door of our neighbor, and knocked. She came to the door.

"I haven't received my milk today," the woman said.

"I don't understand it, ma'am, nobody in the neighborhood got their milk today, and I know I delivered it."

It was all Bob and I could do to keep from laughing. Of course, we and four of our friends had followed the milkman around the neighborhood that morning before the sun came up and stole all the milk.

You see, Mom and my stepdad had gone off to California on vacation for a week, and I had the house all to myself.

Let me explain. The previous spring, when I quit the band, Bob and I started a gang. In today's game, I guess we were pretty mild. We got into fights with other gangs from other high schools, and we had our connections, people over twenty-one who would buy us beer for parties. That was about as racy as it got. Anyway, we'd had a good one the night before, and when everybody had sobered up, around 4 A.M., we decided to make pancakes for breakfast, but we were out of milk. That's when we heard the milkman delivering next door.

We had been in the Civil Air Patrol and had been on camp-outs where we dressed in army fatigues and played jungle war-fare with our faces blackened. So this time, we dressed up for a real mission. Charcoal on our faces, our army fatigues on, off we went to covertly gather the milk. By the time we were done, there was enough milk in my kitchen to make pancakes for the Pacific fleet as well as chocolate milk and orange juice. What a breakfast we had.

We never did get caught for that one, but others eventually caught up to us. Skipping school was one of them. And then there was the time Bob and I had packed our bags and were sneaking out to run away from home in late November 1966. Bob had his stuff packed in the back of my car, and we were both over at my house. He was supposedly spending the night. The plan was to wait for everyone to go to sleep, and then we were going to sneak out.

Right after nightfall, Bob's parents showed up at the door and wanted to know why all of his things were gone if he was just to spend the night. We were busted. He went home with his parents, and I was confronted with "Why? How could you do this to me, your mother?"

I remember thinking, That's a good question.

I hated school because I never got any help or support from home and never got any recognition. I saw my mother as a loser, I saw my father as a loser, I saw my stepfather as a loser, and I couldn't stand the way they were raising my little half brother, Sam Jr.

That's a typical seventeen-year-old's outlook on life, isn't it? We know it all, and those old folks don't know shit.

It was to be years before I realized that I was wrong. The real reason I was running away was that I wasn't happy with who I was or where I was headed—jail probably—and I knew I wasn't going to change that by sticking around.

I never have been much for waiting around for things to happen. I've always been one to focus on what I wanted or who I wanted to be and go for it. The problem was, most of the time I failed miserably. That was because of my terrible self-image. My *choice*.

My fantasy self, the Action-Adventure Hero, was alive and well. I just had a serious problem making that person become real. There was a big gap between my fantasy and my reality. I wasn't confident that I could close that gap. However, I am Irish and very stubborn. I could not, and would not, let go of that dream.

Anyway, Mom was very understanding, much to my surprise.

"Okay, dear, what do you want to do?"

"I want to go into the service," I told her sternly. I was expecting a yelling match to break out at any moment.

"What branch?" she asked calmly.

"The Marines."

Staying calm, she answered, "Okay, I'll make a deal with you. I'll give you all the help and support you need to make this happen if you promise to go into the navy or air force instead. That way, I don't have to worry about you going to Vietnam."

I agreed. My *choice*.

She actually accompanied me to the recruiters. That's the

first time I can remember her ever doing anything with me. Well, that's not totally true. She did teach me how to drive. Later, as responsibilities grew along with the challenges in my life, I realized how much positive support I had had from my parents.

We went to see the navy recruiter first. I was so anxious to get going that I jumped at their deal. A *choice* that would put me on a whole different path. They promised me something they called an "A school," a technical school where I'd learn electronics, or something else technical. I was later talked out of it in boot camp because a petty officer said I'd like on-the-job training (OJT) better. But we'll talk more about that later.

After I was all set up to enter the navy, I had to take the GED test; you couldn't enter the navy unless you were a high-school graduate or had received a GED. I needed my mother's signature to take the test, because I was still just seventeen. But by the time I was sworn into the navy, I would be eighteen and wouldn't need her signature.

The recruiter told us that we would have to go through the University of Texas to schedule and take the test. Mom signed the authorization, and the recruiter made the call and set up an appointment.

It wasn't anything you could study for; you either knew the material or you didn't. The recruiter said that the test had three parts and that if I failed a part, I could take a course at the university and then retake that part of the test. Once I passed the test, I would ship out to boot camp. The recruiter told us that wouldn't be until August of 1967.

About three days later, I went to the university and took the test. A very long test, it took most of the day to complete. Then I had to wait on the results. I hated waiting on anything. Several days later, the recruiter got the results and called me with the good news: I had passed all three parts. God had answered another prayer. Remember, I wasn't very smart, and the odds of my passing that test the first time hadn't been very good. Let me rephrase that. I was smart, I just didn't believe it.

Next on the list, I had to check out of school. High school did not hold any good memories for me, so it was happy days to say good-bye. I'm sure Reagan High School didn't miss me either.

I have to say that I now regret dropping out of school because I have no high-school reunion to attend, and it would be nice to see some of the old crowd again. I would have graduated in '68. There are some good memories about Reagan, too. I just didn't want to admit it.

The next month, I spent working in a toy store. Around the middle of December 1966, the recruiter called and said there was an early opening for boot camp in Chicago at the Great Lakes facility. If I wanted it, I would be sworn in and ship out on January 15, 1967.

I was ecstatic.

More *choices*. If I had said no and waited for August, that choice would have put me on another path.

"You bet I want it," I told the recruiter.

I hung up the phone, looked up, and said, "Thanks, J.C.!"

Mom was standing there. She was real happy for me.

One more thing was left to get done. The physical! I had to pass that in order to finally be sworn in.

The date was set. I went down to the recruiting office and met a bunch of others who also needed their physicals. We all got on a bus for San Antonio. My big fear was that I wouldn't pass because I had such flat feet. When it came time for the doctors to check, I faked an arch by curling up the bottoms of my feet slightly. I passed with flying colors. Then it was a matter of just waiting out the few weeks before getting on that plane.

During that endless waiting period to ship out, I gave my entire Beatles record collection to Liarakos. I also gave him my car. Later, after I had been in the navy for a while, I heard he had used the car to run away from home and join the navy.

My stepdad and mother saw me off at the airport on a beautiful afternoon. I remember I was wearing brown suede Beatle boots; light-colored blue jeans; brown belt; yellow, short-sleeve, button-down-collar shirt; light blue, sheep's-wool-lined blue jeans jacket, and a Beatles hair cut. Per the recruiter's instructions, all I had was a carry-on bag with toiletries because I would receive everything else I needed at Great Lakes Naval Training Center.

The temperature in Austin was a cool sixty degrees. In Chicago, I got off the plane in thirty-five-degree weather. Damn, it was cold!

Once in the main terminal building, I found my way to the bathroom. As I stood there, a very large man came strolling in. He looked to be in his late thirties or early forties and had a dark blue sailor pea coat on over what looked like a navy uniform. He picked a spot two places down from me and started to relieve himself.

I had learned all the ranks of the military when I was in the Civil Air Patrol, and I could tell by the three red chevrons on his coat he was a first class petty officer. I've never been hesitant to start a conversation with a stranger, so I struck up a conversation with him. I asked him where he was headed, and he said he had put in twenty years and was retiring. He was headed home. I told him that I was headed for boot camp in the navy. He laughed and said that I was going to love it, but he was glad that he was done. He wished me well.

Exiting the men's room, I made my way to the front of the airport terminal, then outside into that cold northern wind. A bus was waiting for new recruits. Boarding, I met guys who had come from all over the country. We didn't have to wait long. I guess I was one of the last recruits they were waiting for.

The ride was a long one. It was after dark when we landed at the airport, and it seemed like two more hours passed before the bus reached the Naval Training Center. I was cold and tired. But that was just the beginning.

Upon arriving at the base, we filed off the bus, navy petty officers hollering at us, telling us where to go and what to do. It was *so* cold.

We were rushed into a building and issued all military clothing, right down to our underwear. My first navy uniform! Boy, was I proud. To this day, I remember the strong smell of mothballs that first night. Our civilian clothes would be stored for us while we were going through basic training.

Finally, they put us in a holding barracks for the night, and we got to go to bed. Sleep, glorious sleep! My head hit the pillow, and I was out for the count.

The next morning it was to the barbershop for the traditional haircuts. Morning, hell—it was still dark outside. Our wake-up call consisted of a first class petty officer and a chief yelling at the top of their lungs for us to get up and get dressed. Somehow I managed it.

Once dressed, we were all led outside, where a line of buses was waiting to take us to the barber. My beautiful Beatles haircut was doomed.

At the slaughterhouse, we lined up to wait our turns. To my surprise, the line moved quickly. Then I saw why: the place reminded me of a film I saw in school, all these guys lined up with cutting shears just manhandling sheep, then shearing them naked. It didn't take but a few seconds, and my hair was gone.

After we had been run through the hair-disposal factory, we were transported by bus, for the last time, to an auditorium for assignment to the various company commanders. Once that was accomplished, we were assigned the company barracks that would be our homes for the next few months.

We then filled out forms asking questions like what kind of hobbies did we have, were we ever in the Boy Scouts, and had we had any type of military experience. This was so our company commander would learn something about each of us. I mentioned my time in the Civil Air Patrol, and that was how I got appointed as leader of 1st Platoon. A job I would come to regret.

Then we took tests to determine what kind of work we would be good at—office work, electrician, auto mechanic, jet mechanic, radio, etc. The list of occupations was endless. One thing I had heard about the navy, and that was their training schools were the best in the country and that the other branches of the armed forces loved to have former navy men reenlist in their branches because of it.

We attended classes on how to find our way around a ship, tying knots, military commands, and the Uniform Code of Military Justice, when to salute, how to wear the uniform, and how to fold clothes, how to shave, how to brush our teeth, how to sew, how to wash our clothes, how to iron our clothes, how to make our beds, how to stand at attention, how to march and all the commands associated to marching, how to salute, how to shine our shoes, physical fitness training, how to shoot, and even how to write letters home. We had classes on nuclear warfare. We had classes on the navy career opportunities. We were even taught to go to the crapper at the same time every day. One thing about boot camp. It was *very* thorough.

One day during classes, a SEAL gave us a presentation that really impressed me. He talked about the PBR, patrol boat river. He talked about BUD, basic underwater demolition. Then he talked about a new navy program, an outfit called the Seawolves—helicopter gunship teams that were created to work with the SEALs and PBRs. We saw films from Vietnam on all three, and all looked very exciting, but if I had to choose one, I would have to go with my first love, flying.

We were advised that before volunteering for any of these three schools it would be a good idea to spend at least one year with the regular navy. That would get us trained in a main job specialty and give us a year of maturing in the navy before trying for the hard stuff. However, if we thought we were ready to go for it then, we were welcome to try. I decided to be conservative and wait the year. My self-confidence wasn't yet what it should be.

That winter at Great Lakes Naval Training Center was the winter of the worst blizzard in history. We had to hang our wet laundry on the clothesline in the blowing snow, with nothing on but our undershorts. I'll *never* forget that cold! When we brought the laundry indoors, we had to beat it against the clothesline poles to get the ice off it. To our surprise, they were dry underneath!

As 1st Platoon Leader, I was responsible for marching alongside the company and calling out the marching commands. The company commander, a first class petty officer, would give me the orders for the company to perform, and it was up to me to administer those orders. That involved just about everything, not just marching. The worst of it was having to be the one to make sure everyone was up in the morning after sleeping just six hours. I was used to having a lot of friends. All of a sudden, I found myself with no friends. I hated that.

I remember the one night's liberty just before graduation. We retrieved our civilian clothes just for that night, then caught the train into Chicago. Since I was only eighteen years old, there wasn't much to do except go to the USO and be bored all night. Plus, I was 1st Platoon leader. It was a very lonely night. This whole situation was very out of character for me.

On graduation day, we all got our orders. Three guys got orders to PBR school; one guy got orders to BUDs; I got orders assigning me to VA-122 at NAS Lemoore California, an A-7 Corsair II squadron. The Corsair was a single-seat jet fighter-bomber.

I had one week's leave before reporting, just enough time to take a bus from Chicago to Iowa to see relatives and visit my older brother and my dad for a couple days. Then from Des Moines, I flew to Austin, Texas, and spent a few days there with my mom, stepdad, and my little brother Sam. Then I flew to Fresno, California, and went by bus from Fresno out to NAS Lemoore.

When I landed at the Fresno, California, airport, it was the first time I had ever been to California that I could remember. I was born just north of San Francisco at Hamilton Air Force Base in 1949, but before I was old enough to remember anything of those days, we had moved to Iowa.

Stepping off the plane, I was mesmerized by the terrain and the smell in the air. Palm trees everywhere I looked. The mountains in the distance. I had never seen the mountains before. It was all so Hollywood perfect! I don't know how else to describe it. It was just like I expected it to be from watching the movies. I was not disappointed.

The bus ride out to the Naval Air Station in Lemoore was just as spectacular. Desert, real live desert with cactus and more palm trees. It was all so beautiful. I guess I had led a very sheltered life. When all you've seen in your whole life is Central Texas and Iowa farmland, then I guess you could get pretty excited about this kind of stuff.

The bus dropped me off at the main gate to the base. I checked in with the duty officer, who sent me to VA-122's barracks to check in and get assigned a room. There I met the man who was going to end up being my boss for almost a year. He was a very large first class petty officer who had been in this man's navy for about sixteen years and was in charge of the upkeep and management of the barracks for the squadron.

When I moved into my cubicle, I met David Welch and Rick Abbott. They had arrived just a few days earlier from boot camp. We spent the rest of the evening looking around the base and getting to know each other. Welch was the same age as I, eighteen, and was a real live hillbilly from the backwoods of Arkansas. A supernice guy, but you didn't give Welch any shit or you'd get a truckload back. Abbott was a West Texas boy, from Abilene, twenty-one years old, and also a big guy who got respect. Both these guys were over six feet, and I was five feet nine.

It was too late in the day to go out to the squadron hangar and check in, so I was told to wait until morning and ride out on the work truck with the rest of the guys. The hangar was about five miles from the main part of the base.

Getting out there to see our A-4s and A-7s for the first time was a very exciting experience. The ride alone was unforgettable: it was like a cattle truck, painted navy gray with wood seats in the back, and all of us jammed in shoulder-to-shoulder.

It took a few long minutes to cover the distance between our housing and where the hangars and planes were located. I was so excited, I couldn't stand it. I immediately went upstairs in the hangar, where all the offices were, and I found my way to the personnel office.

Reporting in, I was assigned to something called "first lieutenant duty." That sounded important! This is going to be great! I thought to myself. Boy, am I glad I got OJT, instead of that A school thing. I asked what I would be doing but was told that I'd be informed when I'd checked in back at the barracks. Sounded okay by me.

Once all the paperwork had been completed, I boarded the truck back to the other side of the base. When I walked into the lobby of the barracks, papers in hand to present to the barracks petty officer, I saw Abbott and Welch mopping the floor.

"What are you guys doing?" I said with a shocked look on my face.

"First lieutenant duty!" they said.

Oh shit! I gave up one of the navy's best technical schools to be a janitor! I was pissed. If I could have gotten my hands on that first-class son of a bitch back at Great Lakes . . . That's right, join the navy, see the world, and clean up after everybody. Believe me, it was a "character-building" experience. Another scar on my self-image.

Oh well, I figured, if I was going to be screwed, I might as well be the best screwee there is. Believe me, I was the best janitor that barracks ever had. We passed every inspection with a perfect score.

Of course, if they hadn't talked me out of the schooling, I would have gone straight to work on jets and would have gotten buried in all that learning and high-tech stuff and probably wouldn't have given the navy special forces another thought.

Anyway, for the rest of that year, all three of us were stuck in first lieutenant duty. The only excitement we had was to hitchhike into L.A. or San Francisco for the weekend. It was the most frustrating time of my life. It had to be close to being in prison.

The times the three of us went into L.A. were a lot of fun. Abbott would buy the beer because he was the only one who was twenty-one. We rented Honda 90s and rode around Beverly Hills. Just seeing the sights was a blast.

One weekend, I wrecked a rental Honda 90, and I almost broke my leg. Had to check into the base hospital when I got back because there was internal bleeding. They had to perform surgery to relieve the pressure.

By the approach of Christmas, 1967, when we had had all we could stand, we put in papers requesting orders to the special forces school at Coronado, California. After all, I could never be much of an Action-Adventure Hero with a mop in my hand. It took about a month to get an answer back. I'll never forget that day. Of course, we had finally been transferred out of first lieutenant duty and sent to the hangar working on the A-7s in electronics. I was just starting to learn and get excited about what we were doing when we were informed that our orders had come in. We were to report to the Naval Amphibious Base at Coronado, California, for training in preparation for assignment to HAL-3, Helicopter Attack Squadron 3, Vung Tau, South Vietnam.

We were excited. *I* was excited because I was finally going to get to fly. I remembered those films they showed us in boot camp, and I had grown up watching "Twelve O'clock High" on TV. My fantasy world was alive and well.

There was one thing on my mind, however. I had a cousin who'd been a navy fighter pilot in the Korean War, and he got shot down on his first mission. That made me think of one of my favorite movies, *The Bridges at Toko-ri,* about a navy fighter pilot, like my cousin, who got shot down and killed in Korea. He even flew the same kind of plane.

We got one week's leave before going to Coronado. We took that leave to go home before checking out of VA-122, so we had to return to NAS Lemoore, pick up our orders, then check out and proceed to Coronado.

All the kids I grew up with were still in high school, halfway through senior year. I remember thinking about how, if things had been different, I'd be playing football and chasing women instead of going off to war. I knew I had the ability, but I lacked the confidence, the opportunity, and the encouragement. We can't think about the past, though. Just what we can *make* the future hold for us by *choice*.

Once my week at home was over, I bid farewell to Mom, my stepdad, and little brother Sam, and boarded a plane heading into my future. I was *choosing* to make it better than my past!

Chapter 2

The winter of 1967–68. My first time in San Diego. The Greyhound bus came over the mountains and followed a winding highway down the other side. The view was incredible. All of San Diego lay out before us, down to the edge of the Pacific Ocean.

We were all eyes as the bus made its way through the traffic into downtown. Once we arrived at the station and dismounted the "Big Dog," we started looking for a way to the Naval Amphibious Base at Coronado. We couldn't help being distracted by the girlie bars everywhere. However, it was not a time to get sidetracked; we had no idea where we were going, and getting to the amphib base to check in had to be our number one priority.

My pocket had been picked in Fresno, so funds were kind of limited. Welch and Abbott decided that we'd just get a cab, and I'd pay my part later.

We hailed a taxi, tossed our duffel bags in the trunk, and piled in. There was no way, back then, that you could take a direct route to Coronado. It was either one hell of a long ride on a highway, or you took the ferry across the bay; we opted for the ferry ride. It was a lot cheaper because the taxi would drop us off at the ferry, we'd ride across, and just catch a bus for the short ride out to the base.

Before long, we found ourselves standing in front of the main gate to the amphib base. As we paused to take in the view, I noticed right across the street was the UDT/SEAL base. I felt strangely torn between the two gates, one across from the other, because of my love for the water and my love of flying.

When I was a kid, my favorite pastime was pretending to be a navy frogman. Or a waist gunner on a World War II B-17. So, you see, this was not an easy choice. My whole life revolved around a fantasy self that I had been creating back as far as I can remember. I believe we all do that, but a lot of us forget that as we grow older, become more mature and more realistic. I believe we forget because people often don't succeed at achieving their fantasy selves, and so they give up. So far, I hadn't.

The crossroads lay before me. Flying in helicopter gunships, hanging out the door, wheeling that M-60 machine gun, just sounded like a little more fun than scuba diving. Besides, you could see more, and I was into seeing as much as I could.

The Seawolves won out. They were my first *choice*.

Upon checking in, we were assigned a barracks and given a time for that afternoon, and a location, for an orientation meeting. That was our first introduction to what we had gotten ourselves into.

After getting settled in the barracks, we ate lunch, went to the administration building to get some money issued to me to replace what had been stolen. I paid the guys back my share of the taxi fare and got to our meeting just in time.

Our instructors were not dressed in navy uniforms as we had expected, but in what looked like Marine fatigues with their pants bloused inside combat boots. We would be turning in all our dungarees and would be reissued clothes like theirs. More in line with Vietnam duty.

Our schedule outlined the training we would receive over the weeks to come. Every morning, we would run on the beach in combat boots and fatigues, beginning with one mile and adding to it as the weeks progressed. Eventually they would roll us into an obstacle course and swimming. Next was intensive classrooom study of Vietnamese language and customs. Following that, further classroom time on such things as booby traps, disease, personal hygiene, hand-to-hand combat, and survival, escape, resistance, and evasion tactics (SERE).

After all that was completed successfully, we would be transported to Camp Pendleton Marine Corps Training Base, where we would be introduced to jungle warfare tactics, special weapons, and explosives.

Upon returning to Coronado we would be separated from the PBR sailors—who would go on to their own school on the boats—and sent to a school on the UH-1B helicopter gunship.

Last and definitely the worst would be the practical experience with SERE school. We all had heard a lot of nasty rumors about that part of our training and had decided that nothing could be as hard as it was said to be.

After they had finished reviewing the training schedule, we were separated into two groups. One was for PBR sailors, and the other group were Seawolves. There were fewer of us than PBR sailors, so we were moved to a smaller room down the hall where a projector had been set up.

We were shown, I believe, the same movie the SEAL showed us in boot camp, but the lecture that went with it was much more informative.

HAL-3, Helicopter Attack Light Squadron 3, was created out of HC-1 and was supplied with UH-1B model helicopters by the army. They were commissioned in 1966 for the purpose of flying close air support for the PBRs and SEALs and for insertion and extraction of elements of SEAL teams. HAL-3's services were desperately needed because most army pilots were not trained to fly in bad weather or at night, and it was felt that they could not be counted on to pull SEALs out of a hot LZ, landing zone. The PBRs and SEALs operated at night most of the time, and definitely in bad weather.

The addition of the Seawolves to the navy's special forces

made them completely self-contained, and their operational success increased greatly. Team unity and integrity made the difference. Our instructor told us that almost any SEAL in Vietnam would say that he owed his life to the Seawolves, and if we made the team, we should always remember our commitment to those on the ground: "When the SEALs call, we go and get them out, no matter what! Don't soil our reputation. Keep it intact at all cost. The Seawolves are the SEALs' *first choice* for help, and we intend to keep it that way!" Our instructor went on to say that the Seawolves had amassed such a reputation in their short life that all forces in the Delta region chose to call on them first.

After the talk we got, I was pumped! I had to be part of that team! Besides, we were told that we could quit at any time, and we'd be sent back to the duty stations we'd come from to resume whatever we were doing before. Of course, that was the last thing I wanted. Join the navy, see the barracks, and clean 'em! That would not help my self-image or help me to become my fantasy self.

Mornings came early during training. Still dark outside, our instructors would come crashing into the barracks, slamming garbage cans and their lids around, making all kinds of racket. We'd be up and in our new fatigues and boots in no time. After falling into formation out front of the barracks, we would run across the base, out the main gate, across the street, down and around the UDT/SEAL base, and onto the beach. There, we would run for what seemed much longer than a mile.

The run would end up back on our base and in front of the chow hall, for breakfast. The food was outstanding. Definitely up to navy standards. On the first day, by the time we got back to the barracks to shower up for class, I already had a broken blister on one of my feet. There would be many more to come.

I loved the classroom part. I got writer's cramp constantly from taking notes. I just couldn't write fast enough. All that good information. What I wouldn't have given for a tape recorder.

The language came rather easy to me. I'm not quite sure why, because in school I was terrible at English. My instructor said I even picked up the Vietnamese accent perfectly.

When they covered venereal diseases in class, we watched films that made me swear off sex for the duration. Unfortunately, my resolve would not hold true. I tried, but failed miserably.

Booby-trap school was frightening. We learned that we could get a hand blown off with what looked like a simple ball-point pen; about kids who would walk up to you on the street and blow themselves up to kill you; about punji pits filled with poisonous stakes. That school made me swear off leaving the barracks for the duration. Unfortunately, my resolve would not hold true. I tried, but failed miserably.

Hand-to-hand combat—good old-fashioned judo mixed in with several other martial arts that I couldn't pronounce, but very useful if you wanted to kill the neighborhood bully. I always loved time in the gym, lifting weights, swimming laps, and wrestling on the mat, and hand-to-hand combat just seemed a natural extension of all that.

The survival part was very interesting. How to find food in the field. Knowing what you could and couldn't eat. How to protect yourself from the elements. It was amazing the things you do, the things you could eat without getting sick. When to travel and when not to travel, and why. How to travel. The cross-country navigation part was similar to things I was taught in the Civil Air Patrol.

All the classroom stuff was great, but I wanted to get out and *do it*. Actually put it to practice. I had quite a collection of broken blisters all over my feet by the time we'd finished survival classes and was ready to do something outside besides run for miles, swim for miles, and practice bettering my time on the obstacle course.

We were done and had passed all the classroom stuff. The next morning would be the beginning of our next phase of training. Time to take a break tonight in San Diego.

Taking showers, shaving, brushing teeth, splashing on cologne, and putting on our best civilian clothes, we were ready! Abbott, Welch, and I headed into town. Back on the bus, down to the ferry, across the bay, and into sin city. Downtown San Diego and the girlie bars.

Shit! Shit! Shit! You had to be twenty-one! That really sucked!

"Okay, Abbott, have a good time, you fuck!" I said as I laughed.

We set up a place to meet at later to catch the boat back across the bay. Abbott went off to barhop while Welch and I wandered through the dirty-book shops and arcades.

After browsing through the books and quarter porno machines, we slowly gravitated to a pool hall. Walking in, I noticed this guy who had his back to me who was playing on the snooker table. He reminded me of someone I used to know back in Texas. Of course, Texas was a long way from there. As we walked past him, I couldn't help but stare. This person must have felt me staring at him, because he turned and looked straight into my eyes. We both gasped at the same time.

"Bill Strawser? What the fuck are you doing out here?" I said at the top of my voice.

All he could say was, "Son of bitch! I don't believe it!"

Our dads had gone through World War II together. We had grown up together, just like our dads. Gone to the same schools in Austin. I mean, we were close. The last time I had heard from Strawser, he had gotten out of high school. I didn't know where he went from there. He knew that I had dropped out of school and joined the navy but didn't know where I was.

"What are you doing here?" I asked again.

Strawser told me that he had joined the navy and was going

to radioman school in San Diego and then on to nuclear submarines. Of course, I told him as much as I could about why I
was there. Since nobody'd ever heard of us, and we were kind
of secret, I couldn't tell him everything.

Talk about a small world. Well, we had a great time that
night. Playing pool, laughing, telling stories. He and Welch hit
if off real well. Needless to say, it was late when we got back
to the base.

Man, I hate getting up early. But it was time to board the bus
for Camp Pendleton. Duffel bags packed with just our fatigue
stuff, we got on board. Out the gate, through Coronado, into
San Diego, and north toward my newest adventure.

It was a beautiful ride straight up the coast. On the left, you
could see the ocean crashing on the beaches the whole way,
and the right, gorgeous southern California hills. Here and
there dream homes could be seen on both sides of the highway.

Exiting to the east, we drove up to the main gate at Pendleton, where the Marine guards waved us through. The bus took
us up to our barracks, where we met the Marine instructor
who was assigned to help us complete that phase of our
training. He was a short guy, black, built like a gymnast. Nice
guy, but you could tell he could get very nasty in a heartbeat.

We got settled in the barracks, pointed in the direction of the
chow hall, and cut loose until early the next morning. The
advice we got was to take advantage of the time and rest
because it would be the last we'd see for a while. Abbott,
Welch, and I took that advice and crashed early.

Lights on! Still dark outside and *way* too early! Morning
already? Boy, was I sleeping good! In the top bunk, with
Welch below me and Abbott in the top bunk across from me, I
remember looking down at that short, black Marine sergeant as
he stood by the front door yelling, "Up and at 'em, ladies!"

And thinking how good he would look as a *dead* short, black
Marine sergeant.

Up we got! Into the fatigues, boots, and Marine hat, and out the door. After falling into formation, we ran to a building, got in line, and were issued combat gear, which included a backpack, belt with canteen, a knife, belt, pouches holding M-16 magazines and ammunition, two Colt-.45 clips and ammunition, a holster, a Colt.45, and, finally, an M-16. I was getting excited!

The biggest thing I had ever fired was a 410 shotgun, and that had been just twice, at a phone book, out in the country with Bill Strawser. My parents wouldn't allow guns in the house.

My excitement slowly faded after we fell into formation again outside. The announcement was that fifteen miles from now would be breakfast. And the breakfast was in the packs on our backs.

These weren't fifteen miles down the beach. These were fifteen miles up and down southern California hills. Where we were being taken was the firing range. Blisters on top of blisters. If nothing else, I'd have the toughest feet in Vietnam. And I was flat-footed.

Arriving at the range, we took a break and had a C ration breakfast. Then came the fun part. We spent the day shooting. Got pretty good with that Colt .45. I could actually hit the target. *Where* on the target, I didn't care. Just as long as I hit it. We were told that if the VC got as close as the targets (probably just twenty-five yards), it was all over anyway.

The M-16 was more fun because it would fire fully automatic. That was a rush! I was surprised at the kick it didn't have; it was almost like shooting a .22-caliber.

Once everyone was done, we had the run back to look forward to. I hated running. Swimming, on the other hand, I could do forever. My feet were not happy. The only thing that kept me going was that speech about the Seawolves. That, and the thought that what I was feeling was just pain. It wouldn't kill you, or they wouldn't let you do it. Others had done it.

Everyone else *here* is doing it. Welch and Abbott are doing it. Who am I to quit now?

Getting back to the barracks, we had a chance to shower, and then straight into class. Time for taking notes again. This time it was on jungle warfare tactics in Vietnam. Very interesting stuff on the VC tunnel system, camouflage, and ambush tactics. How you couldn't tell who the enemy was until they shot at you. I thought they did a pretty good job outlining all the tricks the VC would pull.

The next day was more of the same. Fifteen miles out and fifteen miles back. This time we got to shoot M-14s. A heavier weapon than the M-16, the M-14 fired a 7.62mm bullet and it did have a kick. They wouldn't let us fire them on full automatic, though. What a drag.

We didn't get to shoot the M-60 light machine gun, but we did get a demonstration by our Marine sergeant. The destructive power of that thing was something to see. He did eat up some fifty-five-gallon drums on the hillside he was shooting at.

That evening we were back in the classroom and into our notes about Charlie in the jungle.

The next day we started all over again and repeated the process, range-firing M-16s, Colt .45s, and M-14s. We were getting about five hours sleep a night, and my feet wanted desperately to go on strike. It was getting harder and harder to stay awake in class and take notes.

The last day was spent on a different range where we practiced throwing live grenades and got to play with "light anti-tank weapon" (LAW) rockets. That was the most scared I had ever been in my life. Knowing you're holding a real live grenade that, three seconds after you pull the pin and release the spoon, is going to explode in a way that would easily tear your head off! By the way, it takes three men and a boy to pull out that pin! You can't do it with your teeth unless you want to extract them from your head!

That LAW rocket was something else! When the instructor

set it off, I about came out of my skin. Talk about loud! And you don't want to be standing behind it when it goes off; the blast from the back side of that tube would erase your face!

We finally wrapped up everything at the range, did our fifteen miles back to the barracks and turned in all our stuff, packed up, and boarded the bus for the trip back to Coronado.

During the stay at Camp Pendleton, a few Seawolves candidates dropped out of the class. Abbott, Welch, and I were still going strong. Nice proving ground, being a janitor. Character building.

It was already dark when we got back to Coronado. All we could do was drag our butts into the barracks and crash. It was late, and we were tired after averaging four or five hours' sleep a night for a week while running thirty miles a day. The next day, we were to start helicopter school. It was going to be a great night, because we were probably going to get seven hours' sleep.

Just about the time we were all dropping off to dreamland, the lights came on and all three of the navy instructors came in yelling, "It's time to get up and start SERE school!"

I couldn't fucking believe it! They lied to us! I bet that Marine sergeant knew, too. That's why he told us to hit the rack early that night! He knew!

"What about helicopter school for us and PBR school for the others?" I said.

One of the instructors said, "You'll get that in Vietnam if you make it through the next week."

Make it through the next week? How about if we make it through the night? We lost a few more candidates right there.

Moments later, we were out front of the barracks in our fatigues in formation. Each of us was given a belt with a knife, canteen of water, and survival pouch. We marched across the base, out the main gate, across the street, and around and down to the beach. That's where we spent the night, but not before we did some running in the surf, getting us all good and wet, *then* it was through the obstacle course. Then we could try for sleep the best way possible. No shelter. Just us soaking wet, and the beach. It was cold!

After about two hours trying to get sleep we gave up, got up from the sand, and tried to find some wood for a fire. Way down at the end of the beach was the Del Coronado Hotel, where we found trash of all kinds. After combing the area thoroughly, we turned up enough stuff to have a great blaze going before the sun had come up. Messing around the rocks in the surf with fishing line and bare hooks, we snagged a lot of crabs. They made for great eating after being roasted over the flames.

The sun was up by then, and things were starting to get warmer. We were then told that we had to run back to the main gate of the base where a bus would be waiting for us.

All I could think of was a cushioned seat and sleep. We were all very tired and of one mind, because we broke all records getting back to the main gate. Sure enough, there was the bus. Some guys just kept running right past the bus and back to the barracks. A few more bit the dust.

I remember getting on, settling into my seat, and hearing the instructors—something about a little trip out to the country—before I was out cold.

It seemed as if I had been asleep for just a few minutes when I was awakened by the instructors, who were yelling at us to get off the bus. We had, in fact, been out for a couple hours.

As we filed off, we were separated into groups of six and given one map and compass per group. We then boarded army trucks and were driven out into a serious wilderness area. Each group was dropped off at a different location, and we had four days to make our way from point A to point B using our land navigation training and living off the land as we went. A few more people quit.

We weren't going to get any sleep out here either, because it was going to take all the time we had to make it to point B. The terrain involved climbing over mountains, around and through a lot of trees, and up and down hills. It wasn't easy. The food we had for those four days consisted of cactus. We tried catching rabbits, but they were too quick. I wish that I had a picture of the six of us trying to run down a rabbit on the fourth day out!

The evening of the fourth day, we arrived at our destination, tired and hungry. When you peel a cactus, it's impossible to get all the stickers because a lot of them are microscopic, so we all had sores in our mouths from them.

Once everyone had arrived, each group was given one live rabbit that we were to kill with our bare hands and eat. Then we were told that the escape and evasion phase would start immediately.

All eyeglasses were collected, all jewelry, anything of value. Then we were told that if we successfully evaded the enemy for the next twenty-four hours and made it to the other end of the course, we would be rewarded with an apple. Well, by that time it sounded like they had Thanksgiving dinner waiting for us. And just think, it was only a few miles up the road. Twenty-four hours? No sweat!

If we completed that period of time without getting captured, then we were to turn ourselves in at the prison camp and go through the interrogation phase, another twenty-four hours.

The instructors had us all line up along a fence. As soon as a whistle sounded we were to climb over the fence and disappear in the woods. The game would be on. Just like hide-and-seek back home.

Standing there at the fence, I noticed that the guy next to me was squinting real bad as he looked past the starting line into the woods. I asked him what his problem was, and he said that he couldn't see without his glasses. Great! Why did he have to end up by me?

Just seconds before the whistle blew, I gritted my teeth, turned to my blind neighbor, and told him to take my hand and I'd lead him through the course. Well, to make a long story

short, he got us captured fifteen minutes into the exercise by
letting go of my hand and walking out into the middle of an
open field. That meant we'd be in the prison camp an extra day
longer than anybody else. The thought crossed my mind that
he might have been a plant.

Getting into the prison camp was an experience I'll not soon
forget. We had to crawl into a barbed-wire cage that was about
twelve inches high and twenty feet square with a barbed-wire
wall all around, a barbed-wire ceiling, and a sloppy mud floor.
Think of it as a mud-wrestling ring.

Once in the cage, we had to take off our clothes, being very
careful not to get caught on the barbed wire. Once we were
naked, with our clothes mixed in with the mud, our captors
sprayed us down with a cold-water hose. I was already freezing
to death. I got the shivers so bad it was like a giant vibrator
mixed in with the mud. Then we had to crawl across the mud-
swamp floor, dragging our mud-soaked clothes behind us, and
out into the main part of the prison camp, where we could stand
up. We were made to put on our clothes, which, by then, were
caked with mud inside and out. The outside clothes themselves
weren't that bad; it was the mud-caked underwear and socks
that bothered me.

After we fell into formation, the interrogations began, and
the interrogators looked like the real thing: they wore Communist uniforms, carried East Bloc weapons, and spoke with East
European accents.

We then endured beatings and all manner of verbal abuse as
the interrogators tried to get us to tell them more than name,
rank, and serial number. They put us in boxes that barely fit us
in the prone position. The lid was then closed and locked. And
there we would stay for up to an hour in the dark before being
taken out and bounced around some more.

After the first day, I started having fainting spells that would
last about a minute at a time. It was the strangest thing. I'd be
standing in formation, and all of a sudden I'd wake up lying in

the mud. As the hours went on into the second day, the spells came closer together. The last night, it was happening every few minutes. Even the guards started getting nervous because they didn't know what was wrong with me. It got to the point that they decided to take me out of the exercise to the medical facility to check me out.

With me in the passenger seat, a guard drove a pickup out of the prison camp and on down the road. It was after dark, and the exercise was to be over at first light. As I looked out the front of the truck at what the headlights exposed, I could see that the dirt road wound through trees. As soon as I could muster up the nerve I yelled, "Escape!" and opened the door to the moving truck. I leaped out into the trees and darkness. Then it was my turn to be surprised: I blacked out as I left the truck! The last thing I can remember was thinking, Oh shit!

The rules of the game were, if you came up with an escape plan, you'd yell "Escape!" and then explain the plan to the guards. If they judged that it was good, you would be rewarded with a cookie or something. Fuck that, I remember thinking. I wanted out of there.

I woke up in the infirmary much later that night, in bed, all cleaned up, and an IV in my arm. There were bandages on my head, arms, and legs but no broken bones; I was going to live. They never made me talk!

After all the other men had boarded, the bus came by to pick me up. Before I left, the doc advised me not to party too hearty when I got back to Coronado because my body would not be able to take the strain for a while.

I was glad that was over!

After resting up for twenty-four hours and eating some good food, the three of us took liberty back in San Diego once again. We met up with Strawser and had one hell of a good time. We couldn't tell him our stories, but he had a good one for us.

Evidently, while we were finishing up SERE training,

he'd been busy stealing the admirals flag. And he got away with it, too.

After a lot of laughs and not a few games of snooker, we said our good-byes and went our separate ways. I wouldn't see him again for several years. But I learned later that after graduating from radioman school, he went on to nuclear submarines.

Back on base the next morning, it was time to receive our orders and move on. Welch had to report to Travis Air Force Base right away for his flight, but according to our orders, Abbott and I had a week to kill. We spent the week back in Texas at home, me in Austin and Abbott in Abilene.

Time in Austin flew by, and I soon found myself getting off the plane in San Francisco. The usual hippie crowd was present and protesting. Once outside, I ran into some more, right where I had to wait for the bus to Travis AFB, but they didn't attempt to bother me there, probably because there were about twenty of us waiting for the same bus, army, air force, and some Marines. I was the only navy guy. We didn't have long to wait before the bus arrived. As soon as we were on the bus and it started moving away, the hippies started yelling obscenities at us. I always wondered what they would have done if the bus driver had backed up and let us off. Instead, ignoring them, we continued on to Travis AFB.

Once on base, the bus dropped us all off at the staging area for all military personal headed for Vietnam, a huge building that seemed to be spread out from one end of the base to the other.

It was a cold winter day in northern California, and I was glad to be wearing dress blues and a navy pea coat. I had a long cold walk ahead of me to find out where I was supposed to check in. Once I entered the building, I got directions. It wasn't much warmer inside.

The place was like an anthill, alive with movement everywhere you turned. Soldiers, all in uniform, from all branches. Some walking in a hurry, some just seemingly walking aimlessly around, some in groups talking, some huddled up in corners sleeping, some just standing by themselves, staring into space. It was a very strange atmosphere. As I walked, I noticed a familiar face coming my way. It was Abbott. He was laughing.

He called out to me, "Just wait till you check in!"

"Why?" I asked.

"You'll see."

Of course, the navy desk was the farthest one away. Approaching the first class petty officer on duty, Abbott yelled out, "Here's your other AWOL!"

Sure enough, the yeoman who'd typed up our orders had made a mistake; we were supposed to have gone out with Welch a week earlier, so both of us had been turned in for being "over the hill." Of course, once our orders were examined, we were in the clear. Since we had missed our scheduled flight a week before, we had to travel on standby. Our names were put on a list, and we had to wait for space to become available. We found ourselves, like a lot of the others, just sitting in a corner, smoking and bored.

After three hours had passed, Abbott's name was called. I walked him to the door and said good-bye. Five hours later, my name was called, and I had to report to a specific gate. The building was huge, the ceiling several stories high. There was nothing on the walls, all of which were just blank white walls except for one that was glass from floor to ceiling. It had doors every few feet, and in front of each set of doors was a long line of soldiers. All I could hear was the loudspeaker calling out names, and the hustle and bustle of thousands of guys going here and there. The atmosphere was cold, eerie, lonely.

Beyond the doors what looked like miles of concrete stretched into the cold night, seemingly all of it occupied by Boeing 707s from just about every commercial airline imaginable. They were scattered everywhere, running lights flashing, jet engines running, as lines of soldiers filed out to each of them.

At my gate, I fell into line along with everyone else. I was already nervous with excitement, and the cold breeze added to my shakes as I followed the guy in front of me out across the flight line. It was a long, quiet walk across that concrete. Just the sound of jet engines was running in the background, then even that seemed to slip away. It was so strange.

To my right, off in the distance, on another part of the flight line, there were several big C-141s with odd-looking buses backed up to them. People there were off-loading something into the buses. I remember trying to figure out what it was they were unloading. The view was so black and white down at that far end, just big gray-and-silver C-141s and the strange gray buses backed up to them. That was a real contrast to all the color at our end, with all the wildly decorated 707s and the soldiers lined up in their relatively colorful uniforms. I wanted to know what they were doing down there, but I didn't think much more about it.

Once on the plane, my awareness of sound seemed to come back, and everyone was talking excitedly, rummaging around, putting their gear up, and getting settled in for a long flight. Once in my seat, I noticed something else rather strange. A few men scattered around the cabin seemed a lot different from the rest of us. They had a calm about them that stood out. A strange stare or gaze that was hard to describe, but noticeable. Unlike the rest of us, they didn't talk to anyone around them. That bothered me for a moment, then I shrugged it off.

Settling back and fastening my seat belt, I peered out the window and stared into darkness punctuated by nothing but runway and taxiway lights of blue and red. My nose was pressed against the window so I could see as much as possible.

Once everyone was in place, the engines grew louder as the plane started to move forward. It was a long steady trip, taxiing out to the runways. We moved out into takeoff position and didn't wait a moment. The pilot was already running up the engines to takeoff power before we were even faced straight down the runway. Ahead of us I saw a plane lifting off clear down at the end. The 707s were taking off as fast as possible day and night, taking troops to Vietnam.

We slowly hit takeoff speed, and I felt the front wheel come off the ground and the rest of the plane followed. As we gained altitude, more and more lights became visible. We made our final exit from the good old United States of America over San Francisco and the Golden Gate Bridge, which was all lit up. It was a beautiful sight. I felt the big bird turn north. Our journey to Saigon, South Vietnam, would take us to Alaska and Japan before landing at Tan Son Nhut AB some twenty-four hours later.

Nearing the end of that twenty-four-hour period, I was beginning to think I had an airplane seat permanently attached to my butt, and it felt like the circulation was failing. My whole body felt dirty and bruised from being confined in such a small space for so long. Would we ever get to Vietnam? I didn't think anywhere on Earth could be so far away.

The No Smoking signs came on, and the pitch of the engines changed as the pilot cut back the power and dipped the nose of the 707. The stewardess announced that we should return to our seats and make sure our seat belts were tightly fastened because these landings were usually a "wild ride."

Boy, was that an understatement! About the time that I could see buildings, several thousand feet below me, we started making a series of sharp turns. The flaps were lowered and the engines revved as the pilot maneuvered into a very sharp dive while still turning. We were losing altitude fast, and my ears were popping like crazy. I looked around the cabin, and everyone else was "white knuckling" their armrests, too, except for those few I mentioned earlier. They seemed detached, betraying no sign of concern at all about our clearly perilous situation.

The plane pitched one way, then the other. All of a sudden, I saw approach lights under us. The runway came up fast! Then the pilot set the plane down so hard that the oxygen masks fell from the overheads into our laps.

I was tempted to take a drag or two of oxygen after what we had just been through, but thought better of it. I wondered if the landing was any indication of how my tour was going to go.

Chapter 3

The engines shut down and the door opened. It got hot in there fast. I'm talking sauna here, not just hot. For the first time in my life, I thought I was going to get heatstroke before I even got into the sun.

It took forever to get up that long aisle to the door and outside. And there it wasn't much better. My dress blues had to go! All I needed was a place to change, but it looked like that was going to take a while because we had to be processed into the country by our people and by the South Vietnamese authorities.

Stepping down the high metal stairway that had been wheeled to the side of the plane, I threw my pea coat over my shoulder. By the time I got to the concrete flight line at the bottom of the stairs, sweat was dripping from the end of my nose.

An air force NCO was holding the stairway in place. As I passed him and proceeded out across the flight line toward the terminal, I heard him saying to everyone, "Welcome to Vietnam."

I remember thinking, What does he think this is, Hawaii or what? But it was a nice gesture. I looked over my shoulder and said, as I kept walking, "Thanks."

We all came to a stop outside the door to the terminal because they couldn't fit us all inside while everyone was going through customs.

Posted at each side of the door were two little Vietnamese kids in some kind of uniform that looked like they had gotten them out of a Cracker Jack box. As I got closer, I noticed they had .38-caliber revolvers strapped to their hips.

Looking behind me, I noticed one of those guys I mentioned earlier who seemed so detached from what was going on. He was a Marine.

I asked him, "What's with the little kids with the guns on?"

That was the first time I'd seen him make any kind of facial expression.

He burst into a laugh and said, "Those are your full-grown Vietnamese police officers, son!"

"No shit!" I answered. These guys were small. Just my size.

Working our way finally into the terminal, I picked up my duffel bag at luggage claim and worked through customs. More of the little kids in uniform with badges. After that, another air force dude gave us directions. I and a few other navy types were directed to a bus stop out front. A navy bus had been called to pick us up.

Once outside, we set our duffels down and lit up smokes. Talking to the others, I found out that they were all yeomen (clerks) headed for desk jobs in Saigon. I told them that I was headed for Vung Tau and the Seawolves. None of them had heard of Seawolves or the SEALs, so I didn't attempt to explain.

Wiping the sweat off my forehead, I flipped my used-up cigarette butt out into the dusty street.

While waiting for the bus to show up, we rehashed the trip. The flight into Alaska and the fuel stop in Japan were rather strange because we never saw anybody at those locations except for ourselves and the people who were doing the refueling.

A loud noise that sounded remarkably like a hot rod from back home caught our attention. As we stopped the conversation to see what that was, a gray school bus rounded the corner to the terminal drive and headed our way. It was going like a bat out of hell, but the bus slid to a stop on the dusty concrete road in front of us. As the cloud created by our transportation dissipated, we noticed that bars and chicken wire covered all the windows.

The door slammed open, and a voice from within called, "Welcome to Saigon, boys. Enter at your own risk. The management assumes no responsibility for lost body parts!"

Jesus, what a greeting! After waving the dust away, I looked up and peered into the bus at the driver. He was a young guy, twenty or so years old. Wearing fatigues neatly bloused into his combat boots, a Marine fatigue hat, and a half-smoked cigar hanging out of a dirty face. A bandolier of magazines had been thrown over his shoulder, and an M-16 hung from the back of his seat. He had a halfway grin on his face as he spoke.

"You guys sure know your fashions—we're going to the tropics, so let's wear our winter dress blues!" He laughed.

"Well, fuck you very much. How fast can you get us somewhere to change?" I laughed as I got on board.

"Grab a seat, and I'll show you," he said. He popped the clutch, the big back tires spun wildly in the dust, and away we went.

"Let's see how many zipper-head gooks we can hit on our way," he said as we raced through the main gate to Tan Son Nhut AB and out on the street headed into Saigon. Obviously not a prejudiced person, our bus driver!

"Where are we going?" I asked.

"Well, that depends," he said.

"Depends on what?" I said as I braced myself to keep from falling out of my seat as we raced around a corner, almost taking out three motorcycles and a rickshaw.

"Depends on where you're headed."

Shit! We aren't getting anywhere. I just started to laugh.

The others told him where they were going, and he said that he'd be taking them there personally. Then they told him that I was a Seawolf and was going to Vung Tau. The whole time they were talking, I was laughing. I couldn't help it; the guy just tickled me. The way he drove. The way he answered questions. I guess I'm easily entertained.

"Seawolf, huh?" he said.

One of the others asked him, "Have you ever heard of them?"

"Oh yeah!" he said. "If it hadn't been for them, the Tet offensive would have been a whole different story around there."

"I'll be taking you to the Meyer Cord Hotel." He said it with raised eyebrows.

I stopped laughing. "What's with the Meyer Cord Hotel?"

"That's where the CIA are. Plus, when the USO has bigwigs come in-country, that's where they stay. Last year, we had Floyd Patterson, Jonathan Winters, and John Wayne stay there."

"How long will I be there?" I asked.

"However long it takes to get other transportation set up for you."

Well! That all sounded very interesting. I had to sit back in my seat and ponder on all this input. What had I got myself into? I was getting excited and intrigued by the whole deal. It's kind of hard to explain, but as that fantasy self and reality got closer together, it was just a little scary.

I tried to relax and watch the sights as our kamikaze driver raced through the crowded streets of Saigon. There were crowds of people everywhere, and a smattering of little motorcycles, taxis, and rickshaws.

Leaning back, so the breeze coming in the window, through the bars and chicken wire, would hit my face, I got some relief from the heat as I daydreamed about what the future would hold for me.

One of the others broke the silence with a stupid question. "What's the bars and chicken wire on the windows for?"

"That's so Charlie can't toss a grenade in the bus as we're going down the street," the driver answered.

The bus got quiet again.

Everywhere I looked, there were soldiers, with and without guns, mixed in with all the civilian Vietnamese. There was a lot of barbed wire, sandbags, and jeeps with machine guns mounted on them that reminded me of the TV show "Rat Patrol," but this was all *very* real. At last, I was in South Vietnam!

The driver wheeled the gray school bus over to the left side of the road and slid to a stop in front of a building about six stories high. He opened the doors and said, "Here's your home away from home, Seawolf."

Grabbing my duffel bag and throwing my pea coat over my shoulder, I stepped off the bus and told the driver I'd see him next time around. The other guys called their good-byes, and the bus door closed behind me. He wound the motor and popped the clutch, and the big back tires spun like crazy as he sped off once again, dodging Vietnamese and motorcycles as the bus disappeared down the street.

I turned and faced the building standing in front of me. Six stories, with no glass in any of its windows and no visible doors, just clean, white exterior walls. Balconies ran around the entire building on every floor. The structure was surrounded by a five-foot-tall sandbag wall with barbed wire across the top. There were .30-caliber machine-gun towers made out of sandbags at the four corners of the building, and one more by the entrance. The place reminded me of the kind of Wild West fort you'd see in a western back home.

Two Marines and two Vietnamese policemen guarded the main gate to the building. I didn't notice any grass, just dirt. Dried dirt, a reddish brown, like Oklahoma in a drought. A strange fish smell permeated the air. For me it was a smell native to Vietnam.

Approaching the Marine guard at the gate, I told him I was in transit to HAL-3 Seawolves.

He checked my ID and said, "Go right on into the lobby and give your orders to the OD, at the desk."

Walking on through the gate, looking around at the sights as I went, I noticed the small clouds of dust that were raised each time one of my boots touched the sidewalk. Turning and looking up as I walked toward the front entrance to the hotel, I saw that .30-caliber machine guns were mounted on each side of the gate behind sandbag towers built higher than the wall surrounding the compound. Continuing my 360-degree turn as I kept moving toward the big doors to the lobby, pea coat in one hand and duffel bag in the other, I noticed one of the Vietnamese police officers going through the bag of a Vietnamese woman who was trying to gain entry into the compound. She looked like a maid. By now I had made my circle of the area and found myself wandering through double doors and into the main lobby. The registration desk was straight across in front. Stairs and an elevator were off to the right. There was a seating area to the left for lounging with a cold drink, magazine, and cigarette. And last, but not least, the registration clerk behind the desk. That, of course, was the OD, otherwise known as the officer on duty, or duty officer.

Walking up to the desk, I dropped my duffel bag to the floor and threw my pea coat on top of it. I pulled my orders from under my arm and handed them to the first class petty officer behind the desk.

"I'm here to get transportation arranged to Vung Tau and HAL-3 Seawolves," I said as I lit up a smoke.

"Welcome aboard," he answered.

"Thanks. Say, how long do you think it'll take?"

"No tellin'. Sometimes an hour. Sometimes a week. You'll get to learn that things in the Nam have their own kind of schedule, and it's usually a surprise!"

"Have you seen a guy by the name of Rick Abbott come

through here? Blond hair, about six foot tall, good-lookin' West Texas boy?"

"Hey, Shorty!" I heard come from behind me.

"I think I remember him. I believe he came in this morning," the OD said, jokingly.

I spun around, looked up, and there was Abbott, standing straight in front of me. He had on his fatigues already and looked very comfortable.

A big smile washed over me. I said, "Damn, it's good to see you. A familiar face at last."

Returning the big smile, he said, "No shit! Let's get you settled in upstairs and out of those damn clothes!"

I wheeled around and asked the OD if he needed anything else.

"No. Everything is in order. I'll get on the horn and try to get you two out of here ASAP. When I get a ride lined up, I'll send for you. By the way, if this takes more than twenty-four hours, you'll have to take your turn standing guard at the gate."

Abbott and I had no problem with that. He handed my orders back, and Abbott and I took the elevator to the top floor. Abbott had already procured a room for us with a great view of the city. Except for the CIA, the hotel was basically empty. They had the entire third floor to themselves. With them was something called the Oceanographic Air Survey Super Constellation Squadron.

The beds were comfortable, and our being on the sixth floor gave us a nice breeze. At least, that's what I thought. But not so! The air was just as still up there as it was down on the deck.

After I picked out a bed next to the balcony, it was time to change. I couldn't get my blues off fast enough. As I undressed and pulled fatigues out of my duffel bag, Abbott said something that made me move even faster.

"Everyone here can legally drink—you don't have to be twenty-one!"

I froze for a moment. "What did you say?"

"I said, as soon as you get ready, *we*, meaning both of us, can go to the enlisted men's club behind this building and drink. All the beer we want. You're legal as long as you're in Vietnam."

All of a sudden, I had a burst of energy. I was unpacked, in my fatigues, and out the door with Abbott in a matter of seconds. On the way to my first cold beer in South Vietnam with my best friend. What a way to finish up a long, tiring, twenty-four-hour trip.

Stepping off the elevator, we made a hard left and went out into the front courtyard. Waving a half salute to the Marine guards, out the gate we went. Right turn followed by another immediate right, down the side of the hotel, right again into the back alley behind our building. All the way down to the end of the alley, we turned left and went up these outside stairs on the building behind ours. The second floor was the EM Club. Hitting the top of the stairs, turning left again, and in the single door to a smoke-filled room of GIs from every branch, all of whom were guzzling cold beers. Ah yes. I couldn't wait.

We found an empty table, and Abbott bought the first round. God bless him.

We put down a bunch of beer celebrating my being able to enter the clubs with Abbott and drink. I don't remember when we headed back to the hotel, but it was late, and the club had pretty well emptied out. Reaching the bottom of those stairs, turning right, and looking down the long *dark* alley that we had to walk down sobered us up somewhat.

"Don't worry about the VC, Abbott; I've seen 'em. They're little tiny shits. Like little fucking leprechauns. If there's any in this alley, I'll take care of 'em," I said as I leaned on Abbott and he helped walk me home.

Stumbling into our room, we got undressed and crashed in our beds. The night was still. A hot-air balloonist's paradise. As I lay there with my eyes closed, I listened to the strange sounds of the night in Saigon, South Vietnam. Faint automatic-weapons fire off in the distance, and artillery fire. No motor vehicle sounds or people; there was a curfew, and the streets were empty. It was like I was on another planet. The occasional gunfire in the background was interrupted by a very large mosquito buzzing around my ear. And to my big Irish ears, that was quite a disturbing sound. Nevertheless, the beer had done its work. There could have been several dozen mosquitoes, with me as their main course, and I wouldn't have known it. I was exhausted and drunk. That just spells one thing: a good night's sleep.

The next morning was terrible. I woke up in a sauna, my eyes glued together with what Mom called sleepy dust. I was soaking wet with sweat. My bedsheet was on the floor, obviously kicked off during the night. As I sat up and cleared my eyes so I could see what time it was, I noticed itchy bumps all over me. Jesus, the bugs ate me alive, and I slept through it all.

I looked at my watch and was shocked—*1130* hours? I hadn't slept that late in years. I wondered where Abbott was.

Sitting on the side of my bed, I fumbled around, looking for my cigarettes and lighter. Shit, the sun was bright. Couldn't somebody turn that thing down? Found my cigarettes. Good. Now where's the damn lighter.

I usually sleep naked, especially when it's hot. I stood up, grabbed my pants, and started rifling the pockets for the lighter. Ha! There it is!

Out of the corner of my eye, I saw this little Vietnamese lady come strolling into our room like it wasn't any big deal. She was just cleaning up a storm. A little yellow tornado.

I, on the other hand, jumped like I was shot, throwing the lighter clear across the room, grabbed the sheet from the floor, and sprang up on the bed, like I was some kind of faggot that just saw a mouse. You see, I've always been very bashful.

"What the fuck?" I yelled out.

She giggled but kept right on working.

Abbott came strolling in as she finished up. By this time I

was just sitting in the middle of the bed, Indian style, in shock, an unlit cigarette hanging from my mouth. Abbott just busted out laughing at me. He knew how shy I was, and some of the others had told him about the people who worked here before I had arrived. So he knew what was coming, the rat.

I couldn't get too mad at him, however, because he had found us tomato juice and a couple of beers for breakfast. There isn't anything in the world better than a tomato beer to settle the system down after a hard night of drinking.

Finally the cleaning lady finished and exited, but not before giving me one last giggle. Recovering my lighter, I finally had that smoke. Then I pulled on my pants and headed for the shower. Everyone shared the same bath area. It reminded me of the locker room back in school. The first thing on the agenda was to take a dump. Where's the shitters?

"Hey, Abbott, where's the shitter at?"

I could hear Abbott laughing from down the hall. That was never a good sign.

Abbott yelled back, "Go around the back side of the showers!"

"Okay, I'm here. Now what?" I said.

"Do you see the holes lined up against the wall?"

"Do you mean the ones that are on the floor?" I said, hopeful that it was a mistake.

"Yup, that's it!" he yelled back.

"What's it?" Trying to confirm that this was all a terrible mistake.

"The hole in the floor is the shitter. What I gotta do, draw you a picture?" he yelled.

This really sucks! They didn't show us that part in the navy special forces recruiter films. Oh well. Taking my pants off, I squatted over the hole and began the very precarious operation.

Suddenly, the Vietnamese lady was back, strolling through the bath area as if my unclad squatting presence was no big deal. Maybe, if I cover my face, she won't notice me squatting here, I thought. Then she started giggling again. That experience was certainly not helping me heal my self-image.

Not many *choices* there. You just shit and take it!

After the bath-area experience was over, I caught up with Abbott downstairs in the lobby. The OD told us that it was okay to go explore as long as it was within a one-block radius so he had a good idea where we could be found.

Leaving the hotel compound, we started to recon the thriving city of Saigon. Or at least one square block of it. The people were incredibly nice to us, well mannered, and eager to make us feel welcome. If it hadn't been for the sandbag walls on every corner, armed soldiers walking the street, and all the jeeps with .50-caliber machine guns, I would have described the place as a beautiful mysterious city somewhere in the Orient. A great vacation spot.

As we rounded our second corner, we found our first Vietnamese bar. A little cautious at first because of our training, we finally entered and grabbed a table that gave us a good view of the street. My first Vietnamese waiter came over and took our order.

"How can I help you sirs?" he asked in excellent English.

"Toi muon mua hai cha bia 33 lam, Cam Ong (We would each like a cold beer, please, sir)," I answered in Vietnamese.

You should have seen his face light up. Obviously pleased with my answer. How about that. My first time using the Vietnamese language. Also my first time to drink *Ba Mui Ba* Vietnamese beer.

Returning with our drinks, he poured the warm beer out of the bottle over a glass full of ice. Another first. Wasn't bad, actually.

We spent the major part of the day there just watching the sights, drinking *Ba Mui Ba*, and talking. What a beautiful place it was. Too bad it had been marred by war for centuries. I was surprised that the people were so nice, considering that they lived in such a violent country. They had incredible character and a great can-do attitude.

Returning to the hotel, we retired to our balcony to watch the sunset from a couple of chairs we had "borrowed" from the lobby. We had sneaked out some Budweisers from the EM club and stashed them in a garbage can full of ice we bought from our new Vietnamese friend back at the bar.

Leaning back in our chairs with our feet up on the railing, beers in hand, we couldn't have been any happier if we'd been a couple of international adventurers on vacation. Gee, that's kind of what we were, wasn't it?

The conversation covered a variety of topics ranging from cars to what we were going to do while over there, and what we were going to do when we got back home. I planned on staying in the service for life. Abbott couldn't wait to get out.

The sun went down with a show of color that would stop traffic, and our conversation slowed as the stars came out. The noise volume generated by the busy city slowly decreased to the usual silence, broken occasionally by the sound of artillery and automatic-weapons fire in the distance. Still as death, the air was. The smoke from my cigarette just hung in the air as if it didn't want to leave. Time to turn in and do battle with the bugs of the nights as we tried to sleep in the black sauna. It had been a great day of rest.

For the next two days all we did was pull guard duty, drink beer, sweat, catnap, and kill bugs as we waited for news of transportation to Vung Tau.

Vung Tau, on the coast, was used as an in-country R & R location, as was Saigon. R & R stands for rest and relaxation; that is, it's a vacation from combat or whatever, without leaving the country. Vung Tau also was home to a major military base, the headquarters for most of the units involved in the Delta region of South Vietnam.

On the third day, another hot, still, dusty, sauna day in Saigon, Abbott and I were standing watch at the main gate when two Marines ran out and said that they were relieving us of guard duty, that we were to report to the OD immediately.

Passing our M-16s, flak vests, and extra magazines to these guys, we ran into the lobby.

"What's up?" I said.

"I just got a call from a buddy of mine out at Tan Son Nhut Air Base who's in charge of the navy mail delivery. He said that a navy C-47 is leaving for Vung Tau in about forty-five minutes. I've already called for the bus, so you guys better shit and git if you're going to make it!" the OD answered.

That didn't leave us much time. Up in the elevator we went. We hit our room in a frenzy, grabbing everything and cramming it into our duffel bags. We clipped them shut at the top, threw them over our shoulders, and flew out of the room and down the hall. Damn it! Of all times for somebody to be using the elevator. The place had been like a ghost town. Why did it get busy then?

We couldn't wait. Down the stairs we dashed. Moments later we emerged from the stairwell, sliding across the tile floor of the lobby as we tried to get traction for the turn to the door into the courtyard.

As we arrived in the courtyard, we heard the hot rod from home—the big navy-gray school bus was just sliding to a stop in front of the main gate. The door slammed open, and as the dust settled, we saw that friendly smile wrapped around a half-smoked cigar.

"Hurry up, jump aboard, grab your ass and a seat, this rocket's leaving Dodge, boys!"

With a grunt, I tossed my duffel bag up onto the landing by the driver. He grabbed it and hurled it down the aisle behind him. Jumping up to the landing myself, I spun around just in time to catch Abbott's bag; tossing it back on top of mine, I fell into the seat behind the driver as Abbott dived into the row across from me.

Winding the engine out and popping the clutch, the driver

launched the big school bus forward. We were off once again, for another ride of a lifetime with the kamikaze driver from hell. Dodging unsuspecting Vietnamese, little motorcycles, and bicycles, we screamed toward Tan Son Nhut AB.

Rounding that last corner, approaching the main gate, the driver slowed way down, transforming himself into someone fairly normal. Pulling up to the air police, he got approval for entry onto the base. Clearing that, we were off again.

The bus raced between hangars, passing F-4s being loaded with bombs or undergoing maintenance, rows of helicopters in revetments, and parked A-1 Skyraiders. We rounded the corner of another group of hangars, and past a C-123, two Caribous, and three C-130s, there it was, out on the taxiway, a navy C-47 with its engines running. The back door was open, and a crewman was waving wildly at us to hurry up.

The driver maneuvered the bus behind and to the left of the plane and drove up next to it. Abbott and I grabbed our duffel bags and, passing our chauffeur, slapped his hand, said adios, and jumped off the bus.

Fighting the prop wash from the big radial engines, we ran to the aircrewman who was hanging out the back of the plane to help us get aboard. There were no stairs, just an open door and a helping hand to lift us up. Abbott was the taller, so I gave him my bag to pass up to the crewman after his was on the plane. He also went first, getting pulled up and in. Then two hands groped downward and little five-foot-nine 150-pound me went flying through the open door and almost into the other side of the interior of the plane.

"You guys Seawolves?" the crewman said.

"Yeah," I answered.

"Meyer Cord Hotel is where you were. That's one of the nicer places in Saigon."

"No shit?" Abbott said. He and I looked at each other in shock. I know he was thinking the same thing I was: What does that tell us about the rest of the country?

"You two are going to have to strap in for takeoff. We got no seats, so you're stuck on the floor. Once we're airborne and I give you the nod, you can take those belts off, move around, and get comfortable."

The back of the plane was full of strapped-in crates. No seats at all. Trying to get as comfortable as possible, we made ourselves secure. It wasn't long before the engines roared and the plane was picking up speed. That familiar feeling in your stomach as the C-47 lifted off the ground told us it wouldn't be long before we'd get that nod and we'd be able to get up and look out the windows. I was dying to see Vietnam from this point of view. We were airborne, headed for Vung Tau.

The aircrewman came back and gave us the signal. I couldn't get up off the floor fast enough. Pressing my face against the little window, I looked out. Wow, jungle and swamp everywhere. We were probably at about three thousand feet, leveled off, and just cruising.

"Hey, Abbott, check out that swamp down there," I said.

The crewman jumped into the conversation before Abbott had a chance to answer. "That's the SEALs', Seawolves', and PBRs' turf. They call it the Rung Sat Special Zone. You might get a chance to see that close up later."

The flight didn't last long. We soon banked right and the plane started its descent into Vung Tau. We were coming down fast, but the aircrewman gave us a break and let us sit up without our seat belts so we could look out the windows as we approached.

The swamp below came closer and closer, and we saw canals running in all directions, dense jungle lining both banks. A PBR came into view under the wing of the C-47 as we passed over a canal. We must have been at about seven hundred feet by then, because I could make out sailors on the deck manning the .50s. The PBR was barely moving. Just as I was starting to wonder why, another PBR came into view. Then came a dirt road alongside the canal. Out from under the wing, an entire outpost became visible. Then a large boat dock with a whole bunch of PBRs tied up to it. Must be a PBR base. Brilliant deduction!

The sights below started getting busier and busier. Little hamlets or groups of thatched huts lining the road that we were flying along started to multiply. More buildings appeared, and there were more people on the roads with bicycles and mopeds. The road merged with a larger one that was paved. An occasional bus was visible traveling down the road. Then I saw army jeeps with machine guns mounted in the back.

We were definitely getting close. Other aircraft were flying around us, helicopters, Bird Dogs, even a Caribou off in the distance. About then, we banked sharply to the left, came in real low over a neighborhood of huts packed so close together I could hardly see between them. We passed over another busy paved road, a large dirt wall, a sandbag wall, then a huge barbed-wire fence. It seemed like our wheels were going to get caught in that last fence.

Then, there it was! The runway. A metal one, made out of PSP (perforated steel planking).

We touched down, moving rapidly. My heart was pounding as I looked out the window and saw a whole line of army-green UH-1B helicopters, each surrounded by a wall of sandbags and "Navy" painted in white on the side of the tail boom! The excitement within me really started to climb!

It didn't take long for the plane to come to a stop. I was bouncing from one side of the aircraft to the other, looking out the windows, trying to see all I could. Then the engine revolutions per minute increased once again as the pilot made a right-hand turn, and we slowly pulled up before a structure that looked like the kind of covered area you use at a park to protect you from the rain. There were a lot of Vietnamese waiting under it, sitting on benches. A few soldiers mingled with them.

As we slowed to a complete stop, the engines were shut down, one at a time. Those big old internal combustion radial engines on a C-47 stopped in a hurry, with the props following close behind. I was already standing up with duffel bag in tow waiting for the crewman to let us out.

"Well, boys, this is it. Keep your trays in the upright and locked position and thanks for flying navy, now get the fuck off my plane," the crewman said.

He swung open the big double doors at the rear of the plane. An army truck was already waiting to be backed up to the aircraft for its cargo. I handed my duffel to Abbott and slid my butt gingerly over the edge and down to the metal-covered flight line below. Wheeling around, I caught my duffel and then Abbott's. He lowered himself down to Mother Earth, and we both waved to the crewman, then walked toward the covered area.

A counter area had been set up at the far end of the open-air terminal. We headed straight for it since we had no idea where we were going from here. Behind the counter stood an army sergeant we hoped had the answers to our questions.

Approaching the counter, I said, "Hey, Sarge, where's the Seawolf HQ?"

He looked up from some papers slowly, glanced in our direction and then off to his right. "Straight over there, about one hundred paces, up those wood stairs, and into that air-conditioned trailer," he said disinterestedly.

Even though he was looking back at his papers and never did really look at us, I still smiled at him and cheerfully said, "Thanks, Sarge! Have a good one!" And we turned and headed for that trailer.

Rule Wiley, a childhood friend back in Austin, Texas, helped me get my first job at a gas station. He taught me that if you're nice to everyone you come in contact with, it will always come back to you later, no matter how they might react at the time.

The terminal structure was on a concrete slab, but as soon as you left it, you were back on the PSP stuff. Just underneath the metal was what looked like sand. Matter of fact, everywhere we looked, all we saw was sand under everything. It was as if the whole base had been built on a very large beach.

Completing our one hundred paces brought us to the foot of five wood steps that led to the porch in front of the door to that air-conditioned trailer sitting on the PSP. *Air-conditioned trailer!* That's all I could think of by that point.

Abbott and I stood on that wood porch, thinking about the A/C inside and how far we'd come to that point. No more janitor work. Opening that door was going to put us in another whole new world. Part of a team that had some respect. That had such a nice ring to it after where we'd come from. *Come on, Mr. Action-Adventure Hero!*

Entering into that wonderful air-conditioned space, we just stood for a few seconds, unable to say anything to anybody. Talk about being spoiled Americans. Oh well.

Straight across from us was a counter where everyone was to check in with their orders. A second class petty officer behind the counter was staring at us with a smile on his face. Coming out of our daze, we walked over to the counter and handed over our orders.

He welcomed us to the squadron. "Congratulations, you made it to the armpit of the world. The A/C will wear off in a minute. It hits all of us the same way when we first get here. Have a seat on the bench over there. I'll give your orders to the lieutenant, and he'll call you when he's ready." Turning and looking at the guy sitting at a desk behind him, he said. "Hey, Jones! Get these two guys a Coke, will ya?"

As I backed up to the wall and slid down on the bench, setting my duffel bag between my legs, I asked, "How long have you been here?"

"Oh, going on nine months now, and I'm glad to say it's all been spent right here in this cool trailer. Ain't nothing like being a yeoman."

Jones came up with our Cokes, we thanked him, and they

lasted all of fifteen seconds as we gulped them down. Abbott and I leaned our heads on the wall behind us and just closed our eyes, trying to recharge our batteries.

"Abbott! Kelly!" the lieutenant yelled out.

Jumping to attention by our duffels, we answered, "Yes, sir!"

"Come in here and take a seat," he said.

Walking through a swinging door at the counter to our right, we proceeded to the end of the trailer where the lieutenant had his desk. Pulling up two chairs, Abbott and I placed ourselves front and center.

The lieutenant sat down, leaned back in his chair, and, rubbing his chin, said, "I've looked at both your records, and frankly, I'm baffled at what I see. Do you two know a David Welch?"

At the same time, laughing, we both said, "Yes, sir."

"Well," the lieutenant went on, "his record said the same as yours. All three of you spent a whole year in first lieutenant duty, yet all three of you have perfect 4.0 records. Can either of you tell me what in the hell is with this VA-122 squadron?"

"No, sir," we said at the same time.

"You guys do know that you shouldn't have been there for more than a few weeks, then transferred to a job-training program, don't you?"

"No, sir."

The lieutenant went on, "This kind of treatment is used for disciplinary matters only, gentlemen. I'd say you've been had. I've never seen this kind of treatment in this man's navy before, and you can bet VA-122 is going to hear about it!"

He was visibly pissed. Pausing to regain his composure, he then went on, "I'll tell you what. I'm going to do the same for you as I did for your friend, Welch. You can pick any duty you want. You're both E-3 airmen. You don't have any kind of training for a major job description, so it's wide open. You pick your job, and I'll make it happen."

Shit, I thought. That's easy. I didn't even hesitate. My

excitement blurted it out. "I want to be a jet mechanic and get assigned to a combat team as soon as possible."

The lieutenant sat back in his chair again. "I said you could pick *anything*!" he said, shocked.

"Yes, sir. That's what I want." My *choice*!

"What about you, Abbott?"

"I'd like to be assigned to airframes, sir."

"Okay, boys, I guess you're set. Abbott, we'll have you report to the airframes shop first thing in the morning, and they'll assign you a shift. Kelly, you report to the line shack, also in the morning. They'll start your training on the UH-1B. You have to be able to fix anything on it, plus study jet engines. Once you've completed all your studies on the aircraft, you'll be assigned to one of our seven detachments. It will be up to the team on that Det whether or not you make the grade. All I can do is give you your shot. Fair enough?"

"Yes, sir! Thank you, sir!" I answered smartly, feeling very pleased with myself.

"Oh, one more thing, here's your first black berets. Congratulations and welcome to the Seawolves." He pulled two berets from a drawer in his desk and handed them to us.

Putting his hand out, he shook both our hands. I think that's the first time I ever had an officer shake my hand.

"Jones will show you how to get to the barracks and assign you bunks, okay?"

"Yes, sir! Thank you, sir," we said as we got up, our duffel bags in tow. With our berets under our arms, we turned around, walked back through the swinging door and on to the front door, where Jones was waiting for us. Placing the berets smartly on our heads, we exited the A/C and went out into the bright sun and heat, right on Jones's heels.

Walking straight ahead from the front porch to the trailer, parallel to the terminal, we weaved between some other trailers, also on PSP, and over to the far side of them, to a main gate that opened up on a paved road to our right. Turning right and going through the gate, we made our way to what looked like a main street through the base.

On our left was the chow hall and on the right the exchange, which sold just about everything—stereos, clothes, alcohol, fans, etc. There was also a restaurant, for those who didn't like what was being served at the chow hall across the street. Behind the exchange was the hangar area where the various squadrons were located. That included the Seawolves.

After pointing all this out to us, Jones made a left turn and headed around behind the chow hall, off the sidewalk and into the sand, past a community bathroom area and shower, on around behind it, to our barracks, a two-story wood structure with stairwell and sandbag bunker for mortar attacks at each end. There was an office space at the end closest to us, on the ground floor, for the barracks administrator and his compartment cleaners, or should I say, first lieutenant duty personnel? That's where we were headed to check in and get a bunk assignment.

Stepping into the barracks and taking a left into the administrator's office, Jones bid us farewell and headed back to work.

"Kelly and Abbott reporting in for a bunk," Abbott said to the second class petty officer sitting behind the desk.

Looking up and noticing that we were just airmen, he asked, thinking he had us for first lieutenant duty, "Where you two newbies reporting for duty?"

"I'm going to airframes, and Kelly here is going straight into team training!" Abbott answered.

Standing up with a surprised look on his face, he said, "Okay, grab two bunks down at the far end on the first floor and get settled in while I check with admin."

I'll be damned, he didn't believe us! Oh well. He'd find out soon enough. We just backed out of the office, grabbed up our duffels, and meandered down the aisle between all the bunks in the open barracks toward the end.

"Hey, Abbott, isn't that Welch sleeping in the top bunk next to the end on the left?"

"By damn, I think you're right!" he answered

Picking the very end bunk on the top, I threw my duffel bag up in the rack and turned around just in time to see Abbott planting a pillow square in the middle of Welch's face like he was swinging a baseball bat. Welch jumped like he was shot out of a cannon and swung, just missing Abbott. We both moved back, laughing, while he got his bearings and realized what had happened.

When he saw that it was us, he laughed.

As we got unpacked and settled in, we brought Welch up to speed on what had happened. In turn, he told us that he had been assigned exactly what he wanted as well—the night shift at the line shack working on the APUs, the auxiliary power units that were used as external power supplies in starting the jet engines on the helicopters. Plus, he gave us the grand tour of the base, which included the EM club for a beer or three. So there we were, back together again, three peas in a pod, working at making our dreams come true.

On our way back from the EM club, I had to stop off in our new community bathroom out in front of the barracks. Walking in through the screen door, I saw a long urinal trough. Across from them were stalls with doors on them.

Hmm, I wondered . . . Taking a slight detour over to the stall doors, I opened one and peered in. Hallelujah, toilets, real live toilets. Not just holes in the floor, but toilets, just like back home. With toilet paper hanging on the wall and everything. I stood there, laughing and playing with the toilet paper.

Looking up as I was still laughing, I noticed that someone had wandered in and was standing at the urinal and staring at me like I was some kind of nut.

I looked back, still laughing, and said, "Hey, toilets, with seats and everything!"

"What did you expect, a sofa with color TV?" the stranger answered back.

Looking back at the toilet and then back at the stranger, I slowed my laughter rather abruptly as I realized how stupid I probably looked. Without another word, I walked over to the urinal.

We checked in to our various jobs the next morning. Welch slept in because he had been up all night at his job in the line shack. Rick was on days, in the airframe shop in the main hangar, our only hangar. I started school on the UH-1B gunship, spending a week in each shop to learn as much as I could and as fast as I could. I had to be able to fix anything that went wrong with it. More time would be spent in an on-the-job format later on, out with the team I would be assigned to.

In between, we had time to go into town, Vung Tau, and party with the natives. Believe it or not, it took a lot of coaxing by Welch and Abbott to get me into town, because I took those navy films they showed us in training very seriously. I was content to stay on the base and get drunk at the EM club.

But they kept coming back with stories about this beautiful place on the beach, a resort area of sorts, that was like something in Miami. After about a week, I broke down and left the base for the first time. Jesus, what an incredible place it was. I had the time of my life. Good-looking women everywhere.

These ladies were French and Chinese, which made for some very beautiful women. The eyes were like something out of a dream, somewhere between slant and round. Very sexy indeed. Enough said about that.

You could also rent Honda 90 motorcycles in town and have a blast riding around Vung Tau. I really enjoyed my time there, learning about helicopters and other things. But I was getting restless. I was ready to be assigned to a detachment so I could complete my training.

It was exciting when one of the combat teams came in from their detachment for special maintenance or supplies, because

I'd watch the way they were treated. Like they were really somebody.

When I saw them, they usually hadn't shaved for several days. Some wore flight suits, some wore striped fatigues; some had beards, some had long hair, some had no hair at all; some wore jungle hats, some wore berets; and nobody saluted anybody. They could walk in anywhere, and nobody would mess with them. They even got to go to the head of the chow line. I wanted to be part of *that* club.

After a couple of weeks, Abbott got transferred to a new barracks on the other side of the base where a lot of the airframe people were. So he had to take a bus to and from work. The only time we saw him after that was at the club or in town.

But by then, Welch and I were working on the line together on the evening shift. We got off around midnight and usually went straight to the EM club for a beer before we went to bed. A typical night was one during which we would have just enough beers to help put us to sleep, in spite of the bugs, heat, and no breeze. That could definitely become habit forming. I was getting into a routine and enjoying it, but was still anxious for some action.

My helicopter training was over, and I did very well. It makes a big difference in your learning potential when you're doing something you're interested in. Plus, I was beginning to discover that I wasn't as stupid as my early teachers and my parents had convinced me.

God was closing that gap between fantasy and reality a little at a time. My self-image was climbing. Now I was just waiting to be assigned to a detachment, to complete my training and, hopefully, make the team.

One night, my mind was wandering through all that had happened to me to date and what the future could bring, as I lay in my bunk. I was smoking that last cigarette for the night, and the smoke was drifting straight up to the ceiling with no waver because of the stillness. The beer was affecting my eyelids and they got heavier. I put the cigarette out in the ashtray on the two-by-four frame around the screen window by my bed. Rolling over on my side, I slipped into dreamland, thinking of that Harley-Davidson motorcycle I'd be driving up in front of my parents' house, and the ticker-tape parade welcoming me home as a real live hero.

About 2 A.M., for no apparent reason, I woke up from an unusually sound sleep. I heard a sound of some kind, off in the distance, that I had never heard before. We always had the usual artillery going on during the night, but that one was different.

Boom! Another one like the one before, but louder and closer. That one made me sit up in bed. I looked over at Welch. He had sat up in his bunk also. I continued to look around and noticed that the guy across from us was still fast asleep. But everyone else was sitting up or standing up.

Then we heard another sound, but not like the other two. It sounded like a freight train coming into the barracks, and it was followed by an incredible explosion. Welch and I were both jumping out of our bunks, heading for the bunker just outside.

As I jumped from my top bunk I yelled out, "That's it, boys, we're out of here!"

I hit the back door first. Welch was a close second, and everyone else was behind him. Just outside was a six-foot fence that went around a patio area, and you had to go out and around it to get to the bunker. Another freight train could be heard coming in at us.

To this day, I have no idea how or why. I don't even remember thinking about it. It just happened. I cleared that six-foot fence without touching anything, and was diving into the bunker.

We were all in our underwear and barefoot as everyone else was scampering and tripping through the sand and into the bunker. It was black as an inkwell inside. You couldn't see the hand in front of your face.

Boom! That one felt like it was right next to us. The blast felt like it went through me, but in actuality it was across the street from us.

"Anybody have any idea where we can get a gun?" I said.

"Are you kidding!" someone said. "Charlie could be coming over the wall right now, and we'd be fucked!"

Welch said, "Who in the hell is running this war? This is bullshit!"

Another person spoke up. "I think they've stopped."

Sure enough, there weren't any more explosions or freight train sounds.

"Hey, Welch, how come this whole place seems to be built on sand, and we're standing in mud with it coming up between our toes?" I asked.

"No shit!" another voice said.

As our adrenaline slowed down and our senses started to return, so did the odor of crap to our noses.

" 'No shit,' my ass!" Welch yelled. "We're up to our ankles in it."

All at once you could hear forty guys screaming like a bunch of little girls trying to get out of that bunker and over to the shower. Nobody cared about the VC; we just wanted that shit off our feet. Evidently the mamma-sans had been using the bunker as their bathroom. Needless to say, we made them clean it up that very day.

Once we got all cleaned up and heard from the hangar that all was well, we made our way back to the barracks and tried to get as much sleep as possible before work.

When we walked back inside, I noticed that one guy was still asleep in his bunk. He'd never moved! I asked one of the others about him. He said that the guy had been a team member and was at the end of his tour. He'd seen a lot of action, including mortar attacks, which didn't seem to bother him anymore. His attitude was that if it was his time to go, there wasn't anything he could do about it, so why worry.

That was the first 122mm rocket attack on Vung Tau, and it put a nice scare into the personnel there. It was pretty good shooting also. With just four rockets they completely destroyed an OV-1 Mohawk, a Caribou, and a fueling area.

That same morning, when it got light enough, we got up to that crazy guy on the Armed Forces Radio saying, "Gooooooood-*morn*ing, Vietnam!" and listened to some great rock music as we all went around taking pictures of the damage. My first taste of live action.

Oh well, with the adrenaline down to normal levels, it was time to get back to work. Still playing the old waiting game, I spent my time working in the line shack with Welch, inspecting helicopters and killing time in town, partaking of the old Irish spirits and poontang.

One night I had stayed late, all by myself with a good-looking girl who was half Vietnamese and half French. Beautiful long legs. That's the only thing that would keep me late. The other guys hadn't gotten lucky, so they went back to the base.

Nobody was supposed to be off the base at night after ten because of possible VC activity. Well, it was past ten, and I had just stepped into the street from the bar. Noticing the lack of activity—the place looked like a ghost town—it dawned on me that I was in trouble. It was a little after ten, and it was a long way back. The usual army trucks that picked us up, and Vietnamese taxis, had stopped running their routes at curfew. I had no choice but to use good old American GI Joe foot power. We're talking three miles here.

It wasn't too long before I realized I was going to be really late. What excuse was I going to use at the main gate, and how much trouble was I going to get into? Boy, the problems women can cause! Many years later, I came to realize that it wasn't the women but my dick that was the problem.

No moon out; it was dark. There were streetlights from town out to the base, maybe one every two hundred yards, so it was very dark and dismal out. No noise at all, other than 105s going off in the distance. Then I was on the main road that went straight out to the main gate. I had about two miles to go.

A sound came to my attention that didn't belong. It was the racing of an engine of some kind. Someone was coming up the street behind me. I turned as I was running, and looked over my shoulder to see what it was. One lone, very weak headlight was coming toward me. It was a small motorcycle. The kind we would rent in town, like a Honda 90.

I almost froze in my tracks, because I had heard stories about VC on motorcycles attacking GIs. I had thought my heart was racing before because of my running; well, it was *really* going now. I started running faster. What am I going to do? No weapon. I can't outrun them. What am I going to do?

I had just passed under a streetlight when I noticed, lying there in front of me, was a beer bottle or something. Reaching down, I scooped it up like a shortstop grabbing a grounder. The motorcycle was almost upon me. I turned around real fast, in the dark, just outside of the last streetlight I had passed under. I got a good look at the motorcycle as it passed under the light. It was two Vietnamese guys, and the one on the back had a board or stick or something. They were coming at me really fast.

Too scared to think, I threw the bottle at the guy driving as hard as I could. Then I ran as fast as my legs would go to the opposite side of the street but still headed in the direction of the base. The bottle broke into pieces, and one of the guys yelled in pain. That was followed by the sound of the motorcycle careening into the ditch on the side of the road where I had been when I threw the bottle.

Later I thought, Hey, that could have been a gun. Why didn't I leave the street and hide when I heard them coming? You can always think of things to do after the fact.

I had covered about a half block when from a side street that was not noticeable because it was not under a streetlight, a pair of tiny headlights appeared that I immediately recognized as "friendly" because of the way the headlights were half painted out. The motor roared to life as the army deuce-and-a-half started up and pulled out in front of me.

It was an army truck picking up some friends at a hootch off the base and bringing them back. They were just loading up when I came running along. Although it was about a block away, the driver had seen what had happened. The best he could tell, he saw this GI turn and throw something at this motorcycle that was speeding down the road toward him, and whatever it was hit the driver square in the head. The motorcycle riders went tumbling into the ditch about forty or fifty miles per hour.

I jumped up on the running board of the passenger side of the truck as it roared around the corner, headed back to the base. Now I didn't have to worry about an excuse to get through the main gate. I had a free ride with this sergeant and his crew.

Back on base, I went straight to the EM club and got shit-faced. Fearing that I might get in trouble, I figured the less said, the better. Loose lips sink ships, and I ain't taking any chances this close to accomplishing my goal.

The next day was a big one. I got notification that Det 1 was coming in to pick me up. They'd be in that evening, and we'd leave the next morning. That was the good news.

The bad news was, they were coming in to pick up a new helicopter because they just had one shot down, over a place called Dung Island. All four crewmen were killed.

We all felt some loss, but not until years later did I really feel the impact, after I had married and had children of my own. There have been quiet times when, in bed alone, or napping on the sofa, awake yet not awake, I've thought of my own children over there, and how I would have felt to get that telegram. My heart really goes out to the parents of the heroes who didn't return. But at that point in my life, I just shrugged the deaths off. I had to pretend death was just part of the game.

Now would come the hard part. I had to be able not only to perform but to fit in with the guys of Detachment 1. That would be the final part of my training. What would they be like? Would my personality fit in? Would I still be the geek from Austin, Texas, or had I grown into the mold I have been trying to make for myself?

The combat teams were special. You didn't get thrown in, handed an M-60 machine gun, and told to go for it. You had to be good, and everyone had to know that, under fire, you would perform well and not get any good guys killed. This wasn't football where, if you dropped a pass, you said oops. You dropped a pass over here, and people died.

We worked with a lot of different units in combat besides our own. The 9th Infantry, Koreans, Australians, the Vietnamese Army (ARVNs), Marine Corps Recon, and the Green Berets. Our reputation with them was high, and we wanted to keep it there.

However, most important to us were the river patrol boats (PBRs) and the SEALs. These guys were good and were always getting in very close-quarters deep shit. They were our main interest because supporting them was why we were created.

So the first thing a new guy had to do was ride middle seat in the gunship on several missions until he got used to getting shot at, all the while taking mental notes on what was going on. While he was doing that, when he wasn't flying, he would be cleaning his M-60 and firing it off the deck of the LST at debris floating downriver.

LST means "landing ship, tank," an old World War II–era flat-bottom boat that had been updated for use on the rivers of Vietnam as a base for the river patrol boats, Seawolves, and SEALs to run operations from.

Once he could shoot and hit anything on the river, and keep hitting it without fail, no matter how small, then he would get to shoot it from the door of the helicopter, one thousand feet in the air, while moving. Once proficient at that, then from three feet in the air and moving. Moving means at about 110 miles per hour and holding the M-60 freehand, no mounts of any kind, just holding it up on his shoulder and shooting, at the same time fighting the wind blast.

After that had been accomplished successfully, then he'd get the chance to fly a real mission in the door with his teacher flying middle seat. When he'd completed fifty hours of successful flying time *and the team accepted him*, then he'd made it. He'd get his wings and "pass."

It was very important that the team like you, because the job was a team effort. It was also a brotherhood. There was no room for out-of-control egos; too much was at stake. Everyone would go home, or no one would go home.

A lot of guys didn't pass. When I stop to think about it, that was some filtering process we went through. First, all the crap we had to go through at Coronado and not quit. Then the schooling at Vung Tau. And, finally, the assignment to a detachment. A guy could go through all that training with the team, only to be scratched because he was an asshole.

Oh well! I just hoped I wouldn't prove myself to be an asshole!

Chapter 4

It was late evening and I was sitting in the line shack with the other guys, waiting for a call that a chopper needed to be pulled into the hangar to be worked on or that one was finished and needed to be taken out to the flight line in preparation for a morning test flight. We were doing the usual things—sitting around smoking cigarettes, drinking coffee, playing cards, reading car magazines or *Playboy*, dreaming, telling stories, or just napping.

Five of us plane captains were in there at the time, about the usual amount for night duty. We heard a chopper come in but didn't give it any thought because choppers came in and went out constantly, twenty-four hours a day. Not to mention C-123s, C-47s, C-130s, CH-54s, OH-6 Cayuses, OV-1 Mohawks, Air America's Fairchild AU-23s, the Otters and Beavers, the Caribous, Chinooks, Beech U-21s, Cobras, Cessna O-2s, and Bird Dogs (O-1s). Just to mention a few. It was a very busy airport, and our line shack was right next to the runway.

As I was blowing smoke from my cigarette into my coffee cup, I took a drink and glanced out of the corner of my eye at the *Hot Rod* magazine on the bench seat next to me. The still air in the room was disturbed by the unexpected opening of our door. I looked up to see who was fixing to disturb us.

There stood a guy about five feet eight or nine, dirty faced, unshaven for at least a couple days, short hair, tiger-striped fatigues, no rank insignia anywhere, a .45-caliber automatic in a shoulder holster, and wearing brown, navy steel-toe flight boots. He was a stocky guy, very solid looking, about twenty-five years old. This was my first meeting with AE2 Searle.

He was married to a girl in the Philippines. That was his home now. Definitely career navy all the way. He was a super-nice guy, but very disciplined. I never saw him really let his hair down. It was like he was always concerned with being a good example to others around him. Don't misunderstand me, he wasn't stuck-up. He laughed and joked like the rest of us, but with a certain amount of reserve.

"Which one of you is Kelly?" Searle asked.

I jumped to my feet in my usual excited way and identified myself. I had a smile on my face a mile wide, and my eyes sparkled with excitement. He gave me a half grin and introduced himself as he told me to come with him to supply for my flying gear and gun.

We'd be leaving early the next morning at sunrise. He told me to say my good-byes to everyone because it was going to be a while before I came back that way, unless I didn't make the team. Then it would be a short trip.

Once I got all my stuff, finished packing, and said my farewells, I was to meet him and his gunner at the EM club. They had to get the new helicopter ready that was to go back with us. He said I wouldn't have any trouble finding them at the club because his gunner was six feet two.

By the time I reached the club, those of my friends who weren't working were already there, getting drunk. As I walked into the club, Page and Schaffernocker were tipping beers. They had already heard the news and had started to cele-brate without me. At the time, they were the only ones of the group who were jealous. The others, including David Welch and Rick Abbott, thought I was crazy. Abbott changed his mind months later and got hungry for the action. We both ended up extending for another tour and we spent our first R & R together in Bangkok. A weeklong party.

It didn't take me long to spot Searle and the other gunner either. They stood out in their two-day beards and dirty tiger-striped fatigues.

I walked over with my usual joyous smile and introduced myself to the bigger-than-life aircrewman. He really was bigger than life. His personality was very much like mine. Out-going, colorful, happy all the time, and serious only when he had to be, Nimmo was an ATN3. A real good-looking guy with dark hair, dark eyes, dark complexion, and hair all over him. He was from San Diego and obviously had to beat the women off with a stick. A very modest person but very confi-dent. The kind of guy you meet and instantly like. The kind of guy I always wanted to be. We hit it off real well.

Searle knew what he was doing when he told me to meet them at the EM club because you can find out a lot about someone by getting drunk with him. We had a good time that night.

The morning came early. We were up before the sun and out on the flight line doing the preflight of the aircraft. That was back when I could get drunk the night before and get up early the next morning without its affecting me. It's great to be young.

The team was also picking up two new pilots as well as me, the new gunner. The pilots were Lt. (jg) Bill Wallen and Lt. (jg) Noel Campbell. Bill was kind of a chunky guy and real nice.

One thing I learned real fast was that the pilots were regular people like us. I mean, they didn't have that ego that said they were the officer and we were the enlisted, so they were better than us. The relationship was more like that of a big brother. We were like a family, a team unit as opposed to a military unit. The team loyalty was very strong, and that really became obvious during the firefights down the road when we were cov-ering the PBRs and the SEALs.

Campbell was tall, dark, and good-looking. I was starting to feel out of place with these GQ (*Gentleman's Quarterly*) types. Anyway, Campbell was also nice, and he was very colorful. Because he always wore sunglasses and strutted his stuff wherever he went, everybody called him Hollywood.

I met our team O in C, Lieutenant Commander Bill Harker. O in C (officer in charge) means the boss of the team. He was like our dad. About thirty-four or thirty-five years old, five feet nine or ten, slender build, always positive, a very strong Christian but not the kind who preached to you and tried to shove the Bible down your throat. Very good-natured, Harker liked to joke around, but he was serious when he needed to be, and an excellent pilot. He seemed very well educated. Harker hailed from Florida. I used to sit out on the flight deck on the LST at night and listen to him talk. He spent time with the enlisted, and talked about whatever we wanted to talk about.

The other pilot with Bill Harker was Lt. (jg) Dave Minahan. He was another real friendly guy but quiet. Unfortunately, Harker is the only one I remember real well. I guess because he had such a large impact on me, that and because he turned out to be my pilot almost all the time.

Harker and Wallen were going to fly the new helicopter with me and Nimmo. Minahan and Campbell were flying the other chopper with Searle. Our luggage was in the back.

As the pilots started to get in the choppers, Nimmo and I put on our flight suits, strapped on our .45s, put on our Mae Wests, and over all that, our bulletproof vests.

Nimmo went to the new helicopter with Minahan, Campbell, and Searle and untied the main rotor blade from the tail boom. He walked it around front, where the pilot could see him, while Searle made sure all the luggage was secure.

The gunner's job was to hold on to the rotor blade until the jet engine was turning fast enough to make the torque pull it out of his hands. That way, it starts to turn faster, and there is less chance of the wind's catching the big blade and blowing it up or down with enough force to damage the rotor head, which would make the helicopter unsafe to fly.

I was at our helicopter doing the same thing at the same time.

We were in revetments surrounded by sandbags, one in front of the other, lined up next to the runway. Both helicopters started their jet engines. As the whine of the turbine increased, so did the pitch of the sound, right in sync with my adrenaline flow. This is it! My next step.

Finally, the rotor blade was pulled from my hands, and I ran around to my side of the aircraft and climbed in, strapped the safety harness on, and pulled the flight helmet over my head. The swooshing blades turned faster and faster until proper rotor revolutions per minute was reached. I plugged my internal communications system cord from my helmet into the radios, rested one foot on the rocket pod outside, the other foot inside, and my hand on the radio button.

The radio in the back had a selection switch on it. One position was for talking inside the aircraft, and the other was for transmitting outside. The crewman in the back used the transmitting position for emergencies only—for example, if the pilot and copilot couldn't talk. The internal position was used so that we could talk among ourselves inside because of the wind noise during flight and the extremely loud jet engine.

As we leaned out our respective doors, we made sure all was clear on both sides of both aircraft, and Nimmo and I, in turn, pushed our buttons and cleared our sides for the pilots to do a hover check.

After each chopper had slowly lifted into the air about five feet, Harker called the tower for permission to take off. The tower cleared us. We moved sideways out of the revetments and onto the runway. Harker slowly tipped the helicopter forward, and we started moving, gaining speed as we went. Looking behind us, I saw Minahan pulling out and falling into formation on our six o'clock. We were gaining speed. Faster and faster. My stomach dropped as Harker pulled up on the collective, thrusting us skyward, out over the end of the runway, over Vung Tau below, and finally, over the beach club, the site of so many parties when I was in school.

Moving on out over the ocean, it wasn't too long before Harker turned the team to the southeast and headed back over land, or should I say swamp. That slowly changed to rice paddies and swamp, then to rice paddies and jungle, and waterways and rivers. I remember thinking how beautiful it was and what a great place to build a resort.

Fifteen hundred feet and just cruising. There I sat, with my face in the wind, visor pulled down so I could see without hindrance. It took us about forty-five minutes to make the flight down to the Bassac River where LST-821 *Harnett County* waited. The trip took us over Dong Tam Army Base where Det 6 was and over the Mekong River where our other two LSTs were with Dets 4 and 5. Nimmo pointed them out to me as we passed over them.

A complete team on a detachment was sixteen men, so you could fly twenty-four hours on and twenty-four hours off. A pilot and copilot, crew chief and gunner per helicopter, and there were two helicopters per team. With every Seawolf team, there was a PBR base. However, there were more PBR teams than Seawolf teams. That always made the PBRs very vulnerable.

The SEAL platoons jumped around the Delta doing their thing, and we were positioned so that there was always a Seawolf team nearby. If the SEAL operation called for a location that wasn't covered, then we picked up and moved to where they needed us. That occasionally put us in some real unusual places.

Det 1 was located on the Bassac River (actually the Hau Giang this far south), the Det farthest south. Upriver was Det 7 at Binh Thuy and Can Tho. At that location were also a large air base and the largest PBR base, where they made all the repairs on the boats. The Seawolves had just seven detachments in Vietnam. Det 2 was at Nha Be, just outside of Saigon; Det 3 was at Vinh Long; Det 4 was on an LST on the Co Chien River; Det 5 was on an LST on the Ham Luong River; and Det 6 was at Dong Tam.

The Seawolves were spread out that way so that response time to the SEALs and PBRs was as short as possible. At each Det location, there was a spot for the SEALs to base out of as well. The naval special forces objective was to jump around the Delta region, hit, and run, with the VC never knowing where we were going to strike next. We gathered our own intelligence, had our own insertion and extraction teams, our own sea and air support, and planned our own operations. We relied on no outside groups. That also made for fewer leaks. That made the navy special forces very effective.

Once we started closing in on the Bassac, Harker took us down to one thousand feet. He circled over the *Harnett County* and called to have the ship turn so we could land coming into the wind. It took them a few minutes to slowly reposition themselves. Once that was done, we came down from our holding pattern.

My first landing on a ship. My eyes were probably popping out of my head as I took it all in. We came in over the jungle very high and then out over the river, dropping down fast and turning on final approach to the LST. I was stretched outside, with my foot on the rocket pod, my body half in the chopper and half out, watching the LST get closer and closer.

My face was in the wind like a puppy dog in a car going down the highway with his head stuck out the window. I looked down, the brown rushing water in the river going by, and up at a small figure standing on the open flight deck of the ship, dressed in yellow. He had a flag in each hand to guide Harker in for the landing.

The deck got larger and larger, the chopper got slower and slower. Coming over the deck, we were moving so slowly I felt the water spray from the river below as it was blown up and sucked down through the rotor blades. What a rush!

Off to my right were four guys in fatigue shorts, no shoes, no shirts, and unshaven. All of them looked to be in very good shape and had been tanned golden brown by the tropical sun.

One was about six feet or so, in his mid-forties, dark hair, with a hairy chest. That was Chief Petty Officer Walsh. He was very quiet except when he had a few beers in him or when you screwed up, but generally he was a very happy guy. The chief was very patient and very professional. He was an excellent father figure for us. An excellent fighter, too.

A second guy was about five feet seven with dark hair. He was a pure-blood Indian with a little bit of a potbelly on him, but he could still kick ass. That was ADR3 Engavo. He told us great stories about being back on the reservation when Hollywood came out to film westerns with John Wayne. He had a good sense of humor and was easy to get along with.

The third guy was AMS3 Fred Record. Dark hair, dark eyes, good-looking, and he knew it. Record was very quick-witted. He kept us laughing. Had a great personality and got along with everybody.

The fourth guy was AN Gibson. The only guy who dangled his M-60 from a bungee cord. He was very serious about his job, and we could always count on him when the shit hit the fan. He was okay to party with but always seemed to hold something back, perhaps because of the friends he lost before I came along—the four who'd gone down on Dung Island and another whose head was blown off over the Zigzag tree line. If you fucked up the slightest little bit, he'd be on your ass. And rightly so! A true professional all the way.

Harker brought us to a complete stop, hovering about three feet off the deck. The guy standing in front of us with the bright yellow jacket on signaled him to set the chopper down and the skids slowly came in contact with the metal of the ship beneath us. As Harker kept dropping the collective, the weight of the helicopter put visible pressure on the skids, and they slipped from side to side, spreading out underneath us as more and more weight was put on them. When the spreading of the skids stopped, the helicopter was completely down.

Once the rotor blade had stopped and had been secured, it was time to clear the deck so the other bird could land. While waiting, Nimmo took care of the introductions. I'll never forget how nice everyone was. It was like I had already become part of the team.

But nothing could have been further from the truth. And I wasn't about to let up when I was so close to achieving my goal. My mother taught me never to assume anything. I had to stay on top of things. Knowing that I was an underachiever meant that I couldn't afford to be down at all. Keep working extra hard, no matter what, and it will come back to you—that was a lesson I learned from my childhood friend, Rule Wiley.

While the others took care of the next bird, Nimmo gave me the grand tour of the LST. I had never been on a ship before, so I didn't know my way around other than what I had been taught in boot camp. He got me settled into our compartment, which was up forward on the LST, up by the anchor storage and away from the regular ship's crew. A hatch from the flight deck opened to a ladder that went straight down, one level below deck, to the middle of our compartment. Forward, between three-tier bunks, was a dead end, the front end of the ship, where stereo equipment hung from the bulkhead. They had speakers that were big enough to make any living room proud.

Doing an about-face and walking back in the other direction, past the ladder that led back up to the flight deck, we came to a door that opened into the bathroom and shower area separating us from the regular navy people. Speaking for the enlisted only, that was the extent of the Seawolves' area.

The officers, or pilots, as we called them, had their own place upstairs, by the wardroom, where the officers hung out.

Of course, off the record, they spent most of their time with us downstairs.

The SEALs, Seawolves, and PBR people were kept separate from the regular sailors on board, and we always got head-of-the-line privileges in the chow hall. That made me feel special. More food for the ego.

In actuality, I don't think the captain of the LST wanted his sailors getting their ideas on proper etiquette from us. The ship's crew was regular navy all the way, with salutes and everything. We, on the other hand, were anything but!

Once I got settled in and unpacked, Nimmo said it was time to start my training and that he had been assigned to be my instructor. That meant I was to eat when he ate, sleep when he slept, and fly when he flew. I was to be his shadow until otherwise notified.

Nimmo took me up on deck, and the training began.

The two UH-1B-model gunships barely fit on the deck next to each other, with just eighteen to twenty-four inches between the rotor blades when they were fully extended. Lining both sides of the flight deck were long steel beams that extended out over the water. Tied to them, down below in the water, were the river patrol boats. The PBR sailors were busy cleaning their .50-caliber machine guns and servicing the boats.

The first thing we did was to go over the armaments on the gunship and the procedure for loading and doing a "quick turn-around." Each chopper carried fourteen 2.75-inch rockets, seven on each side, in rocket pods that were aimed and fired by the pilot. The pods were always loaded with the fourteen rockets, but the electrical contacts on the back of the rockets—the devices that made them ignite—were not clicked down in the ready-to-fire position. Because there had been situations when radio transmissions had set rockets off, the contacts were only clicked down just before liftoff on a mission.

Four M-60 flex machine guns, two each on pylons extending from each side of the gunship, were mounted above the rocket pods and swiveled via a remote-control sight operated by the copilot. The flex guns were fed 7.62mm—or .308s for you civilian types—ammunition through a flexible metal track that ran from the guns outside to ammo trays inside that were located on the floor between the two gunners. Each tray held one thousand rounds. The trays were larger for land-based detachments because they didn't have our weight problem. When you're going over the side of a ship, you don't have the same room to get transitional lift going that the others do.

A canvas seat was mounted in each door on aluminum legs, backed up to the back of the cabin wall. A quarter-inch-steel plate was suspended by wire beneath the canvas. The steel plate was there to keep us from getting shot in the butt.

Our only seat belt was an extended single belt that looped around the gunner so that if he fell out, he could climb back in. It also allowed the gunner mobility inside the back of the gunship since he didn't have to take it off to move around. It was just long enough to let me stand up on the rocket pod, with one foot inside, and still keep the rest of my body outside so I could swing my freehand M-60 around and shoot in all directions. With the belt on, if I slipped or we hit an air pocket, I wouldn't fall to my death. Just get the shit scared out of me.

Halfway between the back of the door and the front of the door, splitting the opening in half, was what we called the pussy pole, because it was there to grab in case someone started to fall out. A can attached to the pussy pole held a smoke grenade with the pin already pulled. The wall of the can held the spoon down and kept the smoke grenade from going off. When the action was hot, the gunner could just grab the grenade and toss it out the door at a moment's notice. The spoon would fly off instantly, the smoke grenade plummeting to the ground and leaving a smoke trail as it went. When we heard a popping sound—a gun or guns on the ground shooting at us—we grabbed the smoke grenade and tossed it outside, and for some strange reason I never understood, the grenade would land on the ground where the enemy fire was coming from. The gunships then circled around and put a strike on the smoke. Most of the time, we got a good enemy body count out of the strike.

Sitting in front of the gunner's seat was a .50-caliber ammo can that had two thousand rounds of belted 7.62 ammunition for the gunner's M-60 machine gun. Lying on the two seats, one on each side, was the gunner's M-60, the ammunition belt inserted into it but with no barrel attached. That was for safety reasons. Without the barrel being plugged in, the gun couldn't be fired. The flex guns mounted on the pylons were the same way. The barrels were locked in place only when we were getting ready to go on a mission.

Each gunner's armor-plated vest lay in the seat as well. Above the seat, on the back wall of the chopper, hung each gunner's flight helmet.

On the back of the pilot's and copilot's seats were racks with spare barrels for the M-60s. That's because when the barrels got white-hot in a firefight, they had to be changed out. If they weren't, the barrels warped, and they wouldn't shoot straight. So in a battle, we rotated the barrels and let the hot ones cool while using others.

Also on the back of the copilot's and pilot's seats were two M-16s, bandoliers of 5.56mm ammunition—or .223 caliber for you civilian types—for the M-16s, and one M-79 grenade launcher with a bandolier of M-79 grenades. These were all backup weapons in case we got shot down.

A quick turnaround was like a pit stop in a car race. We did one only when we were in the middle of a big shoot-out and were running out of gas and ammunition but the battle was far from being over. Usually the LST wasn't far away, so one of the two choppers could break away and rush back while the other orbited the area and put in door-gunner fire. This would provide some protection for the ground troops while the chop-pers rotated.

Once both were refueled and reloaded with ammo and rockets, then they would continue rocket strikes. Usually one gunship wouldn't carry out rocket strikes on its own because the other one was needed for cover. With two gunships, there were enough gunners to keep the enemy's head down while the ships rotated rocket strikes.

Anyway, for a quick turnaround, the ship's crew came out to help the aircrewmen. The chopper came in and landed, but the pilot kept the gunship turning up full speed while guys with a rocket in each hand ran up and slid them into the back of the rocket pods. The gunners jumped out and pulled out their empty .50-caliber ammo cans, replacing them with full ones loaded with 7.62 belted ammo, and reloading the flex-gun trays while another LST sailor pumped fuel into the chopper's fuel tank. After the gunners refilled the flex-gun trays, they dumped all the expended ammo casings out of the chopper; it was usually scattered everywhere around the cockpit and could be hazardous to the crewmen in the back when moving around.

By this time, all the rockets have been reloaded, and they are now just waiting on the fuel. The gunners are back in their positions ready for combat; the LST sailor finishes fueling and gives a thumbs-up to the gunner, who tells the pilot, "Go!" And they're off.

After Nimmo went over all that with me, it was time for shooting lesson number one. Nimmo pulled out what was going to be *my* M-60, grabbed a barrel, and told me to grab an ammo can. A .50-caliber ammo can is a big can, and when it's got two thousand rounds of 7.62 belted ammo in it, well, it's *real* heavy.

My heart was pounding as I struggled with that can to get it over to the side of the ship. It wasn't pounding from the weight of the can, either. It was pounding because of the excitement. The last time I had seen an M-60 fired was at Camp Pendleton.

It was the loudest thing I had ever heard until I went through the rocket attack at Vung Tau.

The LST was moving upriver by that time to another location where it would anchor for the night. We did some target practice off the side of the ship, shooting at things that were floating by in the river. Nimmo stuck the barrel in, flipped the barrel lock down, stuck the belt of ammo in the gun's tray, and closed the feeder cover down on the belt. Flopping the belt over his left arm, he tucked the gun under his right and cut loose on some floating sticks.

The sound was so loud it made me jump. His target was only about twenty yards away. The water shot way up in the air, and the sticks just shattered into oblivion. Nimmo said that I had to be able to hold the M-60 on my target indefinitely from the LST before I could even think about going upstairs and doing it from the door of the helicopter.

Then he showed me how to test-fire it after every cleaning, to check and see if it was going to feed properly. He held the M-60 in his right hand, tucked under his arm, and held the ammo belt in his left hand and shot the M-60 into the river, tugging on the belt with his left hand trying to get the gun to jam. He was shooting an M-60 with one hand! I couldn't believe it. He said I had to be able to do that also.

Wait a minute. Nimmo was six feet two and probably 190 pounds. At the time I was five feet nine and 140 or 150 pounds. There was no way I could one-hand an M-60 while pulling on the ammo belt with the other.

Nimmo said, "Oh yes, you can, and you will. Or you won't make the team!"

He said that it was all in the balance and how you used the kick of the weapon to your advantage.

He handed me the gun, got me set up, and cut me loose to shoot whenever I was ready.

It took about a minute for me to get ready. I'm the kind of guy who will sit there and think about what I need to do and how I'm going to go about it before I do it. That's because I had failed so many times at other things in my life, and I didn't want to mess this up. I wanted Seawolves bad! It was finally my chance to shine. I had come that far; nothing was going to stop me.

I braced myself and leaned into the gun per Nimmo's instructions. Slowly I squeezed the trigger. Away we went, me and the M-60. All over the river, and I mean *all* over the river! Splashes going eight and ten feet in the air as those .308s did everything except stay in a small group.

I was thinking, I'm out of control. Nimmo was yelling at me not to stop, just keep holding the trigger down until I gained control. Slowly the splashes started to come into some sort of focus out in front of me. They were actually starting to come together. Not near as good as Nimmo, but better than it was at the beginning.

I wasn't going to stop shooting until Nimmo said so. I guess it took a while until he figured that out. Finally he yelled, "Okay, that's enough."

And I stopped. He pointed out to me that we weren't flying up in the air at 120 miles per hour in an open door to cool the barrel off. I needed to change barrels. Using an asbestos glove, I pulled the hot barrel out and put a cool one in. He gave me a few pointers, and away we went again. If there were any VC on the bank, watching, I'm sure they were getting a good laugh. But Nimmo was very encouraging as he gave me instructions. That settled me down a lot.

We spent the afternoon shooting off the side of the ship, then it was time to clean guns. That was the next learning experience. We had to be able to take the M-60 apart, find out what might be wrong with it, then put it back together, blindfolded. That was because on night missions there wouldn't be any light in the chopper. At some time in a firefight, the M-60 is going to break, and I was going to have to take it apart in the dark and fix it.

We had a fifty-five-gallon drum that had been cut in half, mounted on legs, and turned into a large sink full of jet fuel that we used as solvent for cleaning guns. After I had cleaned my M-60 it was time to practice taking it apart and putting it back together again. That's how I spent my first afternoon.

That evening, I was scheduled for the regular patrol, a strike on a known enemy position. Nimmo and I were flying, me in the middle seat to see how I would react to getting shot at—and to get used to the feeling.

That movie *The Bridges at Toko-ri* and the cousin who got shot down on his first mission in Korea started to haunt me. I'd be glad when the mission was over.

It was twilight; the sun had gone down, but it was still light out. Everyone was busy getting ready to go, and I was watching Nimmo, taking mental notes on everything he was doing and why.

After strapping on his Colt .45 automatic, followed by the Mae West life vest and then his armor-plated vest, he was ready. Now it was the helicopter's turn. Nimmo put the barrels in the copilot's flex guns on his side. Record took care of the other side. Then they both swung around to the back of the rocket pods and put all the contacts down.

Harker and Wallen had already gotten in and were preparing to start her up. As Nimmo headed back for the tail boom to untie the main rotor blade and bring it around front, he told me to go ahead and climb into the middle and sit on the flex trays that held the ammo for the flex guns.

I already had my .45, Mae West, and armor plating on. All I needed to do was get situated on the flex trays, pull my helmet on, and plug into the ICS (intercom system). Record was already in position.

By the time I was ready, Nimmo was standing out front of the chopper, holding the rotor blade. In the other bird sitting next to us, Minahan, Campbell, Chief Walsh, and Engavo were all set. Chief Walsh was standing outside, holding their rotor blade, waiting for us to take off.*

Harker's voice came over my headset. "Clear?"

Record said, "All clear!"

Harker, reaching both hands down on the collective, turning the throttle, and pulling the starter trigger, said, "Coming hot!"

I heard the faint sound of the jet engine starting to come alive. Getting louder and louder as the whine got higher and higher. Out in front, Nimmo held the rotor blade. Finally it was pulled from his hands, and around it went, faster and faster. As the revolutions per minute increased, so did the wind blowing through the chopper. Nimmo got settled in his seat, plugged in, and gave Harker the okay.

Harker pulled up on the collective slowly, and the smooth sound that the rotor blade was making changed to a load *pop, chop* sound as the rotor took bigger and bigger bites of the air, driving it down under us and pushing us slowly skyward. As we pulled up into about a three-foot hover, Harker backed us up as close to the edge of the deck behind us as possible. He wanted as big a run as possible so as to get more transitional lift as we went forward across the deck in front of us and over the side.

Harker pushed forward on the cyclic, pulled up on the collective, and we nosed over, moving forward toward the other side of the ship, gaining speed, and out over the side of the flight deck and the PBRs below.

Holy shit! We dropped like a rock about eight feet or so! I thought we were going to hit the tops of the PBRs! River water was blown up by the wash of the rotor blade, and a cool mist

---

*With such close quarters on the deck, only one chopper could turn up at a time, so it took longer for us to scramble. Sometime later we started turning up both choppers at the same time, with just that eighteen-inch space between the moving rotor blades, so we could leave at the same time and cut our response time. As far as we knew, we were the only fire team to do that. We also learned to do our quick turnarounds at the same time, which put us back in the firefight a lot quicker.

rained down on us as the water vapor was pulled back down through the blades above our heads. Much to my surprise, we kept moving forward, faster and faster, above the water, about fifteen feet in the air. Then transitional lift started to take effect, and we were gaining altitude again. My asshole was back, but I didn't think I'd be able to shit for a week. I just *knew* we were going to hit the tops of those PBRs. Wow! What a pucker factor!

Anyway, I was listening intently and almost shaking, I was so excited. My teeth were chattering. That always happened when I was excited beyond description. The movie *The Bridges at Toko-ri* kept replaying in my mind. I remembered again about William Holden, as the navy pilot, getting shot down in Korea, and Mickey Rooney, the helicopter pilot trying to rescue him but getting killed, then William Holden getting killed by the North Koreans. My cousin, the navy pilot, was killed on his first mission over Korea, flying the same kind of jet William Holden flew in the movie. Suddenly, there *I* was, on my first mission.

We climbed to one thousand feet and orbited around the LST, waiting for our other bird to join us.

Harker's call sign was Seawolf One-six because he was the boss. Seawolf One-five would be second in command, and so on. Seawolf One-four was Minahan, our trail bird, for that mission.

Over the radio I heard, "Seawolf One-four is off at this time." Minahan had taken off and was headed on up to join us in formation. When Harker heard that, he turned the chopper onto the heading for our strike mission. Minahan would fall into formation behind us, off to one side or the other.

We tried never to fly directly behind anybody because we would be in the same line of fire as the one in front, which meant if someone was shooting at the first bird and missed, they could hit the trail bird by accident. We didn't need any accidents.

It didn't take long for us to reach our target, because the mobility of the LST on the rivers allowed it to get fairly close before we took off. That really was the ideal situation for combat in the Delta.

As we approached the strike area, Harker started giving Wallen instructions on what to do with the flex guns once we started our run—when to shoot and where to shoot and when not to shoot.

Instead of orbiting the target area and giving the VC a warning, we approached the target from the direction Harker wanted for the first strike. That was done in order to surprise the enemy. We would put in three rocket runs, each from a different direction, so the VC couldn't get a line on us from the ground. If we'd put in a strike from the same direction every time, the VC would target that approach and improve their chances of shooting us down. Over the eighteen months I was there, I learned that they could get set up very fast, triangulate our position, and actually ambush us in the sky.

Approaching the enemy position, Harker called out the strike. The pilots already knew the target from the premission briefing. The gunners would lean out the doors and shoot straight forward, wherever the copilot was shooting the flex guns or wherever they saw muzzle flashes and tracers coming back up at us.

"Seawolf One-six, rolling in two nine zero degrees. Three darts, break left."

That gave Seawolf One-four the heading for the first run and a three-rocket fire mission followed by a breaking off of the attack by turning left. Seawolf One-four would put her strike in beneath Seawolf One-six just before we started our break. Shooting her rockets underneath and the flex guns and door gunners firing their M-60s into the jungle would keep the enemies' heads down while we left the area. When Seawolf One-four broke left, our door gunners would be in position to fire their M-60s beneath them to cover her exit from the strike.

Here we go. My first strike. The chopper nosed over abruptly. I felt us gaining speed as we descended toward the target. My heart was pounding. It was almost dark, but I could still see the jungle below.

Wallen opened up with the flex guns. Nimmo and Record started firing forward as well. The expended cartridges ejecting from Nimmo's and Record's M-60s were hitting me from both sides. They were hot little pieces of excitement adding to mine as they pelted me everywhere. The sound of those six machine guns was pounding right through my flight helmet and into my ears. I was so scared that everything started to go out of focus, then I heard Nimmo say over the ICS, "Receiving fire! Receiving fire!"

He had a press-to-talk button on the floor so he wouldn't have to stop firing his machine gun to key his mike.

I began to focus on these red and green flashes of light I saw passing our door in the other direction!

Just when I didn't think it was possible to get any more scared than I was, Harker punched off a rocket. I had never heard that sound before. Loud! And the darkness of the cockpit was filled with sparks from the rocket engine as it exited the tube underneath the pylon and rushed toward its target below. Then another one, and the third.

When Harker fired the third rocket, something hit me in my cheek and stung just a little. What the hell was that? Was I shot? While I put my hand up to my face to feel if there was any blood, I was checking out the possibility of sucking my ass up over my shoulders. Nope! Wasn't going to work. I couldn't hide. There was no place to go. My hand came down from my face with nothing on it. I was okay.

I was scrunched up like the catcher behind home plate, sitting on those ammo cans, trying my best to be invisible, and replaying that damned movie in my head. My first mission. Was I going to die like my cousin did?

We came off the strike without a hitch, and the trail bird put its strike in, with no problems.

I'd made it! My first run, and still alive. A feeling came over me, something that I couldn't explain, something that told me I was going to be okay. We came around from another direction.

"Seawolf One-six, right hand break. Three darts."

"One-four, roger!"

This time, I was like a rubbernecker on the freeway looking at a crash. I couldn't see enough. It was incredible. I could actually see the muzzle flashes of the enemy guns in the jungle below, followed by those tracers coming my way. Some of them were red, and some of them were green. Green tracers seemed most popular with Communist weapons.

Anyway, at night, when they got close, you could see the tracers were the size of basketballs. And we had to remember there were probably four other bullets we *couldn't* see coming at us between each of the tracers we could.

Well, we had more tracers going down at them than they had coming up at us. There went the rockets! This time, I saw them hitting the ground out in front of us. That was better than any Fourth of July show I can remember. The sparks coming into the cockpit didn't bother me this time because they didn't seem to bother the other guys.

We broke off and came around a third time and put in our final strike with a whole bunch of rockets. Harker pretty much had the main group pinpointed by this time because of all the fire we were taking. At night, we could see muzzle flashes real well and tell where the main group of bad guys was and where the tracers were coming from. You should have seen that last run! Eight explosions grouped tightly together, almost hitting at the same time. Wow!

As we broke off the attack and headed home, the questions started flying.

"One-six, One-four. What did the new guy think of that?"

Harker looked over his shoulder, through the clear visor on his helmet. Even today, I remember that Harker smile.

I was laughing with excitement and pushed the ICS button. "Is there anything else we can go blow up? I want to go blow something else up! This is great! What a rush!"

They all started laughing at me as Harker passed the news back to One-four. Wallen and Campbell stayed calm because they were the officers, but I knew inside, they were going crazy, too.

Upon landing back at the LST, checking for damage, and finding none, we cleaned guns and got ready for the rest of the night in case we got scrambled, and the usual morning patrol. In addition, we had a miniature celebration because I had earned my first two points toward an Air Medal.

Air Medals were awarded on a point system. Half a point for flying a combat patrol, one point for putting in a strike at a known enemy position, and two points for receiving fire from the enemy. You couldn't receive more than two points on any one mission. So, once you collected twenty points total—a minimum of ten combat missions—you qualified for one Air Medal.

Before turning in, I remembered that thing hitting me in the face. I asked Nimmo about it, and he said it was probably a rocket cap, the electrical contact for the firing mechanism. When the electrical charge ignited the rocket, the cap flew off, and you never knew where it was going to go. It was red-hot as it came off, but didn't take long to cool.

He and the other guys showed me the scars on their legs where they'd been hit by red-hot rocket caps. When we were shooting forward, that's where we usually got hit because the leg was always hanging outside or braced on top of the rocket pod.

It was time to turn in for the night. Our bunks were steel framed, attached to the steel wall of the ship by hinges and, when folded down, suspended from chains to the outside of the frame. A very thin mattress lay on the steel-frame rack. Springs and canvas were strung underneath. They were mounted there high on the wall, one on top of the other with very little space between them.

But the compartment was definitely not lacking for entertainment facilities: they had fantastic stereo equipment that had been bought at the duty-free stores in-country and on passing ships. Reel-to-reel tape decks, tuners, amps, and speakers that we could turn loud enough to entertain the troops at Vung Tau.

Hanging from the ceiling were strobe lights that were originally intended for Mae West life vests in case we were shot down at night. The idea was that we could turn them on and give the rescue chopper a way to see us. Of course, they also alerted the VC. In addition, the strobe's light looked just like a muzzle flash from the air, so Charlie would start shooting up in the air, and our own guys would end up shooting at us. That's why we took them off the Mae Wests. If we got shot down at night, the plan was to sit tight until light and then be rescued. It was either that or we'd walk out.

Anyway, it made for a cool atmosphere when we were listening to Jimi Hendrix, and all the lights were turned off except the strobes. The shipboard compartments were sealed tight so no light got in at all. That made for a great light show. But we didn't turn the strobes on that night; it was time for some serious sleep.

The guys had forewarned me about the shipboard-sailor night watch, which walked around the ship all night long, dropping concussion grenades over the side. That was done to keep the VC from swimming in under the ship and planting a mine. Back in Vung Tau, it was the mosquitoes and humid heat that kept me from sleeping. On the river in the LST, we had air-conditioning, but we also had an incredible explosion every few minutes just on the other side of the steel bulkhead. I'd take the explosions over the bugs and heat any day.

As I lay there going to sleep, I was thinking about where I had come from to get to that point, about my home life and how everything seemed to go bad as I got older, and now how everything was coming together. There I was with a dream coming true. My *choice*, and God was doing his thing to close the gap between my fantasy self and reality.

It seemed like I had hit it off real well with the guys. I hoped they liked me. They were such a neat group.

The ship's crew really treated us well. Everyone seemed to have respect for us, and that really made us feel good. It's amazing what people will do for just a little respect and recognition.

The lights went out except for the red ones. They always stayed on unless we turned them off to party with the strobe lights going.

I lay there looking around at the others in the compartment, wondering what roads they had traveled to get there.

Remember, Seawolves was strictly volunteer duty. You could quit anytime you wanted. Everyone I was looking at was there because they wanted to be. What were their reasons for being there? Maybe they wanted to be somebody too, like me.

The next few days were pretty normal. Me, riding middle seat with Nimmo and Record, Harker and Wallen as our pilots, doing morning patrols and one in the afternoon.

Between patrols, I practiced marksmanship with the M-60 off the side of the ship, entertaining the local VC, trying to keep the spray in the river in one spot.

I finally got good enough that Nimmo arranged, when there were no patrols or operations scheduled, to have me taken up in the helicopter so I could practice from the door at one thousand feet. Once I got that down, he set me up for some low-level passes on floating targets. We're talking three feet off the water here.

That was a whole different deal! With low-level, high-speed flight, you don't have time to follow the tracers down on the deck because you're on the target before they have a chance to light up. If you aim right at the target, you're going to miss every time because of your motion and the target's being stationary. And if both you and the target are moving, well, that's a whole different deal again! Practice, practice, practice. You can get good at anything with enough practice.

That's the only part that scared me, because I was afraid that I wouldn't pass and, therefore, wouldn't make the team. In growing up, I rarely had anybody take an interest in teaching me how to play ball or anything else. If it was going to get done, I had to do it myself! Now, for the first time, someone was taking an interest in me and my accomplishments. That was Nimmo. So the pressure was on. I had to learn; with that kind of help, there could be no excuses!

Thank God, I got it down!

More tricks of the trade to learn. While shooting, we had to be very careful where the brass was being ejected from the gun, because we couldn't let it fly into the tail rotor. Expended 7.62 casings flying out the door of a helicopter doing about 120 miles per hour and hitting a tail rotor spinning at incredible revolutions per minute do amazing things to the leading edge of said blade. That gets very expensive, and the blade is a pain in the butt to change. Consequently, we held the M-60 in a very unusual way to make sure the brass was ejected inside the helicopter: If we held it upside down and up over the top of the shoulder, away from the body, the brass ejected under the armpit and flew around and behind the gunner, inside the chopper. Then the brass just harmlessly rolled around on the floor of the cockpit for us gunners to trip over.

I had been at the detachment about a week and had the shooting down pretty good. It didn't take long when you were shooting about four thousand rounds a day.

It was a clear night and had been pretty quiet since that strike we put in the day I arrived. Everything was actually rather routine. I was sleeping so soundly. Dreaming beautiful dreams, without a care in the world.

Bong! Bong! Bong! A very loud bell went off. So loud, I bounced off the bottom of Nimmo's bunk with a start. As my eyes exploded open, Nimmo's feet flew past me, headed for the deck. The background was lit up in red. My eyes were trying to focus as I tried to get to my pants, when a voice yelled over the loudspeakers, drowning out the bell.

"Scramble the helos! Scramble the helos! Scramble One! Scramble One! Scramble the helos! Scramble the helos!"

It was *loud*.

"Scramble One" meant that only U.S. troops were in trouble. "Scramble Two" meant U.S. and Vietnamese, and "Scramble Three" meant just Vietnamese with a U.S. adviser.

We treated them all as of equal importance. Some didn't. Enough said.

My heart was pumping like crazy. I couldn't move fast enough. Everybody was up, dressed, and fighting their way up the ladder to the flight deck. It probably took us about thirty seconds, and we were on the flight deck untying the helicopter.

The pilots were climbing in, yelling that the PBRs were in trouble, as we were running rotor blades around front for the start-up. The other crew members were putting the rocket contacts down and sticking in the flex-gun barrels. Another two and a half minutes, and we were lifting off the deck.

The ship's captain had already maneuvered the LST to turn the flight deck into the wind while we were getting up. I was in Seawolf One-six with Nimmo and Record. We took off first and were headed downriver to the location of the PBRs in trouble. Harker didn't wait for Seawolf One-four. He just told him to let us know when he was on his way.

It was a clear night with a full moon as we went downriver in the direction of Dung Island. I was in the middle seat and stretching to see all that I could. For the first three hundred or four hundred yards Harker kept us on the deck, low-level, and then very slowly gained altitude, keeping us in the middle of the river. That way it would be harder for the VC to hit us.

The Bassac River, that particular part of it, was very wide. As we broke through five hundred feet, we heard over the radio, "Seawolf One-four is off at this time."

"One-six, roger!" Harker answered.

Our running lights were on, so One-four wouldn't have trouble seeing us to catch up.

The PBRs had been drifting downriver, next to Dung Island, silently trying to sneak up on Charlie, who they supposed might be making a crossing with weapons and supplies to the mainland. For some reason, a lot of supplies for the VC seemed to come from Dung Island. Anyway, the PBRs had stumbled onto something all right, because Charlie opened up on them with a whole shitload of automatic-weapons fire.

The PBR called. "Seawolf, Seawolf. Alfa Bobcat. What's your ETA? Over."

Harker answered. "Bobcat. Seawolf One-six. ETA four minutes. Over."

"Bobcat, roger!"

"Bobcat. Seawolf One-six. Where do you want us to strike? Over."

"Just follow the tracers from our .50s, Seawolf! You can't miss it! We're taking all kinds of fire!"

That was no shit. I could see them from my middle-seat observation post. Tracers bouncing clear up in the air past us from bouncing off of whatever they were shooting at on the ground.

Record, looking out his door behind us, came on the ICS. "One-four is in formation!"

Harker acknowledged Record on the ICS.

Pushing the transmit button, Harker said, "Roger that, Bobcat! Seawolf is rolling in!"

Harker barked out the strike plan to Seawolf One-four as he nosed us over and went straight in without hesitation. "One-four, One-six. Five darts and break right. Over!"

"One-four. Roger!"

As we rolled in for our strike, the green and red tracers stopped coming out of the jungle at the boats. Of course, that didn't stop the PBRs from continuing to fire their .50s. Harker placed five rockets right on top of where the tracers had been coming from. Five very colorful explosions really lit up the clear night sky. The flex guns and two M-60s Nimmo and Record were firing just saturated the target area.

Harker took the rocket run in very close before breaking off to the right. As he pulled power and swung us up to the right and off the attack run, I was pressed into the flex trays I was sitting on. Suddenly the seat became very uncomfortable. But my attention was diverted from the pain in my butt by the *swoosh* and huge blast of Seawolf One-four's rockets as they screamed underneath us. You could almost feel the explosions up in the air. That's the kind of cover you like on the break. Put that with the tracers from six M-60s coming under you, and that really raises the comfort level; you know that Charlie is ducking instead of popping up to shoot you in the ass.

Harker made the second run a little more conservative, using only three darts. Then a final run with six darts. The PBRs didn't take any more fire the rest of the night.

So I logged my first scramble.

The big day came for me to start flying in the door with my M-60. Nimmo rode middle seat, keeping a watchful eye on my performance.

It was a normal patrol in conjunction with the PBRs. The PBRs were stopping sampans as they crossed from one side of the Bassac to the other and searching them for arms and supplies.

The biggest concentration was around Dung Island. Intelligence reports told us that's where a lot of supplies were coming in for the VC.

We got a call from a PBR that had seen a large sampan crossing from Dung Island to the mainland, but it was too far downriver to catch before it disappeared into the jungle at water's edge. They wanted to know if we could chase it down and hold it until they got there.

We were clear down at the other end of the island with another PBR, but we could probably get there in time. Lieutenant Soto was the pilot that day, Bagley was copilot, and Record was the other gunner. Soto told them we'd head that way.

Turning, and heading for the coordinates of the sampan's location, Soto glanced over at me out of the corner of his helmet and said, "Kelly, we're going to bring them up on your side. Get a bead on 'em and be ready to grease 'em if they move wrong."

I responded with a nod and started to get nervous, my M-60 at the ready, waiting for this sampan to show up. We crossed over Dung Island at one thousand feet and headed toward where the sampan was supposed to be. Once we were out over the river, Soto dropped us down to about three feet over the water as we approached the sampan. I could see it now, coming up in the distance. It was more than halfway across the river, and I could make out the people in it. It was a big sampan, but didn't have a cover or roof on it.

I remember thinking, I've never been hunting, never killed anything other than your regular house-and-garden-variety bugs. I knew the day would come when I'd have to kill someone but was so caught up in my dream that the reality of what that meant had never set in. I had to be able to do it. I was starting to sweat. I began to feel like I was coming down with the flu. I thought that I was going to puke, but I couldn't, I just couldn't. I had to be able to do my job. I kept saying to myself that lives are depending on me, depending on what I do over the next few minutes. I had to focus. I didn't have time to try to justify anything.

Please God, get me through this. This isn't going to be from eight hundred or one thousand feet, but up close, face-to-face.

My finger was tight on the trigger, ready for anything at a second's notice. If something happened, I *had* to shoot first.

I had seen what an M-60 could do to a log floating down-river or a fifty-five-gallon drum. It would literally blow that sampan in half and rip a human body to pieces.

The sampan was coming up fast now on my side. Soto told me to be ready for anything and keep the occupants in my sights. From close range, they could tear the chopper up pretty badly with just an AK-47; a B40 rocket would flat take us out of the game altogether.

I could feel Nimmo's eyes staring a hole in the back of my head. He was watching to make sure I didn't screw up. We went screaming by, as I followed the sampan and everyone in it with my M-60. I saw an old woman, some little children, an old man, and a young girl. They had a lot of cargo in the boat, but I couldn't tell what it was. They instantly stopped dead in the water.

Soto brought us back around for another low pass. They all were ducking down and looked very scared. So was I. I didn't want to shoot anybody, especially women and children. Our trail bird with Minahan, Campbell, Walsh, and Engavo was on them also. We kept buzzing them real close, and they just stayed ducked down. That gave the PBRs time to get there.

The sampan turned out to be clean, but after that little encounter, I had a whole new respect for the PBR crews.

When we got back, all the guys came out and patted me on the back, saying things like, what a close one that was, and you almost got your first kill, and you'll get another chance real soon to run up your score. They all were laughing and cutting up. So, of course, was I. I certainly wasn't going to tell them I'd almost tossed my cookies. They were all talking about how many kills they had and how everybody kept his own score to see who could get the most kills. It was like a big game, and I actually started to feel better about the experience. Scary, huh?

You are what your surroundings are. You adjust to survive.

That experience was what I went to Vietnam for. It was all volunteer stuff. I could have left anytime. But I couldn't. I went there to become something. I went there to prove something. I went there to make a difference. I went there to get out of being a janitor. This is nuts.

Ironically, the next day, we got a call to go to a small village the team had befriended before my arrival. The village was in bad need of a doctor, and our team had evidently taken one out there on regular visits to help with the sick. Well, the VC didn't like that, so they raided the village. Harker wanted to go check the situation out in person to see if there was anything we could do to help. He thought it best that I go along for the ride even though it was my day off. With Harker was Wallen, and in the back, I was riding between Walsh and Record. Seawolf One-four was Minahan and Campbell, with Searle and Nimmo in the back.

We came up on the village at one thousand feet. A lot of smoke was rising into the clear sunny sky from hootches still burning below. As Harker brought us down closer, I noticed an army medevac chopper shut down at the edge of the village. Green Berets were scouting the perimeter for signs of trouble.

We came up fast and flared, throwing dry reddish-brown dust everywhere. Minahan was right behind us. Pulling into a hover, Harker slowly set us down next to the army chopper.

As the rotor blade slowed to a stop, I was thinking that I wasn't sure I wanted to get out. Something told me the village wasn't going to be a pleasant experience. Everyone else seemed to be okay with it except for Wallen and Campbell. All three of us got out very slowly. The others had already dismounted and were looking around.

With the other pilots, Harker walked over to visit with the senior Green Beret.

I finally climbed out and stood by our bird. I saw Wallen standing out front and in the middle of our two helicopters, standing alongside Campbell. They were staring into the center of the village, just mesmerized. Shuffling my boots in the dust, I floated over to them, staring in the same direction.

There were three piles in the middle of the village. Flies and bugs were everywhere. The smell, one I'll never forget, came from a spot to our left. Crying Vietnamese were everywhere.

The smell was coming from the chief of the village, who had been staked out and burned alive. I struggled to keep from getting sick.

Turning toward the center of the village, we walked toward the three piles. I could not believe what I saw and, furthermore, didn't want to believe it. They'd been children. Tiny children. Chopped up. One pile had the heads. Another, the arms and legs, and last were the torsos.

They did this to their own kind? I couldn't believe it. Half the village had been burned to the ground. I still couldn't believe it. The children! Why the children and the babies?

When the mind is faced with tragedy that is not tolerable, a change takes place within that mind for that person to survive. It's built in. Self-preservation. It's like when you fail at something, and you know that it's your fault, but it's such a hard pill to take that you refuse to admit that it was your fault, so you blame it on something else. That's the best way and the only way I can describe what happened to me.

The transformation was complete. These people needed help. But there just didn't seem to be enough of us around to do the job. The politicians, the hippies, the *world* had no idea what was going on over there. One on one, somebody had to help those villagers. The problem with the war was that it was being managed from the top down instead of from the bottom up.

Harker knew exactly what he was doing by taking us new guys out to see things like that! I have no doubt he saved my life that day. Not to mention the lives that would have been lost if I had hesitated to pull the trigger later in my tour.

After Harker met with the army, he decided that there was nothing we could do there, so we mounted up and took to the sky. Everyone was letting the sights of the village filter in and out to that great file in the brain that says, Open only in case of war.

On our way back from the village, Harker decided to run a regular patrol to help get our minds back on business. Out of nowhere, we get enemy fire.

"Receiving fire!" Chief Walsh yelled out on the ICS. He tossed his smoke grenade out the door.

We rolled around and put in a small strike of three rockets each. Not receiving any more fire, other than the one round the chief heard, we decided that the gunman was probably a lone farmer with an SKS and an itchy trigger finger.

From that point on, it seemed like every time we went up on my day to fly, we got shot at. Chief Walsh started calling me Magnet Ass.

Chapter 5

A few days later, in the middle of the night, we got a Scramble Two from a Green Beret–advised outpost, back from the Bassac River, in a swampy area. While getting everything ready on deck to lift off, Harker had to call Saigon on the radio in the chopper to get permission to help the outpost. Anytime Vietnamese troops were involved, we had to call Saigon for permission to put in a strike. It took a while to get a response back. It always did. So we went ahead with the mission, as usual.

Upon arriving on station, we saw a disaster in process. Another clear night lit up by tracers everywhere. The Green Beret on the ground said that the VC were coming over the walls, and we were the fastest response he could get to help.

"Romeo One, Seawolf One-six. On station. Where do you want us to strike? Over."

"Seawolf, Seawolf, Romeo One! They're coming over the north wall! Hit the north wall! Over!"

"Seawolf One-six, Roger. We're rolling in!" Harker set up the battle plan with One-four, and we started our run.

I leaned out my door and opened up with my M-60, shooting forward. The red tracers lighting up after they left the barrel glowed beautifully in the night. To my surprise, some of them were ricocheting off the standing water that was around the north wall. I didn't know bullets would do that. I could see where the water was because of the reflection of moonlight.

Unfortunately, I couldn't see the VC except for the muzzle flashes.

With pinpoint accuracy, Harker launched four rockets right down the line of the north wall that had been marked by flares, with Seawolf One-four following right behind as soon as we broke left.

Leaning way out my door, left foot on the top of the rocket pod and my right foot stuck under my door seat, I was shooting between the skids, underneath our chopper, down at the green tracers flying up at us. I was trying to give us and Minahan some cover. Between the gravity pushing down on me from Harker's hard left turn and the 120-mile-per-hour wind, plus balancing outside the helicopter and fighting to shoot straight, every muscle in my body was stretched tight as a banjo string. About 374 on a stress scale of 100.

Once again, I felt Nimmo's penetrating eyes on me from the middle seat, waiting to see if I was going to make a mistake. Record was busy wearing out his machine gun because he had a bird's-eye view from his position.

Harker brought us around again for another run from a different direction. As guns blazed and rockets flew, my shin was introduced to its first rocket cap. Shit, that hurt! It was just like being kicked in the shins, but it burned at the same time. Wonderful feeling.

Breaking right that time, it was my turn to have the bird's-eye view as we broke away and started covering One-four. My barrel was getting white-hot, and the tracer rounds were starting to cook off before they left the gun. That made for a blinding red explosion at the end of the barrel as they departed. And it did wonders for my night vision. It was definitely time to change to a cooler barrel. That was my next job as soon as One-four was clear.

We had just about broken their backs with well-placed three- and four-dart rocket runs, the flex guns, and our door-gun fire. There were four rockets left in each bird, so we could do one more run. We pissed off Charlie good that night to the point that they forgot about the outpost and started shooting at us. Then they were on the run, back into the jungle.

Wallen was strafing the jungle below as we finished up the third pass when his flex guns on my side jammed. I had finished up, and had used my asbestos glove to change out for a cool barrel and was getting ready for the next pass.

"Seawolf, Romeo One! We're secure down here. You've got 'em on the run! Over."

"Romeo One, Seawolf One-six. Roger!"

"One-four, One-six."

"One-four, go."

"One-four, One-six. Continue orbiting, putting in door-gunner fire. We have to do minor repairs. Over."

"One-four. Roger."

I looked at Nimmo, wondering what Harker was talking about. Nimmo looked back, as if to say, well?

Nimmo pushed his ICS. "Well? Go fix 'em!"

"Fix what?" I asked, knowing, down deep, what he was talking about but not wanting to admit it to myself.

Punching me in the shoulder, he said with a grin on his face, "The flex guns, dumb-ass!"

"But the door gunner's belt won't reach that far outside. It's clear out on the end of the pylon!"

"No shit, Dumbo ears," Nimmo said.

I could hear Harker laughing. Thus my nickname went from Magnet Ass to Dumbo.

"Take the belt off and go out there and clear that jam!"

Okay, Seawolf! Time to gut it up and join the ranks of the few! I took off my seat belt, unplugged the ICS lead to my helmet, and slowly climbed out on the pylon in the pitch-dark with nothing to keep me from falling one thousand feet to my death. Then I slowly took the M-60s apart to clear their jams so they would work again.

Feeling my way along the pylon, fighting to keep my balance and stay in the proper position so the one-hundred-miles-per-hour wind would be blowing me onto the pylon instead of off into space, I reached the guns. No gloves on, because it was all by touch and feel in the dark, I slowly pulled the first gun open. Great! That one was easy; just a feeding jam. Pulling the bad round out of the feeding tray, I reloaded the gun with the belt of ammo coming from the metal feed line and closed down the top.

Now for the bottom gun. That's the one farthest to reach. Draping my whole body over the top of the guns, I stretched down to reach the problem. Opening the feed cover, I felt around for another feeder jam. No such luck. Now what? Well, I had to pull the back off, letting the insides out, and feel for a broken part. That's very precarious because it's spring-loaded, and if you slip, all the innards of the gun will shoot out the back, dropping into the darkness below, never to be seen again. I was moving my hands by walking my fingers along the gun like a spider, toward the back. The wind was incredible. It was like driving down the highway at one hundred miles per hour with your hand out the window while trying to do something with it.

Anyway, I slowly worked the backplate off, holding the recoil spring in place, and carefully letting the innards work their way out into my waiting hand. Feeling the parts as best I could, I discovered a broken recoil spring. Thank goodness, the insides of an M-60 are real basic. One bolt, the rod, and the recoil spring. Since I had one of each stuck in my armor-plate vest, I replaced the spring and slowly eased everything back into the gun. All the time, I kept flinching from the tracers coming up at us. Creeping backward, ever so slowly, I closed the distance between me and my door. Finally getting within reaching distance of the pussy pole, I turned to face forward and pull myself back inside. Not a smart move. I should have waited until I was closer or kept my face down, because as I turned around to face forward, the wind caught my helmet and blew my face mask up, just about pulling the whole helmet off. The surprise made me lose my balance, and my left leg slipped between the skids. I spun around, my chest hit just below my seat, almost at the floor, and I grabbed the seat with an adrenaline rush that could have snapped a steel rod like it was a pencil. Nimmo reached out and grabbed me by the back of my armor vest and helped pull me on in.

The guns were operational again. I resumed my puckered position in my seat, looked at Nimmo as he patted me on the back, then began blasting away again at the VC muzzle flashes on the ground.

"One-four, One-six. We are operational!" Harker said.

"One-four. Roger!"

We came around and put in one last strike. That seemed to do it. There weren't any more muzzle flashes or tracers coming up at us. Harker headed us back upriver to the LST.

All of a sudden, I got another lesson: a radio communication from Saigon denied us permission to engage the enemy at that location. That meant we couldn't log the mission! Damn! And I'd done so well, too. Well, all I can control is me! So, I did good! So, fuck 'em!

The night wasn't a total loss. When we got back to the LST, it was time to celebrate. I had graduated. Nimmo said that after the night's performance, I was on my own. I'd made it. I was part of the team for real. I was assigned Helicopter 303 and would fly with Harker. Engavo, the Indian, would be my crew chief.

The next day Harker came down to the crew's quarters and gave us a briefing on a special operation we'd be doing with a Green Beret strike force. They were going to be dropped off by a bunch of army slicks (that's a UH-1H-model helicopter that is designed to carry troops) to sweep a tree line separating two rice paddies.

This was a very dangerous area and was known for shooting

helicopters and anything else out of the sky. Matter of fact, a Det 1 gunner had been shot in the head there, Gibson's partner. So this mission was going to be personal. It was known as the Zigzag tree line.

It was suspected that enormous arms caches were in the area because that was where all the weapons coming from Dung Island were supposed to be going for further distribution. The Green Berets expected heavy resistance and wanted us on station as the sweep began in order to catch VC running out into the rice paddies before they could reach the jungle. Also, they wanted us to help point out potential trouble spots. I didn't know what they meant by that, because from the air you could see very little in that jungle. The canopy was just too thick.

Our orders were simple, Anyone who came out of the Zigzag and wasn't a Green Beret was to be killed instantly.

We took off into the blue sky. It didn't take us long to get on station. The Green Berets on the ground were already doing their thing. Those guys were good: not a whole lot of shooting, but a lot of results. They were doing the job, and by the sounds of it on the radio, having great success. There were quickly several Victor Charlie KIAs and many captured B-40 rockets and AK-47s.

The Green Berets had cut off all areas of retreat and had found the other end of the tunnel system that was hidden within the Zigzag, so there was no place for Charlie to go except into the hands of our guys or out in the open, into the rice paddies, and try to make a run for the other side and into the jungle.

"Seawolf, Seawolf. Bravo Three."

"Roger, Bravo Three. Seawolf One-six. Over."

"Roger, Seawolf One-six. Bravo Three. We've got a whole bunch of Victor Charlies *didi*ing [running] across the rice paddies to the south of the Zigzag. Can you intercept? Over."

"Roger that, Bravo Three. Seawolf One-six is on it! Over."

"One-four, One-six."

"One-four, go."

"One-four, One-six. Did you spot 'em? Over."

"Roger, One-six. We got 'em at our five o'clock position. Over."

Engavo piped in on the ICS, "I see 'em! They're at our four o'clock!"

"Seawolf One-six rolling in!"

"One-four, roger!"

Harker gave instructions that we weren't going to use any rockets as he broke into a sharp turn to the right, bringing all those moving black ants down in the rice paddies into our sights. Just the flex guns and our two M-60s. Save the rockets for anything that might pop up and surprise Bravo Three on the ground.

Down we went, toward the black-pajamas. We broke through eight hundred feet, and Wallen opened up with the flex guns. I cut loose with my machine gun, shooting straight forward, the brass ejecting inside the chopper as I held my finger down on the trigger, not letting up for anything, and watching my tracers scream earthward like a long stream of death toward the figures on the ground. Some of the VC were shooting their AK-47s skyward at us, some were shooting back into the jungle behind them, and some were just running for the other side. There must have been better than a dozen of them.

Between our flex guns and the M-60s Engavo and I were using, water was splashing all over the rice paddy where those VC surfaced. Several of them quickly dropped, turning the rice paddy water red around them where they lay. We couldn't tell who hit what because so many of us were shooting.

We came around for a second pass after Seawolf One-four made its run; there wasn't anybody left by that time, only one figure was running for the other side. He had an AK-47 in his hand. We made the turn to my side. Seawolf One-four had already flown over him and missed. Suddenly, while he was looking up at us, he threw his AK into the water of the rice paddy and let it sink, then snatched up one of the beaters rice farmers use to whack at the rice in the field and started to pretend he was a rice farmer. Even funnier, he kept nudging toward the edge of the jungle on the other side.

"Do you believe **that** guy?" I said, pushing the ICS.

"You know our orders, Dumbo! I'm bringing him up on your side. Take him out!" Harker said.

"Roger that! This is for Gibson's friend!"

"Seawolf, Seawolf. Bravo Three. Don't let that one get away!"

"Bravo Three, Seawolf One-six. He's toast!"

I opened up. We were about fifty feet in the air and about three hundred feet from my target. As my 7.62s reached their mark, the Victor Charlie disappeared into the cloud of rice paddy water that sprung up ten feet in the air all around him. But the mist subsided as my rounds were ripping through his body, instead of the rice paddy. Then we were one hundred feet from him, and I could see him jumping all over the place as more and more of my bullets tore through him and body parts flew in the air. I stopped shooting as we came up on him. By then he was just a mangled mess lying on the edge of the rice paddy dike, lifeless, looking something like a rag doll that had been ripped to shreds by a pit bull.

"Roger that, Seawolf! Bravo three, out."

My first confirmed kill. It's permanently etched in my mind along with those poor Vietnamese babies that had been tortured and butchered.

He had to be killed, because it was too risky in that area to land and attempt to hold him. Besides, he could have been booby-trapped. The Green Berets were too far away and would be at considerable risk crossing the open ground to retrieve him. Plus, they'd made it very clear that no one was supposed to get away. Besides, a lot of good Americans had been killed in the Zigzag. Including one of our family members. I had no remorse. Matter of fact, I was excited. War is hell not only because of what it does to us physically but also because of what it does to us mentally.

When we got back to the LST, we had another little surprise. A new gunner had arrived to begin his training. He had been dropped off by a PBR that had come down from Binh Thuy. Steve McAlester—we called him Mack—from Seattle, Washington, entered our life. He was about my height or a little shorter, and had blond hair. Skinny guy, but he could definitely hold his own in a fight. Steve had a great personality and was fun to be around. Searle became Mack's instructor.

Anyway, with Mack on board and all the introductions complete, it was back to work. Well, not all work.

In an attempt to give us something interesting to do, Harker got his hands on a small sailboat from the captain of our squadron in Vung Tau. Harker had a Chinook bring it out to the LST and drop it off. However, it didn't do too well on its first voyage because the current in the river was too strong to sail it. So much for entertainment. A sailboat was sitting in the holding area of the LST, and we couldn't do anything with it.

Chapter 6

Once again, Harker came down to the crew's quarters. Another briefing.

The special operation we'd taken part in with the Green Beret strike force was so successful uncovering arms in the Zigzag that a friend of Harker's, Lt. (jg) Richard Marcinko, was wondering where all these weapons were coming from.

Marcinko, with SEAL Team 2, thought since so much arms came from Dung Island onto the mainland, that perhaps, since the island extends out into the coastal waters, the arms were coming down the coast from North Vietnam by sub and were being unloaded on the island.

Marcinko and his team would be inserted on the end of Dung Island, and they would sit tight to see if they could catch Charlie in the act. When Charlie was caught, then we would be called in to hit him. The SEALs would board the LST that next night in preparation for the mission.

Just after sundown, four SEALs, two for each gunship, would be flown downriver to the southern tip of Dung Island and be dropped off in an area of very tall grass. We would fly low level all the way so Charlie couldn't tell where we were going. It would take just a second to unload our cargo, and we'd be gone. It should happen so fast, Charlie shouldn't be the wiser. He would just think one of our usual low-level patrols at twilight was trying to scare up some action.

Low leveling at that time of the evening, all the chopper's

running lights turned off, anybody trying to see us would lose us in the jungle pattern behind the choppers on the horizon as the choppers traversed down the middle of the river. The way sound travels with helicopters, you can't tell what direction they're coming from or where they're headed in the jungle. You know they're there, but where?

This was my first work with the SEALs. A great bunch of guys. Real friendly to us. They were part of that family I was talking about. I loved their toys. I hadn't ever seen an M-16 with an M-79 grenade launcher attached to it before. Then there was the Stoner. Basically a belt-fed M-16 with a one-hundred-round box magazine. I loved that little thing.

We were all down below having Cokes and waiting for the SEALs to arrive. Engavo was telling us about the time a Hollywood movie studio came to his reservation to make a western.

The deal was, the director told him and all his friends, that they were supposed to ride over the top of a hill, on horseback, and down the other side, attacking the wagon train in the valley below. He would pay them so much per person to do this. And anyone who volunteered to be shot off his horse would get paid double.

All was set. Everyone, including Engavo, came charging over the hill, like a bunch of crazed Indians, and down at the circled wagons. Then it happened! The first shot rang out over the valley. The one and only shot that was ever fired from the wagons at the Indians. Well, every Indian on horseback, including Engavo, fell off his horse, dead! The director had to come up with another plan.

Engavo was full of funny stories.

When all the laughter died down, I decided to go up to the flight deck and have a smoke. The SEAL team would be arriving before too long. It wouldn't be much longer before the sun went down, and we had to be ready to get airborne.

I broke the hatch at the top of our ladder and opened it up onto the deck. The heat and setting sun hit me in the face, and

I felt the kind of shock you get coming out of the movie theater after being in there for ninety minutes. Closing the hatch behind me quickly to keep the cool air inside, I pulled out a cigarette and Zippo lighter. As I lit that cigarette, I noticed three figures across the flight deck at our two gunships.

One was sitting in the door of the chopper closest to me, applying camouflage makeup to his face. The other two were standing next to him, their makeup already on. They were checking each other's web gear, to make sure their grenades and magazines were properly secure. All three wore tiger-stripe fatigues, and each donned separate headgear, a bandanna and two different types of floppy hats. The one sitting in the door had Stoner belted ammo fastened around him like one of Pancho Villa's bandits.

I stood there and watched. Interrupting them didn't seem like the correct thing to do. It was obvious that they were concentrating on what they were doing.

As I stood there, smoking my cigarette, Harker walked across the flight deck toward me, with Marcinko. Both were ready to go. Turning around, I opened the hatch and yelled down to the guys, "Hey, boys. Time to turn up the birds. They're ready for us!"

All the guys came running up the ladder and onto the flight deck. We went through the usual motions, untying the rotor blades, inserting the barrels, clicking down the rocket caps, and putting on our gear. Everyone was real quiet. Keeping the job at hand on the mind. Marcinko and one of his men boarded our chopper, and the other two got in Minahan's. I mounted up, got situated, stuck my barrel in, and flipped down the barrel lock. Looking past Marcinko, who was sitting next to me, and his partner, I gave thumbs-up to Engavo.

The sun had just gone down. We were all waiting for Marcinko's signal. He and Harker knew about how long it would take to reach the objective and how much light we would need to avoid flying into one another as we low-leveled to our target insertion. We knew that Marcinko would want to wait until the last possible second so that on insertion it would be at its darkest, consistent with safety.

Harker looked back at him. We were already turning up, just waiting for the high sign. Marcinko gave him the thumbs-up, and the chopper lifted off the deck.

Harker eased us over the side carefully because we were very heavy with our extra passengers. As we dipped down and almost hit the PBRs with our skids, I hit a seriously high pucker factor once again. We stayed near the surface and kept moving forward to develop some badly needed transitional lift. As we gained speed, we headed around the LST, then in one of the widest parts of the river, so we could orbit with comparative safety. Holding that orbit at about three feet off the water, we waited for Seawolf One-four to take off.

Making one more pass around the LST after Seawolf One-four fell in behind us, Harker pointed the team downriver toward Dung Island.

I kept my eyes on the shoreline constantly, with my M-60 up on my shoulder, looking for muzzle flashes just in case somebody decided to take a shot at us. We had a ways to go, but it didn't take long, as we weaved back and forth, just above the water.

Marcinko and Harker had timed the available daylight well. The deep twilight we were flying in reminded me of one night when we were playing ball as kids, and we were having so much fun, we didn't want to stop, but it was so dark we could hardly see the ball. But it wasn't *totally* dark, so we kept on playing. Then all of a sudden, we realized it *was* totally dark, and somebody was going to get hit in the head if we kept playing.

All senses were at a peak. I could have found the head of a pin with my asshole.

Harker hit the ICS. "Heads up, gentlemen. You got about a minute."

With that, Engavo and I gave Marcinko and his partner the high sign that it was time to get into position. Our passengers moved into the doors on each side. Marcinko was in my door in front of me, his butt resting on the floor and his feet on the skids outside. He was poised like a cat waiting for a mouse to pounce on.

I continued to scan the area, with my M-60 up and ready to shoot, with my third eye watching Marcinko, making sure his dismount was going okay.

Pulling a sharp turn to the right, we hopped up over the jungle and down the other side into a very small clearing that was completely covered with tall grass. I was concerned with the close proximity of the trees to the rotor blades as Harker brought the chopper to a quick flare. The tail dropped way down and the nose came way up. We slid across the top of the grass, blowing it down with the rotor blades, but still not able to see the ground. The chopper kept sliding along, like trying to stop a car on ice, until just before the stop was completed, Marcinko and his partner were gone. They disappeared into the grass below.

Seawolf One-four, close on our tail, was doing the same thing. The Blue Angels couldn't have done it any better, with just a few feet separating our two choppers.

Engavo hit his ICS. "They're clear!"

"Roger that," Harker answered.

Pulling on the power, we were instantly tipped in the other direction, nose down and tail up, zooming across the grass and up over the jungle on the other side of the clearing. I glanced back and saw One-four close on our tail. That was a good drop. Didn't take a half a second. I just hoped our guys were okay, because Marcinko really disappeared into that tall grass as he was falling.

I had no idea how long they were going to stay. Maybe just the night, maybe a week. We weren't privy to the intelligence they had on when the sub might arrive. Harker probably knew.

Our job was done, and Harker had us up to speed again. Unless Charlie was sitting right there watching us, he would never have guessed that we'd had time to drop anybody anywhere. After reaching the other side of the island, we turned upriver, still at three feet off the water. Guns still at the ready, we made a beeline for the LST. Things had gone really well. It appeared that it was going to be a quiet night. I started to let down just a little and rested my elbow on my knee. That M-60 was heavy.

We were almost back to the LST, and Harker was gaining altitude in preparation for approach and landing when we heard over the radio, "Seawolf, Seawolf. Silver Bullet."

My first thought was, Shit, they're in trouble, because that's the only reason they'd call so soon.

Harker, still gaining altitude, answered, "Silver Bullet. Seawolf One-six. Over."

"Seawolf. Silver Bullet. Request extraction, *now*! Over."

"Silver Bullet. Seawolf One-six. Roger. ETA five minutes. Over."

We were at about five hundred feet by then, as Harker pointed us back downriver and really poured on the coals. We were all wondering what had happened; we could tell by the voice that they wanted out yesterday.

It was totally dark, and the only help we had was that it was a full-moon night with clear skies. Finding them was going to be a challenge. Extraction wasn't supposed to take place this way. They were supposed to come out by boat after our strike, assuming they were successful.

I pushed my ICS. "How we supposed to find 'em?"

"Just keep your eyes peeled for some kind of sign!" Harker answered.

Upon arriving at the drop-off point, we stayed at about five hundred feet, which made us sitting ducks. Luckily, we had moonlight so we could keep our running lights turned off and still see well enough so as not to fly into each other. Well, not really, but with God's help, you can do anything.

We made a pass over the general area, M-60s at the ready. I just knew we were fixing to find ourselves smack in the middle of a shit storm. Just as my eyes began to hurt from staring so hard to catch a trace of their location, I saw a light at our five o'clock position. Minahan had already passed over them.

"I think I got 'em. Seawolf One-four just passed over them at our five o'clock. Looks like a flashlight or something," I said.

Harker brought us around to the right and lined on the little light blinking out of the darkness below.

We came in fast, One-four tucked in tight on our six. Sure enough it was them. We flared, and slid to a stop as I gave directions to their exact location. The trees were thicker there. I don't think it was the same place we'd dropped them at. Harker was very concerned with the clearance for the rotor blades as he slowly dropped the skids way down in the grass so Marcinko could reach them. This stuff was tall. Way over our heads. Watching the trees to make sure we didn't hit them, watching for muzzle flashes, and making sure we got our guys back on board kept all our senses working overtime.

Bullets slapped into our tail boom. Fuck me! "Receiving fire!" I yelled into the ICS. It was the first time I'd heard that sound. It was frighteningly clear and very loud.

Engavo and I cut loose with our M-60s, just hosing down the whole area as the guys jumped up for the skids and climbed in. Automatic-weapons fire was coming from *everywhere*. Engavo hit the ICS and let Harker know that our guys were on board and that we could depart anytime he was ready!

Marcinko was also shooting out my door into the tall grass. So was his partner on the other side.

"Seawolf One-six, One-four. We got our guys. Over."

"Roger, One-four. We're outa here!"

As we started forward to get that transitional lift, Wallen was spraying everything in front of us with his flex guns. I glanced over my shoulder to make sure that Seawolf One-four was following us out. They were. Along with their two SEALs, Record and Searle were firing like mad, too.

An occasional tracer flew past us, and muzzle flashes were scattered all around as we slowly climbed out of the area and up to one thousand feet over the river before turning toward the LST. It was a miracle that we didn't fly into each other in the dark with all our lights off. Minahan and Harker were really on that night. No injuries, no bullet holes, except for the ones in the choppers, and good old sheet metal will fix that.

Marcinko was very thankful! Evidently we had set them down in the middle of a bunch of VC. What are the odds? It sounded like a situation of who was the most surprised. But Marcinko was thankful for our quick turnaround. He told Harker, "Anything you want, you just name it!"

Jokingly, Harker mentioned that we had this little sailboat that we couldn't use because the current was too strong, and that it would be great if we had an outboard motor for it.

Marcinko said, "No problem."

About a week later a platoon from SEAL Team 1 came downriver from Binh Thuy in two SEAL team assault boats for a mission. On the back of one of the boats was a new fifty-horsepower outboard motor still in its crate, with "Binh Thuy Air Base" stamped on it. Harker really thought that Marcinko had just been kidding. We really got a lot of use out of that motor. It made that little sailboat really fly. When the LST moved up- or downriver, we'd get in that little thing and race ahead of the ship. When the ship was anchored, we'd use it as a swim platform and play in the water. It really took the heat off. One day, Harker, Gibson, and I spent a whole afternoon playing in our "SWAB"—Seawolf assault boat—and got seriously sunburned. Anyway, we never did find out if a submarine was bringing weapons down.

Backing up a little, I wasn't present when SEAL Team 1 arrived that particular afternoon with the boat motor. I had just finished my shift and was down below sleeping. The LST had moved upriver, closer to Binh Thuy and Can Tho. The SEALs were conducting a special operation up a particular canal that required their further attention.

It was after nightfall when I woke up. Rolling myself out of the rack, I took a shower, brushed my teeth, and threw on some shorts. Climbing the ladder and opening the hatch, I stepped out onto the deck for a cigarette. It was after dark, so I had to light my cigarette without being visible from the jungled shoreline. That would have made me a target for a VC sniper.

I was just taking my first, long drag when a face came out of nowhere, all cammied up, growling right in my kisser! I jumped like I was shot! The guy scared the shit out of me! That was my first introduction to Frank Sparks, one of the smallest SEALs in the teams at that time. Matter of fact, we called him mini-SEAL. A five-foot-two-inch badass motherfucker.

Sparky, as he was called, and I became real good friends over the next week. Between operations, the SEALs would come down and party in our compartment. We had beer hidden away down there for just such occasions. Sparky would swing around on the bunks like a little monkey. He was quite the acrobat, and very entertaining.

He told us stories about his dad and their friends in the circus and in the movies. He mentioned one of my favorites, *The Crimson Pirate,* with Burt Lancaster and Nick Cravat. Nick played Picolo, I believe. It was all very fascinating.

Sparky gave me a tour of one of the new LSSCs (light SEAL support craft). I hadn't seen one of the boats before. It had a radar dome in the middle; the steering wheel up front was also in the middle; an M-60 was mounted on each corner, and the whole thing was powered by two 427-cubic-inch V8s with dual-quad carburetors. They were very fast, and because of their jet pump drives, could do it in very shallow water. He gave me an overview of their weaponry, including the Stoner 5.56mm machine gun. It was a great weapon with an excellent rate of fire. I told Sparky that I wished our M-60s could shoot as fast. That's all it took. We spent an afternoon figuring out a way to make that happen. The solution turned out to be screwing two recoil springs together and installing them in the gun. It worked. Made my M-60 shoot a whole lot faster. I kept it that way the rest of my time over there.

The last night his platoon was there, Sparky asked me if I wanted to go in with them on their last mission. Just on the LSSC. I would take my M-60 and go in for the insertion and then back again for the extraction.

I jumped at the chance! What an experience. I'd seen it all from the air up till then. To see it from the other perspective would be great!

After it got dark, we slipped over the side of the LST and down into the LSSC. Nobody saying a word—me in my tiger-stripe fatigues with my M-60 and my Colt .45, the SEALs with their grenades, Stoners, M-16s with grenade launchers, and all painted up. Some were barefoot, some wore tennis shoes, and some wore jungle boots. Some were wearing hats, and some were wearing scarves. A couple had LAW rockets slung over their backs. They were ready for anything. I was on an adrenaline high.

Once in the LSSC, we headed upriver, still no one saying a word. We were really flying. The boat was fast but very well muffled; you could hardly hear the motors.

We came up parallel to a spot on the shore, then made a sharp left turn toward the bank. I was scanning for any movement and was ready with my M-60. I had no idea where we were going. All I knew was to watch and listen and protect the boat.

As I watched the bank, I noticed that we were heading for shore very fast. Just when I was getting a little concerned, straight in front of us I saw a little canal, not much bigger than the creek behind my house in Austin.

Into the canal we went. The jungle just swallowed us up as we shot up the canal at incredible speed. I looked up in the trees.

Way up in the trees. They were tall suckers, and the jungle was very thick. There was about ten feet between the shoreline and the boat on each side. Where the shoreline started, so did the jungle. I couldn't see beyond that. I almost couldn't see the shoreline.

I don't remember how late at night it was, but it was late. After ten, anyway. Well, the driver brought us to almost a stop, and we slowly drifted up to the bank on the left. I was on the right side of the driver watching the right bank. Sparky and the others were over the side and disappeared into the jungle without a sound.

The driver of the boat used the engines to turn us around slowly. It took him a minute, but he got us pointed in the right direction and accelerated down the canal and out into the Bassac.

It's time like that when all your senses are at a peak. You're conscious of your breathing, your heartbeat, but you're completely unaware of all the bugs and other minor distractions. I guess that's because your system has switched over to other priorities, like staying live.

Once we got out away from the insertion point and were headed back downriver with the throttles wide open, we could relax. The wind in our faces was cool as we watched the radar screen and returned to the LST. It was hard even to see the shoreline by then because it had gotten darker. Like clouds had moved in or something. We were just cruising, watching, and listening to the silence on the radio. Silence on the radio meant things were okay. When the SEALs used the radio, it meant that shit was going down.

It was quiet all night. Just before sunup, the driver and I crawled over the side of the LST and back into the LSSC. Away we went, upriver again to our rendezvous.

It was a different location from where we dropped them off. The canal we entered didn't go in as far as the last one, but it was about as small. The driver placed me on the left side that time because we'd be picking the SEALs up on the right. By the time we got there, it was daylight, and I could see the jungle on the bank.

I could hear the team whispering to the driver on the radio. They were telling him how much farther it was to pick them up.

"Just a little further, slow down, we're just to your right. Stop. Now just drift in."

I was watching the other bank but was also looking out of the corner of my eye, trying to locate them. I couldn't see them!

We slid into the bank, and they all moved at once. Shiiiit! They were standing out in the open on the bank in plain sight, but I couldn't see them until they moved. I was impressed. That was also very spooky.

The last one was in and pushed us off. The driver got us turned around, and out we went. As we cleared the mouth of the canal and came out into the open river, I felt a pat on my shoulder. It was Sparky.

"Well, what did you think of that?" he asked.

"I can't believe I couldn't see you guys. We were right next to you and couldn't see you."

'That's why I like doing this and not what you guys do. You guys are crazy. Everybody can see you!"

"Yeah, well, flying's my thing! By the way, what did ya'll do, anyway?" I asked.

"We left Charlie a little surprise. We booby-trapped one of his favorite things with claymores."

"Oh, the old fight-fire-with-fire ploy, huh?" I said.

"You bet your ass!"

More than a year passed before I saw Sparky again. I missed him and his antics.

Chapter 7

Monsoon season was upon us. The rain was very refreshing, but when it stopped, the incredible heat turned the atmosphere into a steam bath.

McAlester had passed his training and had made the team. He was flying with Searle, but occasionally, he flew with me. Gibson's tour was up, and he was returning to the World. Another new guy, Robert Hunt, had joined us. He was a first class petty officer jet mechanic, and Searle was training him. Record had also shipped out. Chief Walsh also checked out and headed home. He was the guy I missed the most.

That left us seriously shorthanded. Engavo, Mack, and me on one bird. Nimmo, Searle, and Hunt on the other. No problem. We could handle it. Just like we could handle the steam of the monsoon.

The rain had just stopped, and we were all on deck trying to clean our guns before it rained again. Wallen wandered over from the officers' side to inform Mack and me that we'd be accompanying him and Campbell to Binh Thuy to help cover for Det 7's "downed" aircraft. That's what we called a chopper that was unable to fly for maintenance reasons.

Minahan had also left for home, so Wallen had become Seawolf One-four. Campbell was going to be his copilot. Wallen had picked Mack and me for his crew on the trip, leaving Engavo home to relieve Nimmo on the other bird. Not that they could do anything without us, because SOP called for two birds to go on a mission.

Anyway, Binh Thuy and Can Tho were the priority. You see, the air force and the army in that area counted on Det 7 for their primary defense against mortar attacks at night. That's because Det 7 was based outside the perimeter at their own facility, next to the PBRs. The bases were frequently mortared after dark and the Seawolves had to scramble immediately to stop the attack. So it was imperative that a fully operational fire team be at Binh Thuy at all times. So Det 1 to the rescue.

This was going to be fun, because Binh Thuy had a great EM club where the SEALs and PBRs hung out. Our mission had party spelled all over it. Wallen and Campbell knew that, too; it is why they'd volunteered. There probably wouldn't be any mortar attack. They seemed to happen a couple of times a week, and scuttlebutt had it that the "quota" had already been filled.

But before we left, Harker decided that both ships would go. Why leave one gunship behind that was useless? He turned the mission into a little liberty trip for everyone. Smart guy. I guess that's why he was the CO.

We all piled into the two gunships and got to Binh Thuy just before sundown. It was a small place with a PSP pad just big enough for four gunships to sit on. There were two sandbag revetments and two air-conditioned trailers for the duty personnel to sleep in alongside the choppers. One was for the pilots and the other for the crew.

We didn't think it would hurt anything to go have a few beers with the SEALs. After all, it was still light out, and even if Charlie decided to hit the base, it would be much later that night. We'd be ready.

Besides, the likelihood of the base's being hit was pretty small. We'd just have a few beers with the SEALs. Of course, it's a law of Nature that *nobody* has just a few beers with the SEALs. Not in this universe.

Of course, we hadn't figured on the curse of Dan Magnet Butt Kelly either.

It was the party to end all parties. Engavo was really rolling with the stories. So was Nimmo. Our new guy, Hunt, was unbelievable. Mack and I just laughed until our bodies hurt. Searle sat back and, in between trying to stay straight and be a good leader, would let out an occasional scream of laughter. When the SEALs got started, we were all under the table. I think we put away enough beer to float the LST.

We all crawled back to our bunks and crashed. It was about 0100 (one A.M.).

At 0130—*kaboom!* A mortar crashed somewhere close by. Close enough to wake us all up. Then another. And another. Still blasted out of our socks, we staggered out of the trailer. I had my flight boots on and my undershorts, and that was it. Mack was standing next to me, in the same shape.

As I looked around to get my bearings, I saw Lieutenant Fury of Det 7 come out of the pilots' trailer. He had on his undershorts, Mae West, and flight boots with his .45 automatic out and waving it around, trying to keep his balance.

He was yelling, "Scramble the helos! Scramble the helos!"

He was just as blasted as the rest of us. Not a good sign when the pilots are drunk, too.

I looked at him, halfway laughing, and said, "Sir, is that a Scramble One, Two, or Three?"

Mack thought it was funny, but Fury didn't.

About then, Mack and I heard a crashing sound. As we turned around, we saw one of Det 7's gunners trying to get up off the ground with his pants half on and half off. He had evidently tried hopping out the door to the trailer with one foot in his pants while trying to put the other one in at the same time.

We started laughing. He didn't even acknowledge our presence. He just headed for the flight line where the choppers were. Mack and I were on his heels.

Arriving at the choppers, which were only about twenty

yards from the trailers, we started getting things ready for takeoff. At least Wallen and Campbell had their flight suits on. By the time Fury reached his bird, he had his on as well.

I untied the rotor blade and brought it around. Mack was putting the contacts down on the rockets, and the pilots were already starting the engine. Standing there in my undershorts, I looked up at Wallen and Campbell in the cockpit as I waited for the torque to pull the rotor blade from my hands. Both of them were grinning at me as they were desperately trying to concentrate on what they were supposed to be doing.

Once the blade was pulled from my hands, I leaped into my seat, and my almost naked butt came into contact with a very cold and wet spot. I was wearing only undershorts. It was your typical humid, cool night in the swamp, broken clouds with the moon peeking through.

I threw on my Mae West and stuck the barrel in my M-60. To this day, I don't know why I put my Mae West on and not my armor-plate vest. Must have been the drink.

The rotor revolutions per minute increased and so did the cool breeze. At least I wasn't barefoot. No socks, though.

I pulled on my helmet and pushed the ICS. "We're set back here! Clear left."

Mack said, "Clear right!"

Snickering a little, Wallen said, "Roger that!"

We pulled up into a hover check while waiting for Seawolf Seven-six to complete his. I was impressed by both Seven-six and One-four. Their hovers weren't bad! A little wobbly, but not bad, considering.

Seven-six, the fire-team lead, was all set. Away we flew into the night. It wasn't a very graceful departure. I am glad they didn't give tickets for FWI (or is it FUI?) in a war zone; we were all over the sky that night.

We spotted the muzzle flashes from the mortars once we leveled off at about eight hundred feet.

"Seawolf One-four, Seven-six. Over."

"One-four, go."

"One-four, Seven-six. Rolling in at one eight five degrees. Five darts and break right. Over."

"One-four. Roger!"

There were several mortar tubes down there for us to shoot at.

I leaned out and opened up with my M-60. Boy, did I get a surprise! As the machine gun fired, the hot expended cartridges ejected out of the gun and right into my chest, instead of the armor plate, which I'd left on the floor of the gunship. I just gritted my teeth and kept firing at the muzzle flashes below, and the hot brass continued to bounce off my bare chest and onto the floor of the gunship. We broke off the attack and came around for another one. More of the same. Shit, that stuff was hot. But not as hot as it was fixing to get!

On the third and last run, after the mortar attack stopped, I was shooting up a storm. My chest was getting numb from the hot brass, until my mind was completely distracted from that area of my body. Then a lone and *very* hot brass cartridge somehow made its way down my front and into my underwear! Holy shit! My balls! My balls! Shit, that's hot!

We weren't taking any fire, so I stopped and frantically retrieved the piece of brass. A night to remember. That was the first time I met "Mr. Murphy" in person. You know. Murphy's Law, if anything can go wrong, it will. I never made that mistake again.

On the good side, nobody got hurt on the base. All the rounds that were fired by Charlie fell harmlessly in empty places.

The next day, Det 7 got their bird up and running, so we returned to the LST.

Searle's training of Hunt was continued. Engavo was getting ready to head for home, and his replacement, Steven McGowan, from Florida, had arrived. McGowan would have made a great car salesman. Everybody loved him right away. No ego problem, just salesmanship all the way. He had the stuff to back it up, too. McGowan, Mack, and I were all about the same age.

Hunt was being trained to take Searle's place when the time came. Hunt was to become my second mentor, Harker being my first. About my height, or a little taller, Hunt was from Florida and married. He was a good money manager, had all the right habits, and was career navy all the way. He had a great sense of humor and was very likable. He was a natural leader and a fast study.

So now we were down to Searle, Nimmo, Hunt in training, me, Mack, and McGowan in training.

We were on a regular afternoon patrol trying to stir up trouble and get Charlie to shoot at us. I was flying with Harker and Wallen, with Nimmo training McGowan, who was riding middle seat. Searle and McAlester, Hunt flying middle seat, were in the other bird with Lieutenant (jg) Campbell and Lieutenant Commander Jerry Pratt. We received Pratt from Det 5. He was a supernice guy and an excellent pilot. Very good with the men. Definitely another Bill Harker.

There were monsoon rain clouds all around us, and Harker had the fire team dodging in and out of the storms. We were out in the middle of nowhere, halfway between the Bassac River and Vinh Long, when the storms closed in on us; visibility was zero, and we couldn't see our trail bird at all.

Harker ordered us to drop down and try to get under it. We did. About treetop level, we broke out. I'm talking palm tree leaves in the skids low. We found a clearing, an abandoned metal runway in the middle of a rice paddy. We had no idea where we were.

The team landed, and we closed up the doors and waited for the bad weather to pass. The rain was coming down in sheets. It was probably about half an hour before we could see anything beyond our little twenty-square-yard piece of real estate.

I was starting to think that we were going to have to abandon the choppers and swim home.

The storm finally subsided. Once the ceiling got above eight hundred feet, Harker decided it was safe to depart. Especially since we were exposed, immobile targets there, and still had no idea where we were.

Completing hover check, we turned the choppers into the wind and headed down the deserted runway, gaining altitude as we went. That's when it became obvious that we weren't in friendly surroundings! We hadn't been up for more than a few seconds when large volumes of tracers started whizzing by us.

Wallen, displaying his usual droll sense of humor, said on the intercom, "Patrol successful."

None of us bothered calling out "Receiving fire!" That would have been a little redundant. We had found the enemy. However, we were just a little overwhelmed by his response. There were a *lot* of bad guys out there.

Each gunner carried a smoke grenade for throwing when receiving fire. Almost immediately, four grenades were headed for the ground at the same time. It looked like an air show. Harker barked out the strike plan over the radio, and we all went to work. The visibility was better by then, but it was still raining.

"One-five, One-six. One three zero degrees, seven darts, break right. Over."

We were receiving very heavy fire, so Harker was going to get this over fast. He called for "seven darts, break right." Nimmo and I hadn't stopped shooting since the first heavy automatic-weapons fire had leaped up at us. We had to stand out on the skids to keep firing in the direction it was all coming from, because it wouldn't let up. The fire team needed protection as it rolled around into position for the strike.

As we rolled around into position and started our run, the rain on our bodies was like a million needles sticking us all at once. It hurt like a son of a bitch when I leaned out in that rain and fired my M-60.

Harker pumped off seven rockets on the first run. They screamed down toward the red smoke billowing up through the jungle canopy. Those four smoke grenades did the job marking the target. And, of course, we couldn't miss seeing the tracers flying up at us. This whole thing was done at about five hundred feet or so. That ain't far away.

The rockets smashed into the jungle, then exploded. The rockets were half high explosive and half white phosphorus. We broke off our attack, and Seawolf One-five was right behind us, plowing their rockets into the jungle below. But the incoming didn't slow down the fire leaping up at us at all.

Nimmo and I were changing barrels like crazy. Things were heating up in the back of the chopper as well as on the ground. By this time, two barrels were cooling off in my rack, and I was working on the third—leaning outside, shooting down between the skids under the chopper, out back behind us underneath the tail boom, everywhere. As fast as we quieted one stream of tracers, another one struck at us from somewhere else. Our adrenaline would jump in and out of overdrive when we heard the occasional *bang* of an enemy bullet ripping through the aluminum skin of the helicopter.

We put in one more strike. Harker launched the rest of our rockets and broke off to cover our trail bird. By this time, I was completely outside, one foot on the rocket pod and the other pushed under the seat to brace my shin against it. I faced backward, shooting over the top of the pylon that holds the flex guns and rocket pod. I could see the whole target area and Seawolf One-five was finishing up her strike. She desperately needed help in covering her ass on her break, because we were still taking all kinds of fire. Nimmo was blanketing the jungle area underneath her from his side, and I was doing all I could from mine. As I put in M-60 fire right underneath her to cover their break when we hit an air pocket, my foot slipped, and so did my gun. Bang! I hit the pylon with one round of my M-60. And that one round penetrated a hydraulic line.

In horror, I watched hydraulic fluid spray into the air behind us. Quickly, I swung back inside.

"I hit the hydraulics! Turn off the hydraulics now!" I yelled over the intercom.

Harker did so immediately.

That was our training. If we saw a leak like that, we had to turn the hydraulics off to save what fluid was left for landing, because you can't land without it. Well, we could, but we had to do it like an airplane because we couldn't hover.

Well, the strike was over, anyway. We had taken several hits, but they were just cosmetic. Seawolf One-five had exited the area safely. We detoured to Vinh Long to check out the hydraulics.

You see, this kind of thing had happened before. Not by me! Anyway, this is the argument the brass like to use when wanting us to mount our M-60s instead of freehanding them. Those of us in the field, however, knew that the risk of something like that happening was more than balanced by the increased cover we had with a freehand M-60.

If our M-60s had been mounted, probably one of us, if not both, would have been shot down for real in that firefight instead of having to land at Vinh Long. I'd much rather slide in on metal skids at Vinh Long than put it down in the middle of the shit storm we just flew out of.

Harker called ahead, so the field was ready for us when we got there. Fire trucks everywhere. Crash crews all waiting with their fire-retardant suits on. It was almost dark as we made the approach.

Harker had us lined up for a perfect approach like an airplane. We were doing a smooth and level sixty knots, but we had to keep it straight and slide in on the runway with our skids, in case there wasn't enough hydraulic fluid left in the system to keep adequate control of the chopper.

Seconds before we touched down, Harker had Wallen turn the hydraulics on. When the metal skids hit that metal runway, the sparks really flew. But there was plenty of fluid left in the system to help us land safely because we had turned it off so quickly. We slid to a stop, and everybody converged on us in seconds. All was well.

We spent the night in Vinh Long while the chopper was fixed. That gave me the chance to visit two of my old buddies from Vung Tau, Page and Schaffernocker. They had finally received orders to a combat team. That team was Det 3.

We had our fair share of beers that night. Of course, the main topic of discussion was my little mishap. We weren't worried about having to make an early departure the next day, because Harker was meeting with the SEALs on what we had run into. So the order of the day was: Party!

Unfortunately, our sleeping in was cut short by a very large *bang!* About 0800 hours, Charlie hit us with six mortars. Two of the six hit just outside our bunker, which was also our sleeping quarters. Just enough to rattle the new guys. Since I wasn't a new guy any longer, the noise just disturbed my tranquil time. I rolled over, pulling my blanket over my head, and thought briefly of that guy I had noticed back in Vung Tau when I went through my first mortar attack. Couldn't get back to sleep, though.

So I decided to get up, found Page and Schaffernocker going over their bird, and talked them into going to breakfast with me. That didn't take a lot of effort. But we soon found out there was a big difference between army chow and navy chow! At a later date, when I was back at Vinh Long visiting for some repairs, Page, Schaffernocker, and I broke into the army chow hall late at night and made up some *real* breakfast. The army stuff came out of the same boxes the navy got its food from; the army just didn't know how to cook! That was a black op to remember!

After breakfast, I met up with Harker and the rest of the guys. As we pulled preflight on the choppers, Harker told us that the SEALs were going to plan an operation in the area we'd been shot out of to see what they could find.

Chapter 8

Back at the LST, the monsoon season was still very active. Rain was falling like crazy, the river was up and moving very fast. The LST had to move, and it looked like if we didn't do something with our SWAB, we would lose it to the storm.

Harker came down to the crew's quarters and asked for a volunteer to sail the SWAB with him over to the Coast Guard base to ride out this bad weather. Well, I loved the water. Any chance to get wet, and I took it. He had his volunteer.

In our SEAL trunks, barefoot, and each of us with an M-16 and a bandolier of magazines thrown over our shoulder, we went over the side of the LST, down the chain ladder, and into the SWAB. It was in the middle of the day, but it was raining so hard we could barely see the riverbank. The raindrops were huge but very cool and refreshing. The wind was blowing like mad, and the brown river water of the Bassac was churning. It had one hell of a current.

Harker got the motor started and gave me the sign to untie us from the LST. He turned us downriver toward the Coast Guard base, and away we went, like shot out of a gun, going with the current. We would return after the storm had passed and the LST was anchored.

The ride over to the base was exciting. While Harker was steering, I was bailing water as fast as I could. The rain was still coming down hard, and water ran in my eyes constantly.

When we made the turn into the canal that led to the Coast

Guard base, I thought we were going to capsize because the river was so strong.

We drew a lot of attention as we pulled up to the dock out of nowhere, in shorts, M-16s, and a civilian sailboat with a big-ass motor on it. That was fun. I always liked making a big entrance and drawing attention to myself. Once we got the boat secured and out of the weather, the Coast Guard guys had some nice hot coffee waiting for us.

We didn't have to stay too long, just an hour or two until the weather looked like it had passed. Harker had talked to the LST by radio, received its location and found out they had anchored, so it was time to hit the road. We said our good-byes and thanked the Coast Guard for the coffee.

Jumping back in the SWAB, we made our way up the canal and out into the main river. It was really a neat little boat, and I was having a blast. Just cruising upriver with my face in the wind, getting hit by an occasional spray of water and thinking how cool it would be if we were on Lake Travis back home in Texas instead of in Vietnam.

Thirty years later, it occurs to me we weren't being very smart; we didn't have a radio! There we were, a Seawolf lieutenant commander and his door gunner, out in the middle of the Bassac River in a dinghy with a badass fifty-horsepower motor, no backup, and no way of calling for help. Well, what the hell, we were having a good time!

While we were running at full speed upriver, we ran into a school of sea snakes, thousands of them. So many, in fact, that they got tangled up in the propeller and stalled the motor. We couldn't get it started.

So there we were, adrift in the Bassac River, surrounded by thousands of very poisonous sea snakes, and in a war zone with no radio. And what were we doing? Laughing! Trying to decide who was going to put his hand in the water and clear the prop so we could restart the motor and continue the journey back to the LST. The laughter stopped abruptly when from the shore we heard the crack of an AK-47 on full automatic, and the water around us shot up as the 7.62×39 rounds cut into the Bassac River. Harker thrust his hand into the murky river water infested with snakes, worked the dead carcasses out of the propeller, and yanked on the cord, starting the motor. I cut loose with my M-16 on full automatic, pointing it toward the jungle onshore where the enemy fire was coming from.

Hitting the gas and thrusting the little boat forward, Harker yelled, "Next time it's your turn to clear the prop!"

We sped upriver and away from the AK-47s' fire while I went through five of my six M-16 magazines on full automatic. Barrel of my M-16 smoking, I sat back in the boat and looked up at the sky, watching blue occasionally peek through. Harker was focused on the river ahead, anxiously scanning for the LST.

He spoke first. "There she is!"

I rolled back over and looked forward. Yup, LST, dead ahead.

Harker pulled us up next to the chain ladder and our docking spot. I tied us up, and we climbed back aboard.

Now, that was an adventure!

That about did it for the monsoon season. It was back to hot and dry. No more rocket runs with little raindrop nails hitting us in the face for a while.

It was chow time on this beautiful afternoon, and they were having my all-time favorite, hot dogs with chili and cheese, and french fries on the side. One thing about the navy and the LSTs, the food was great.

We Seawolves always got head-of-the-line privileges because we never knew when we would get scrambled. I had just filled my tray with two beautiful hot dogs and garnished them perfectly with just the right amount of chili and cheese. The cheese had melted down around everything, and the fries were salted to perfection. The smell was enough to give me an orgasm. Hunt was standing next to me in line and was making fun of me because he knew how much I loved hot dogs.

"You know what those are made out of?"

"Yes," I said, "and I don't care!"

Bong! Bong! Bong! "Scramble the helos, scramble the helos. This is a Scramble One, Scramble One!"

Shit! I couldn't believe it.

Hunt started to laugh. "Just your luck, Dumbo."

My big Irish ears struck again.

Abandoning our trays, we ran for the choppers. Three minutes, and we were lifting off. Harker briefed everybody on the situation in the air.

A small town nearby was under attack. Cu Lao Rong was a walled village of some size, just off the Bassac. Building-to-building fighting was being conducted. The ground troops were units of the U.S. 9th Infantry and some ARVNs. North Vietnamese regulars had pulled a midday raid. When we got on site, army Cobras were already putting in strikes.

The VC were inside the town and causing all kinds of problems, while the NVA were mounting an attack to hit the main wall to the village. They had moved mortar tubes into the jungle at the edge of town and were hitting the side of town where the 9th Infantry was. The Cobras were working on the mortars in the jungle, so we turned our attention to the main wall, which already had a large hole in it.

This was going to be a challenge for One-six. The town was divided into two parts—a wall surrounded the entire town, and a bigger wall went around the larger of the two parts. So a large wall separated the two halves, and civilians were on both sides of it.

Our guys were in the larger part, taking out the VC, a little at a time. The NVA had the smaller part and were fixing to rush the hole in the bigger wall to enter the part the 9th Infantry was in.

The problem was, no matter which direction we shot our rockets, the aim had to be dead on or we were going to have a lot of dead and injured civilians. And if the NVA were to make it past the wall, part of the 9th Infantry and a lot of innocent people were going to be in a lot of trouble.

Hunt, Mack, McGowan, and I were shooting our M-60s like crazy, trying to keep the NVA rush to a minimum, but there were just too many. Plus, we were taking fire to beat the band. We might as well have been using a paper cup to bail out the *Titanic*.

Harker called out the strike: "Seawolf One-four, One-six. Four darts and break left. Over."

We came in right over the top of the larger half of Cu Lao Rong, shooting straight at the open space in the wall. Beyond the wall were NVA and the other part of the town. If the rocket undershot, we hit the town; if the rocket overshot, we hit the town.

All of us were firing our machine guns forward when Harker squeezed off the first rocket.

Shit! What the fuck was that?

Harker hit the ICS. "Oh no! Jesus, don't let this happen!"

One of the rocket's fins came off in flight! We watched in horror as the rocket dropped short, dived into the village, jinked around a couple of buildings, down a street, around a corner, back up, and then down, right into the mass of oncoming NVA, exploding bad-guy body parts all over the Delta.

Harker quickly regained his composure and squeezed off three more rockets, all of which hit in the same spot. We broke left and kept the machine guns shooting. I believe we all were thanking God for that one! Harker had said the magic word that made it all happen.

After four direct hits, the NVA split. One-four came in right behind us and placed all four of their rockets in the same spot. Charlie sat up and took notice, and one of the army Cobra pilots came up on our push and said, "Seawolf, Bad Dog Three. Damn nice shooting! Over."

We were still taking ground fire, and the NVA mortars were still doing their thing, when a 9th Infantry person came on the radio and said that he had two ARVNs who needed medevac immediately, but there was no army medevac available, and the two soldiers couldn't wait.

Well, the two-seat Cobras couldn't do it, so that left us!

But with all our armament we were too heavy, so we used the rest of our rockets on the area around the wall, doing cleanup work. Then, a bit lighter, we headed for the location in town, on the larger side, where the medevac was needed.

Our trail bird covered us while we landed on a soccer field between several tall palm trees and two large pagodas. We had to come in high and then hover down into a hole. Occasional sniper fire was rather distracting on the approach. As we hovered down into the soccer field, all kinds of paper, trash, and dirt got sucked up by the rotor blades and thrown down through them, all over us. It was a real mess. But what made it worse was that the mortar tubes were dropping rounds on us as well.

Jesus, get us the fuck out of here! I couldn't see where to lay down suppressive fire because of the trash flying everywhere, and the mortar rounds were putting nice divots in the soccer field, tossing dirt all over the place, which really improved my vision. There was a sniper or three out there taking shots at us from somewhere, and I was helping the VN wounded aboard a chopper that probably wasn't going to make it out of the hole because it was too heavy! It's not that I'm into negative thinking, but shit, this was getting ridiculous.

Finally the two wounded were secured in our chopper, and the 9th Infantry guy was backing away from us per my official U.S. Navy hand gestures meaning "get the fuck out of the way so we can get the fuck out of here!"

Time for another miracle, Jesus! We were way heavy with

the wounded, and had no running room to get transitional lift. Pulling up into a hover, Harker slowly backed us up until the tail boom was hanging out over the fence at the end of the soccer field. He was almost cutting a groove in the palm trees beyond the fence with our tail rotor.

Watching behind us, holding my M-60 up at the ready in case I could get a look at that sniper, I finally hit my ICS button. "That's it! We can't go back any further!"

"Roger. Okay, boys, it's up to Jesus from here on!" Harker said.

Pushing the chopper over and pulling all the power that it could muster, we started racing across the soccer field. Faster and faster. All of us adding all the body English we could, to help us up over the tops of the tall palm trees at the other end of the field. I could tell by the way Harker was holding the collective that it wasn't looking good. We got closer and closer. I looked at the two Vietnamese wounded sitting between us. They had this look on their faces, as if to say, "You can let us off anywhere along here, boys. We don't need a ride that bad!"

Finally, we started coming up, but was it going to be in time? The helicopter began to shudder and Harker had the collective pulled up into his armpit. We were out of room! Shit! We're not going to make it!

Just at the last second, something seemed to just give us an extra lift, right over the top of those palm trees. Only one big leaf got hung up in our skids as we cleared them!

Airspeed up to par, Harker brought us around and pointed us in the direction of Binh Thuy.

Of course, as we climbed out, we became a good target again. So, opening up with our machine guns, we started hosing down the muzzle flashes below. My barrel was already white hot. Because I didn't think it would be safe, I hadn't taken time to change it when we went in for the wounded. So now tracers were cooking off in the barrel. After all we had been through, I couldn't handle the thought of us not making it out so I had to make the change in record time! Letting up on the trigger, I flipped up the barrel release arm, grabbed the white-hot barrel, tossed it into the cooling rack, grabbed a cold one, slammed it in, flipped down the barrel lock arm, and squeezed the trigger again, resuming cover fire.

Jeeesus! What did I just do? In my rush I'd forgotten the asbestos glove before I grabbed the white-hot barrel. But I kept shooting and started saying Our Fathers and Hail Marys like a good Catholic boy. I kept waiting for the pain to start, but it didn't come. Moments later, we were cruising comfortably at one thousand feet and out of danger.

The 9th Infantry guy on the radio said that they were just mopping up and that they really appreciated our help!

I sat back, put the M-60 in my lap, and slowly took off my melted flight glove. It came off in pieces. I didn't want to look at my hand, but I did.

Far out! Not a single mark anywhere. I looked over at our two passengers, and they were looking at me with their eyes so big, for a minute I thought that they were Round Eyes! They obviously were thinking the same thing as me. Unbelievable! Yup. No doubt in this soldier's mind. There *is* a God in heaven!

We got the two guys to Binh Thuy Evac Hospital and they pulled through.

Chapter 9

The next morning, we were out on the flight deck, pre-flighting the aircraft in preparation for a patrol, when we heard helicopters approaching. Then a voice out of the sky, as clear as a bell, saying, "Get up, get up. It's time to go get the bad guys!"

It was Det 7 from Binh Thuy showing off its new *chieu hoi* ("surrender") speakers.

During a *chieu hoi* mission, we flew over the jungle and played a Vietnamese tape over the loudspeakers, telling the VC that if they surrendered, we would give them money and food. We'd also throw out boxes of thousands of leaflets, telling them more of the same and where to go to give themselves up.

Laughing, Lieutenant Commander Pratt came out on the deck and told us that our speakers had been delivered the previous night by PBR and that we had to install them.

Well, this sounded like it was going to be interesting, putting speakers in the helicopter that we killed them from, trying to make friends with them, and talking them into giving themselves up. Yeah, sure. And I'm tall, dark, and handsome.

Who in the hell were they kidding? One more thing for Charlie to laugh at. The conduct of the war was just a bunch of bullshit! Let's hear it once again for managing from the top down, boys!

But far be it from us to ignore Saigon's think tank. We

mounted the speakers, big suckers, too, hooked up the tape recorder and microphone, and were ready to patrol.

Some of the time, we had a Vietnamese fly in the back with us. He used the mike to ad-lib while trying to talk the VC and NVA into surrendering. The rest of the time, we used the tapes.

Oh! And we don't want to forget the leaflets. Boxes and boxes of them. They said, basically, the same thing the tape said, but they had a map showing where to go. We just dumped them out the doors as we flew over, littering the jungle.

We did as we were told and used the speakers and "distributed" boxes of leaflets on all three patrols a day for over a week. The only time we didn't use them was when we went on a strike mission. That was the only time that we really disliked the *chieu hoi* mission, because the damn speaker system got in the way.

Returning from a strike mission, we were all down below in our compartment, bitching about the speaker system and listening to rock-and-roll tapes on the stereo. All of a sudden McGowan piped up, "Hey, guys, I got a great idea!"

Laughing, Hunt said, "Oh shit, do we want to hear it?"

"Listen, the next time we got a fire mission, let's take one of *our* tapes along!" McGowan said.

We all got real quiet. Looking at each other, we were all waiting for a response from Searle or Hunt.

Searle was the first. He started to giggle. "Shit, that's a damn good idea!" We looked at Hunt.

Hunt started to laugh out loud. "I like that a lot! Way to go, McGowan!"

We bounced it off the pilots, and they agreed.

The stage was set for some serious fun!

McGowan and I were flying together with One-four, Bill Wallen. One-three was Campbell. We had been called in to help the 9th Infantry flush out some VC they had cornered in a tree line up toward Binh Thuy. The plan was to rattle their cage with a couple of rocket runs.

Well, we rattled their cage all right. But it wasn't quite what they expected.

"One-three, One-four. Three darts, break left. Over."

"McGowan, you ready?" I asked over the intercom.

"Abso-fucking-lutely! Wait till Charlie gets a load of this!"

"Push Play on my mark," Wallen said.

"Roger that," McGowan answered.

"One-three, One-four is rolling in."

"Roger, One-four."

Wallen told McGowan, "Hit it!"

Crisp and clear, the best of Jimi Hendrix blasted out over the jungle as loud as the speakers and our amp could push it! Wallen punched off the rockets right in sync with the beat, and our M-60s pounded out their own tune as accompaniment.

The rockets exploded into the trees; then I saw something that I thought I'd never see. Viet Cong, in a dead run out in the middle of the rice paddies, dropping their weapons as they went. These guys were surrendering. Was Jimi Hendrix more than they could stand? Or was it just a coincidence?

"Seawolf, Seawolf. This is Delta Nine. Over."

"Delta Nine. Seawolf One-four. Go."

"Seawolf. Delta Nine. Is there any way you can corral those folks to give us time to get out there and take control of the situation? Over."

I hit my ICS. "Take control of them! What the fuck does he mean by that?"

"No problem, Delta Nine. We can handle it! Seawolf One-four, out."

Wallen, talking to us in the back as well as Seawolf One-three over the radio, said, "Okay, guys, this is what we're going to do. Use the door gunners to keep them together by shooting short bursts close to them, while we hover down and around them like we'd herd cattle out in Texas. McGowan, you keep that music going back there. One-three, keep our front to them in case we need to use the rockets at a moment's notice.

When I come around, take up a position at my three o'clock. We'll keep this up until Delta Nine gives us the wave-off. Now just follow my lead."

"Roger that, One-four!" One-three answered.

McGowan and I didn't have time to think about what was taking place; we were in it up to our necks!

Guns trained on all the black-pajama-clad characters, Wallen brought us around from our strike run and made a slow approach toward them, keeping the 9th Infantry at our five o'clock position. Campbell came around behind us and slowly moved sideways to our three o'clock, keeping the 9th Infantry on their seven o'clock. That way, if the shit hit the fan, everybody had a clear shot at the bad guys without endangering each other.

We couldn't see any weapons, but just as a safety measure, McGowan and I occasionally squeezed off a few rounds over their heads or along the sides of the group to keep them closely packed together.

It had occurred to us that we were really sitting ducks to anybody who might be in the opposite tree line. The exposed VC might just be part of an elaborate ambush.

Even so, hovering twenty or so feet off the ground for such a long time was starting to make all of us pretty nervous. I, for one, was real glad to see the U.S. Army emerge from the jungle behind us and surround the prisoners. They were all searched one by one and slowly ushered off in the direction of Binh Thuy. What a catch!

As it became obvious that our guys on the ground had things well in control, we killed the music and departed. From that point on we used the speakers to play rock music on all our missions until the navy took them away from us. I guess the word got out what we thought of management's ideas.

Admiral Zumwalt seemed to be the only one on top that was in touch with reality! He saved our asses from stupidity upstairs more than once.

Mel Gibson was in a movie called *Air America*. They played on a similar theme where a tape of war sounds was to be played over loudspeakers from aircraft to scare the enemy. A similar thing was done in *Apocalypse Now*. I liked our way better! It was like killing VC at a rock concert! What a trip. My God! What am I saying? This is not good.

Anyway, trying to get back to the point. The guys at the top got there because they were in touch with the bottom and knew what was going on. But once they'd been on top for a while, they lost touch, and suddenly they started making mistakes! They should have been spending most of their time *communicating* with the bottom, staying in touch. If they'd done that, they certainly wouldn't have spent money on speakers and tapes! In that business, if "they" fucked up, other people died while "they" stayed safe on top.

To make up for the speaker thing, Admiral Zumwalt came up with a great idea of his own. Down south were the Ca Mau Peninsula, Square Bay, Phu Quoc Island, and Ha Tien. No one had really ventured down there before. What if someone could put together a recon team that would be totally self-contained and have that team go exploring just to see what we might be missing?

Harker saw to it that morning arrived early, entering the crews' quarters for another one of his special briefings and telling us that we had to pack up everything because we had been temporarily assigned to an LST in the Gulf of Siam. We would be running missions into an area called Square Bay with the SEALs. Next stop would be Phu Quoc Island to Duong Dong Air Base. Finally, before returning to the Bassac, we would carry out one last project at Ha Tien.

The purpose of the reconnaissance was to look for POW camps. Our latest intel said that the VC were bringing prisoners from the north, through Laos and Cambodia, down to the south and into the areas we were being assigned to search.

It was also a very good day for my self-image to climb up a

few steps. I had gotten some stick time in the copilot's seat, with Harker as pilot. My old training, flying Cessnas in the Civil Air Patrol, helped out a lot because I picked up on flying the helicopter pretty quickly. I wasn't a regular pilot by any means, but in an emergency, I could probably get us down. You had to be familiar with handling the controls in the helicopter to qualify as a crew chief. And Searle felt it was time to promote me to crew chief of my own bird. I was also promoted to third class petty officer. Happy days! Steve McGowan was assigned to me as my gunner, and McAlester was flying with Hunt.

We packed all our stereo equipment and everything. Bill Wallen, Campbell, Pratt, and Soto took our two birds off the deck and orbited the LST so the army could land three H-model Hueys for our gear and those of us who couldn't fit in the gunships. Then our two birds landed, picked us up, and we left.

It was a long trip south to Square Bay and on out to the LST in the Gulf of Siam. We flew in formation with the army choppers the whole trip, making a fuel stop at Quan Long to hand-pump our own fuel into all four choppers. That part seemed to take forever. It really made me appreciate the amount of fuel that went into those birds.

Once we got to the LST, the army choppers landed, and the ship's crew unloaded them for us. Then we came in, landed, and got settled.

It was really cool. The guys on the LST acted like they had never seen sailors like us before. They weren't quite sure what to make of us. We did look pretty ragged. The army pilots and crews had nice neat uniforms on. We Seawolves, on the other hand, never looked the same twice. We wore a variety of camouflage fatigues, mixed and matched. Some wore flight suits, some didn't. Some shaved, and some didn't. Some cut their hair, and some didn't. Some of us shaved our heads and grew Fu Manchus. Any look that would scare Charlie.

The LST was much bigger than the one on the Bassac River. The flight deck was bigger, too, so Harker decided that we

Harker piloting our Huey up the Bassac on patrol.

On patrol north of Dung Island. Note the four hootches visible through the Plexiglas.

The hydraulics after I lost my footing. Note the flex-gun ammunition feeds above the cylinder.

Record (up top) and Nimmo carrying out an early-morning inspection before a patrol along the Bassac.

I'm holding the B-40 launcher captured during the Green Beret sweep of the Zigzag tree line where I got my first confirmed kill.

Me and my pilot, Pratt, the night after we rescued the Vietnamese and I got shot in the hand.

The dock where the sick little girl was handed aboard the helicopter.

Swift boats tied up alongside the LST the day after the battle of the 43 Boat. There are bullet holes in the gun tub and pilothouse of the 21 Boat. The hatch on the 38 Boat was hit by a B-40 rocket.

Some of the orphans on Fuqua Island we gave Christmas toys to.

Me (left) and Hunt (right) cleaning weapons under Searle's watchful eye.

Bagley (right) looking for a good shot for his Instamatic.

Me (left) and my gunner, Valladares, below in our quarters. They make 'em big up north.

Bud Barnes down in the enlisted quarters, as usual. Fine pilot, great leader.

Mack (left) and I in the Gulf of Siam.

Lieutenant Commander Habicht, our fearless leader, ready for action. Super pilot and loved by all.

Rick "Mad Man" Saddler with his usual grin. On the far side, in the pilot's seat, "Wild Bill" Wallen is slouched. Both were great pilots, and we crewguys would have followed them anywhere.

Mack Thomas, without cammo makeup and tiger stripes.

Brocheux in his Cayuse. A very brave man and a guy I'll never forget.

Brocheux flying into Hai Yen, RVN Marines in the foreground.

Me in the movie *Born on the Fourth of July*. I hated wearing the Marine uniform, but I got to spend four days with Tom Cruise.

Me and my partner at work. I'm the short one. I figured if I had only one leg, I'd better compensate by being one strong son of a bitch: that's about sixty pounds of muscle I added since Vietnam.

Belle and I out on the ranch in West Texas. Who says having one leg slows you down?

could turn up both choppers at the same time with no problem. That really cut down our scramble time. Not to mention quick turnarounds.

We had just about settled in when the SEALs came aboard. It was meeting time, but we helicopter crewmen weren't in on the big planning session, just the pilots and SEALs. We would be briefed later.

From what I understood, intel the SEALs had gathered led them to believe that there was a large concentration of POW camps on the Ca Mau Peninsula and that the area was an R & R location for Victor Charlie. The idea made sense, because the United States didn't have anything down there. The area was wide open.

Our two gunships and the SEALs hit the locals fast. Parakeet hops, body-snatch missions, and rocket fire from a rocket cruiser offshore. Then along came the Swift boats—they could kick VC ass with those .50s. We were used to having the PBRs with us all the time, but there weren't any down south. But those Swift boats! Man, they were somethin'! Big suckers. Like the old PT boats of World War II. Good old Admiral Zumwalt! He knew how to throw a party and plan an op, God bless him.

The body-snatch missions were successful. We got wind of a very large POW camp in the area, and serious numbers of bad guys.

A beautiful sun rose over the Gulf of Siam, exposing a clear blue sky. It was going to be perfect weather for the day's operation. We were up on deck before the sun had arrived, pulling preflights on both aircraft. The SEALs were at Hai Yen getting ready. We had commandeered an army H-model Huey and its pilots to carry the entire SEAL squad to the target that morning. We would be meeting up with them in the air over Square Bay. Our target was a very large POW camp in the Nam Can Forest, just off a major canal.

Harker and Pratt walked out to see if we were ready to go, then placed their maps and mission notes in the cockpits and went over the operation with us one more time. There's no such thing as being overprepared.

All things in order, it was time to hit the sky. McGowan and I got Seawolf One-six's flex-gun barrels clicked in and the rocket caps down while Hunt and Mack took care of Seawolf One-five. All the pilots in their birds and situated, the rotor blades were untied and brought around front.

A beautiful tropical breeze was blowing across the deck as the jet engines on both helicopters began to spool up. As I stood there, waiting for the main rotor blade to be pulled from my hand, the thought hit me once again that it was a beautiful place for a resort. It was just gorgeous there. The water in the gulf was a magnificent aqua that sparkled beautifully in the morning sun. My daydreaming shattered when the rotor was yanked from my hands! Time to get back to the business of hitting that POW camp and getting our guys out.

I strapped myself in. We were ready. This was going to be fun. The first time two gunships would take off at the same time from an LST.

Up, up, and away we went, One-six and One-five into the wild blue yonder to rendezvous with the army's Bravo Six. Both gunships over the side of the deck at the same time, turning in opposite directions, banking around the LST and falling into formation, one behind the other on the other side, headed in toward Square Bay, three feet off the water. We were in for a wild ride.

To help pass the time while waiting to meet up with Bravo Six, I kept going over our equipment to make sure everything was in order. All five barrels were in the cooling rack, M-16 loaded and ready, M-60 loaded and barrel properly locked in, spare parts in their proper place and easy to get to, flex-gun ammo trays strapped in solid, M-79 and grenades at the ready, smoke grenade ready, pussy strap fastened around myself, plus our latest addition: two cases of WP (white phosphorus) and HE (high explosive) grenades sitting between McGowan and me. We were ready!

It was about time to try to spot Bravo Six. He would be coming from our ten or eleven o'clock position and low, just like us. We weren't supposed to get above three feet the whole operation.

Leaning back against the fire wall behind me, I tried to relax and scan the horizon for Bravo Six at the same time. Usually, when I'm relaxed and not trying real hard to see something, that's when I see it. Sure enough!

Hitting the ICS foot button: "Bravo Six at our ten o'clock!"

"Roger that. I see 'em!" Harker answered.

We were flying trail bird that day, and Pratt was flying lead. The army slick with the SEALs slipped in between us. We would follow the winding canal the POW camp was supposed to be on.

The jungle line beyond the beach was coming up fast. Time to get set. Bringing my M-60 to the ready, I started scanning the area for movement. Being in the trail bird made for a good view of what was going on. The army slick was in front of us, and One-five was in front of it. Watching, as the mouth of the target canal appeared in the jungle line on the beach, was spectacular.

"Keep a sharp eye, boys. We're going in!" Harker said on the ICS.

McGowan and I said we were good to go.

Swoosh! Up the canal we went. Three feet off the water. We had to look up to see the tops of the trees. What a rush! God I loved that! Every muscle was tight as a banjo string. My M-60 was up and ready as the three choppers dipped and swayed back and forth, following the canal. Around to the left, then a tight bank to the right. The jungle came right to the water's edge on both sides. I had not a single thought of it being a jungle paradise! The only thought I had was total focus on I better see him before he sees me, and how fast can I get my machine gun on his ass!

Another sharp turn to the right, and then we were yanked back to the left, the rotor blades popping loudly with the rapid changes in direction. Still no sign of life. Just solid thick jungle. The canal we were following was about 150 to 200 feet wide. From our briefing, I had a general idea about how far the camp was. We had to be getting close.

Sure enough. We were there. Banking left, up and over the trees, then down into the village, we took up orbiting positions to watch and cover the SEALs while they were on the ground. One-five was to break off and take up an orbiting position, low level to the north, and we would do the same to the south; at the same time, the slick would land, and the SEALs would sweep the camp. One-five had already started its move when we broke into the clear. The slick on the ground was just starting to lift up, and the SEALs were already spread out, hitting the hootches. I kept my focus on the SEALs and their perimeter to be able to give them cover fire instantly as needed.

In order to keep a clear eye on our guys as they continued their moves, Harker had to bring us up a little more than was comfortable. If we stayed right on the deck, the jungle trees would obstruct our vision. And that was just unacceptable! That's why we got paid the big bucks, to hang our asses out at fifty feet off the tops of the trees and be sitting ducks for the VC. We could be taken out with a slingshot at that range.

Sitting there, trying to relax and keep those eyes active, concentrating, holding that heavy M-60 up at the ready, fighting the G forces as we circled, waiting for the call for extraction was tough. That was when all the training at Coronado paid off: I was at peak physical fitness, otherwise I couldn't have done it.

Continually scanning the camp for sign of hostility, I was impressed at the speed with which the SEAL squad had fanned out to cover the area. We had a great view of what was going on. The army slick had gone up to fifteen hundred feet and orbited the area while waiting to be called for pickup.

The waiting period was surprisingly short.

"Bravo Six, Sidewinder. Over."

"Bravo Six. Go."

"Bravo Six, Sidewinder. We've got all we need. Extraction now. Over."

"Roger. Bravo Six en route!"

I was always impressed with the SEALs on the radio. Of all the groups we worked with, they were the most fun to listen to. There was a monotone, whispery stealthiness about them. A calmness and control; imperturbable, like a piece of cold steel. They were not trying to impress, but they did. Even when shit was coming down around their ears. They didn't even have to use a call sign. I could tell a SEAL was on the air by the way he talked on the radio.

The army slick came in low and fast, flared, and the SEALs were on board in a twinkling of an eye. No prisoners! I wondered what the story was; not a shot fired, and we're on our way home.

Our exit took us out low-level, just the way we came in but on a different route. We stayed over the jungle, skimming the tops of the trees all the way to Hai Yen. Once we arrived and landed, the news was out. We had just missed the prisoners. Bowls of soup were on the dinner tables, still hot. Fires burning. Everything was in its place but there were no people, no prisoners. They had been moved out through an elaborate tunnel system that the SEALs discovered at the last minute. Knowing it would be futile to explore them with just seven men, they opted to take what intel they had and visit another day.

What they'd found were schools—four- and five-story buildings hidden under the trees we were flying over so that we couldn't see them. School papers they found showed that they were teaching their children math: one dead American plus two dead Americans equals three dead Americans. Jesus, and our people think TV is bad for the kids.

They couldn't have had much warning. The only thing we could figure was coastal lookouts spotted us coming in or the Vietnamese Kit Carson scout the SEALs were using was a double agent. We'd have to come up with another plan or catch the scout in the act.

Chapter 10

It was dark out, and that big LST was doing its best to rock us to sleep in the middle of a huge storm. It was raining hard enough to make Noah take notice. Welcome back to Vietnam, Mr. Monsoon.

I really liked the season. Of course, I've always loved anything to do with water. Didn't much like doing gun runs in the rain, though. I could do without the needle-strikes to the body when leaning out the door at better than one hundred miles per hour.

The rocking of the ship was great. The red lights were on, and all of us were tucked in tight, dozing in and out of La La Land, dreaming of other places and times. I was cruising the main drag back home in Austin with my new GTO convertible, all my old high-school friends around me helping celebrate my heroic return from Vietnam.

GTOs and teenage beauties falling in love with me dissipated rapidly as I came conscious to "*Bong! Bong! Bong! Scramble the helos! Scramble the helos! Scramble One! Scramble One!*"

Flying to my feet, I jumped into my tiger-stripe cammies, pulled on my boots, and sprang to the ladder. I was first to pop my head out the door and into the red lights of the flight deck. Everyone else was clambering up the ladder right behind me.

It was spooky up on deck. All I could see was what was lit up by the red deck lights. Beyond the deck was darkness like

153

an inkwell. The ship was pitching violently from side to side in the rough seas, and rain was still falling. An occasional wave leaped out of the night and washed over the deck. It was really creepy.

The ship's crew was up to help us on our first scramble since we'd arrived. Not wanting to be washed over the side, I worked my way carefully around to my side of the helicopter. I placed the flex-gun barrels in and locked them down, followed by the rocket caps. McGowan was on his side doing the same. One of the ship's crew worked his way across the deck from the other side and presented me with a case of flares.

"I was told to give you these. They said that you were going to need them for this mission."

"Thanks, man. I appreciate it," I said.

Placing the case between McGowan and me, I couldn't help wondering what we'd really need them for. Pop flares? What kind of scramble is this?

That thought was interrupted by another that had a little more importance to it. Damn, this boat's rocking *bad*. I could feel the helicopter trying to slip over the side, but we had it chained to the deck because we knew that the storm was coming. Well, shit, what are we going to do when we unchain it so we can leave? About then Harker showed up.

He took one look at my face and said, "I have a plan!"

"Somehow I knew you would!" I said.

The "plan" was to have the shipboard sailors stand on the skids after we turned up the aircraft. Then we'd unchain the skids, jump in our seats, and as the pilot lifted the collective, all the sailors would jump off the skids and run like hell out of the way. Then we would take off. Of course, we'd be operating under the assumption that the weight of the sailors was enough to hold the chopper still until we were ready to take off. I sure was glad Harker was close to God. 'Cause that was the only way his plan was going to work. Plus, I could see us losing some guys over the side as they tried to get out of our way. Those boys should have been getting a medal for that duty.

Untying the blade, I walked and slid around to the front of the bird and hung on for all I was worth while Harker turned up the jet engine. McGowan was in his seat ready to go. Wallen, Seawolf One-four, was all set with his crew. This was *not* the time to scramble both at the same time. Once we made it off, then Wallen would go.

Finally, the torque pulled the blade from my hands, and I walked, slid, and stumbled back to my place in the chopper. Rotor revolutions per minute reached takeoff speed, and the skids were unchained. Even with all the sailors standing on the skids, we were slipping a little, but not too much. Harker nodded, and McGowan and I waved everybody off.

Wow! Talk about a slip and slide. We did that and more, but Harker soon had us under control. What a pilot! What a guy! Oh, and thank you, Jesus!

Keeping my eyes on the instruments as we disappeared into the night sky, I could tell all was normal, and we were climbing out just fine. No horizon was visible because of the storm, so we were on instrument flying rules (IFR) only. Harker put us in an orbit around the LST at about seven hundred feet while we waited for Wallen to get airborne. That's when he told us what we had been scrambled for.

Evidently, the Marines were in on this, as well. Leatherneck Six was a recon platoon that had been staking out Square Bay for a while. Watching at night mostly, using their starlight scope. Well, they had caught Charlie red-handed that night. A whole flotilla of junks was crossing Square Bay under cover of the storm. The VC knew that even if they were seen, there wasn't anybody crazy enough to fly in that weather and come after them.

They didn't know us vairwee well, did they! That's what the flares were for. The lead chopper was going to pop flares over the target area so the trail bird could see the bad guys and put in strikes. Once they were done, the other bird would pop flares while One-six went turkey shooting over the barrel.

This is going to be some serious fun! We'd pop flares first. Once on location, McGowan and I would alternate the flares out each side while One-four sent her fourteen rockets and eight thousand rounds of 7.62 hailing down on Charlie's unsuspecting head. Hunt and Mack were going to go nuts.

"Leather Neck Six, Seawolf One-six. We're on station. Over."

"Roger, Seawolf. They're right in the middle of the bay heading away from us. There are no friendlies. I repeat. There are no friendlies. Just a ton of supplies. Over."

"Leatherneck Six, Seawolf One-six. Roger!"

The ceiling was about one thousand feet, and it was still raining. We were over Square Bay, trying to get an eye on the junks or very large sampans. They had to have heard us coming by then. McGowan and I were ready in the back, flares in hand.

"Seawolf One-four, One-six. Are you ready and do you have me in sight? Over."

"One-six, One-four. Roger!"

"McGowan, Kelly; I think I see them. Start popping the flares," Harker said on the ICS.

I went first. Pop! Out it went with a sparkly trailer as it flew down until the parachute opened. Jeesus, did it get bright. There went my night vision! Then McGowan popped one. Man, it was like in the middle of the day. I could see the whole bay. Shit! Including the whole VC navy. To this day, I don't know how many there were, but it was a lot.

Wallen, quick on the trigger, had already sent two rockets into one of the larger boats. McGowan and I weren't doing anything. Just popping flares and watching the show. And what a show it was. Hunt's and Mack's tracers, along with those from the flex guns, were just going everywhere. Each machine gun just picked a boat and did its best to sink it.

I hit the ICS button. "McGowan, did you see that secondary explosion? My God, that was incredible."

"Jesus, Kelly. They probably saw that back on the LST," McGowan answered.

Tracers were coming back up at us, but most weren't even close because we didn't have running lights on anymore. Sure, they could see the sparks from an occasional flare when we popped it out the door, but that wasn't enough to allow them to get a bead on us. One-four was at a slightly lower altitude while putting in his strikes, and he didn't have any lights on either. We really had the advantage for once. They tried hard to escape us, but their boats just kept going down.

The water there in the bay was a lot calmer than it was out in the gulf, and the wind wasn't near as strong either. That made for better shooting. Between the secondary explosions and the flares, we had enough light to see a lot. Which made the shooting go even better.

Finally it was our turn; One-four was out of rockets.

All right, slide the flares out of the way and get that M-60 up at the ready. Harker rolled us around, and we started down as One-four went up to one thousand feet and started popping flares.

It was incredible. I had a hard time picking a target, there were so many good ones. Oops! That was easy. Get the one that has the most tracers coming up at you. I was really whaling away on this one big boat that was giving us a lot of fire, and with all the light, I could see the damage I was doing. Big chunks of wood were flying up in the air mixed with water as my rounds cut through the boat and out the bottom. Then all of a sudden, *swoosh,* there goes a rocket, followed by another close behind. Then there was a huge blast where the boat used to be! Thanks, Harker!

I chose another boat and kept at it.

One thing that dawned on me over there was that you had to keep your sense of humor about what's happening and what you're doing or you'd end up a head case with permanent nausea and persistent vomiting.

We had an incredible field day that night. Secondary explosions touched off everywhere. What a turkey shoot. It had to have been some kind of record for just two gunships. All the rockets were gone, and almost all the M-60 ammunition was expended, and all the sampans and junks were on the bottom. It was time to go home.

Leaving the land behind us, we flew straight out to sea, to where the ship had been when he left it. We had been flying for a while when Harker said, "Hey, anybody see an LST?"

Nobody was laughing. My job as crew chief was to help watch the gauges, and I knew we didn't have much fuel left. We were getting very cold and very wet, and we were flying just under the clouds, looking for lights from the ship. The weather was getting worse, and the ceiling was getting lower. Then we were at about four hundred feet just cruising out into nothingness. I had no idea what kind of plan Harker had for this one, but I hoped it was good. The idea of having to ditch in that weather was not very pleasant. I love the water and all that, but this was ridiculous. Harker turned on all our running lights and the spotlight so we could see the condition of the gulf below us. The swells I was looking at had to be thirty feet or better.

Then we were running on fumes. No fuel was registering on the gauges at all, and McGowan and I were preparing for ditching, ready to throw out the doors everything that's not tied down. That included the rocket pods, barrels, anything that would make us lighter. I was sure that Hunt and Mack were doing the same.

All set. The only things we were wearing were our tiger stripes and Mae Wests. Boy, what I wouldn't have given for some swim fins just then.

Suddenly "Seawolf One-six, One-four. We've got it in sight!" came the call from our trail bird.

Hunt had seen the LST and pointed it out to Wallen. It was way off to our three o'clock position. Could we make it in time?

Thank you, Jesus, we did. If we had to ditch, at least it would be next to the ship.

But the LST was a very scary sight. The flight deck was tossing violently to and fro, more than it had been when we left, and if it was at too high an angle, the tail rotor would hit the flight deck if the chopper wasn't timed perfectly with the rocking of the deck.

Another problem that came to mind was the danger of the chopper's sliding over the side. Once the choppers were on the deck, there'd be nothing to keep them there. Same deal as when we left, but worse.

One good thing was that we were so much lighter than we had been when we left: no fuel, no ammo, no rockets, no rocket pods, no flares, no shit! We'd slide off the deck so much easier.

Harker told the ship our problem, and they got the biggest, heaviest guys they could to volunteer to try to catch us, weight us down, and chain us to the deck before we went over the side. They managed it with two teams. One team would run out to hold us in place while the other team followed with the chains.

Wallen went first as we all held our breath. Watching him try to synchronize his chopper with the rocking of the LST while all those brave sailors ran out at the last minute to strap it to the deck before it went over the side was the most hair-raising experience of my life. Remember, the whole time this is happening, the helicopter is running full speed. These sailors were doing good just to keep themselves from ending up in the drink, let alone catch a helicopter.

Harker kept us in a very small and slow orbit about fifty feet off the water, watching Wallen's attempt to land, wondering if we were going to make it to our turn before we ran out of fuel and had to ditch.

I kept watching and praying the old reliable Our Father and Hail Mary from Catholic school. The night was so dark and cold and wet, it could have been the perfect nightmare except for the fact that it was real. I started to shiver, and the shivers reminded me of Coronado. I wished I was back there instead of looking down at the huge black swells under us.

Then Wallen touched down. He made it! Somehow he made it! The sailors grabbed them and chained the chopper to the deck. Thank you, Jesus!

Then it was our turn. Technically we were out of fuel and should have been treading water or drowning. We were hovering toward a tossing flight deck lit up by red lights. I was still praying, and I was sure everyone else was, too. Harker slowly brought us over the flight deck. What was scaring me was the fact that if the engine quit, we'd get a lot of people killed; we weren't over the water anymore. I could make out the shivering faces of the ship's crew as the men stood on the deck, chains in hand. The wind was howling and blowing the rain almost horizontal. Everyone was soaked, but the other chopper was tied down, the rotor tied in place on the tail boom, and the other crew was standing at the ready to catch us as we landed.

Harker started to rock the helicopter to synchronize with the rocking of the deck. Slowly he matched the rhythm and slid us onto the ship as everyone ran out and jumped on the skids. Even so, we slid several feet before the chains stopped us. Harker cut the power, and I was out in a flash to catch the rotor blade before it was damaged by the wind, only to find that Hunt had already covered that. We made it!

I don't know what your beliefs are, but I know that it was Jesus Christ that brought us safely home that night! If you're not a religious person, you'll find that you'll become one if you're ever in very many situations like that!

A few days after the storms had settled down, Admiral Zumwalt, in person, flew out to assess the situation. He arrived in an army slick and went on a tour of the area, sitting between me and McGowan, with Harker at the controls and Beem flying copilot. Harker and the admiral were talking about all the action we had seen since our arrival. The intel the SEALs had gathered so far was drawing a very interesting picture. The admiral was impressed with our results and was seriously considering a major naval operation in the area.

Phu Quoc Island was our next stop. The LST weighed anchor, and we headed north, toward the island and the edge of Cambodia.

I hadn't ever been on a cruise before. And the water was gorgeous. I'd never seen a color blue like that. The short jaunt up to Phu Quoc turned out to be somewhat of a vacation for us. We just lay out in the sun and enjoyed the cool sea breeze as the porpoises swam alongside.

Once we arrived, it was more of the same. The brass were making plans, while we took it easy. We had anchored at a very large navy base on the southern tip of the island. Our operation was on the northern tip at an outpost in the middle of enemy territory, right next to Cambodia.

This place was great. We commandeered an LCVP from the LST and went for an FGT (fucking good time). We took it out in the little bay we were anchored in and used it for a swim platform. The water was so clear you could see one hundred feet to the bottom. Good swimming that I'll never forget.

After two beautiful days there on the boat, it was time to depart for the outpost on the other end of the island. Another army H-model came aboard and picked up our supplies. We Seawolves followed behind in the two gunships.

The island was a mountainous, gorgeous, tropical paradise like one of the islands in Hawaii. It had a lot of continuous jungle, unlike the rest of the Delta on the mainland, which was mostly rice paddies with jungle between them.

Once we cleared the bay and where the navy base was, it was like we were on another planet. Not a living thing within miles. Just vast mountains and jungle with rice paddies here and there. Some in little areas in a valley, others terraced on the side of one of the hills. Apparently, no one was working in any of the few fields.

Flying on farther north, we finally came across a few small villages. The jungle came right up to the edge of them. I just couldn't get over how beautiful it was.

As we came over this last ridge of jungle, I saw down in the valley before us a stereotypical Special Forces–type outpost cut out of the jungle, right on the beach, with a PSP runway built down the outside of it, coming straight in off the Gulf of Siam. Twentieth-century technology stuck out like a sore thumb in the middle of this paradise.

Not too far from the outpost that we were flying over was a very large village intermingled with the jungle. Harker brought us around right behind the army slick and on final to the PSP runway. The H-model flared and pulled up to a stop, then slowly moved off to the left, facing the entrance to the outpost. He sat down in the grass and shut down his engine. Both our gunships followed suit.

The outpost was manned by air force personnel, a way station for planes to and from Vietnam and Thailand. Essentially, it was a gas station. C-47s, C-123s, Caribous, and C-130s all stopped there. An occasional Bird Dog would show up, too. But I don't think I saw another helicopter come through the whole time we were there. Air America made an appearance on several occasions with Fairchild AU-23A Peacemakers.

The air force dudes made us feel real at home, setting us up in a hootch and handing us a schedule of the chow times. We had to leave the choppers parked outside the outpost, which I didn't like. So we watched them ourselves. It was not that we didn't trust the air force to do it; it was a matter of who flew them. They didn't, and we did, so we'd have been just a little more comfortable if the choppers had been inside the perimeter. Oh well! The extra duty kept us alert.

The air force personnel said that they didn't go into the village much, but that it was supposed to be safe. A very successful Catholic mission operated there, and the mission ran a large orphanage. So Harker and I borrowed a jeep and drove into town to check it out. I hate to be redundant, but that place was just magnificent. Green everywhere, like a fantasyland. And everywhere we looked, we were greeted with a smile.

We found the mission, parked the jeep, and went in. The priest was easy to find because he found us. He spoke perfect English. He gave us a tour of the mission and the orphanage, where the kids were well behaved and very cute. A lot of them were refuges from the mainland, Vietnam and Cambodia both.

He told us that we would be welcome to come back anytime and that they were having a midnight Christmas service that he thought we would find very interesting. It obviously would all be in Vietnamese. We left with very light hearts after talking with him and seeing all those children.

I don't know how Harker pulled if off, but before Christmas arrived, he had crates of toys shipped in on a navy C-47 that we distributed to the orphans on Christmas Eve. All kinds of stuff but no metal toys, just plastic, rubber, and wood. Lincoln Logs, trucks, cars, dolls, rubber balls of all kinds, shapes, and colors. No toy guns, for obvious reasons. The kids' faces just lit up. I've always had a special place in my heart for kids. Couldn't wait to have some of my own. I don't know why. That's just the way I was. A lot of men don't seem to like kids. Not me. I get right down in the dirt and play right alongside of them. That one day's experience with the orphans made everything I'd experienced in the Nam worthwhile.

Harker and I were the only ones who stayed for the evening mass, which was just as spectacular as the priest had promised. On our way home, we stopped at the helicopters and spent some time looking at the stars. Harker gave me a combination Bible/astronomy lesson that was great. I loved hanging around smart people because I always envied them. I'd never thought of myself as being very smart, so I was always in awe of those who were. We finally got unwound from the night's activities and decided that we were dead tired. Entering the outpost, we found that everyone had passed out from overdoing their own Christmas party. But we decided that we had a lot more fun than the rest of them did.

The next morning, it was back to the usual. Christmas Day was just another day in the Nam. I don't think any of us gave it a second thought except Harker and me. I was out on the top of the helicopter inspecting the head while the others were giving the rest of the helicopters the once-over. Harker came walking out into the field and up to the chopper, saying good morning to everybody. He looked up at me, and I looked down at him, and we gave each other that Merry Christmas smile without saying anything. Then it was back to work!

But it was beginning to look like our whole mission there was going to be a bust. The SEALs hadn't called us once, and about a week had gone by. I wondered what Charlie was up to. We hadn't even gotten a mortar attack.

Several days later, when the sun had gone down but there was still light, the old orange sunset was doing its thing. Harker, Pratt, Campbell, and Bagley all came running out to the choppers. We crewmen had been sitting around smoking cigarettes and telling stories while watching the sunset.

Campbell yelled out, "Off and on, boys! The SEALs need us!"

We punched the endorphin dump switch, and the adrenaline hit high as four guys flew over two gunships like bees over a hive, getting them ready for liftoff. There was no wind at all, so we had just untied the rotors and left them alone while we got aboard. By the time the pilots were getting in, we all were already sitting in our seats, barrels locked in and contacts clicked down.

Harker had us up to speed quickly and pulled into a hover. Wheeling the chopper to the right, he nosed us over, pulled power, and we slowly gained speed shooting across the grass field, out across the width of the PSP runway, and up into the air, climbing out steadily, with Pratt right on our butt the whole way. We leveled off at one thousand feet, which had us clearing the mountains in front of us by about five hundred feet.

The SEALs were on the northeastern tip of the island, right next to the Cambodian border. They had evidently taken some small-arms fire from the hills above them and wanted us to saturate the area with rocket fire. They told us that there were Cambodian gunboats in the area, so we had to be careful.

As we came around the last hillside I saw two gunboats just off the beach, waiting to get a chance at shooting us down. They didn't like us very much. Maybe that's because we kept invading them, kicking Charlie's ass against the rules. Oh well! Shit happens!

"Seawolf. Snake Eyes. Over."

"Snake Eyes, Seawolf One-six. Go."

"Seawolf. Marking target with red smoke. Is there enough daylight left? Over."

"Snake Eyes, Seawolf One-six. Roger."

"Popping red smoke, Seawolf. Make strike just uphill from smoke. Over."

Harker brought us around and rolled in on the smoke. We could see it all right, but just barely. McGowan and I cut loose with our M-60s, Campbell opened up with the flexes, and Harker squeezed off three rockets. All of which hit right on target.

Pratt came in on our tail, punching his darts right on top of ours. It was a beautiful run. Textbook.

We came around for a second attack from a different angle. This time we were going to be dangerously close to the Cambodian border. I guess a little too close for the Cambodians, because we had just rolled in and away the tracers went. Big ones right past us and on up into the darkening sky. Jesus, they were bad shots. We just stayed on our heading and placed another letter-perfect strike on the side of the hill.

"Seawolf, Seawolf. Snake Eyes. That did it. Thanks."

"Roger, Snake Eyes. Be sure and ring if you need anything else. Seawolf One-six. Out!"

So much for our time at Phu Quoc Island. Rather uneventful, but stimulating. I'll never forget Christmas there.

The next stop would be Ha Tien, just across the water on the mainland next to Cambodia. We still had to find out where the NVA were coming across the border and heading down to the Nam Cam Forest. Some of the route they were taking was known, but not the part by the border. That was our next step.

It was time, and all was packed. While we were waiting for the army slick to arrive so we could load on our stuff, we found out that the Bob Hope Christmas show had been at the navy base on the southern tip of the island where we had been a couple weeks earlier. It was his last show before leaving the country. That sucked; one of the things I had dreamed about when I came to Vietnam was being at the Bob Hope Christmas show. We would have been able to go, too, because we weren't doing anything at the time and neither were the SEALs. Well, I guess it would have been anticlimactic after the Christmas Eve we'd had.

Our baggage carrier arrived. It didn't take long to get it all loaded. This time the army H-model wasn't coming with us; it was going on back to the LST on the Bassac with the guys who didn't have flying duty that day. They were getting off easy, too, because we would be separated for about a week. The eight of us would be living in the choppers for a week on the runway at Ha Tien, waiting for news from the PBRs or the SEALs. There really wasn't much at Ha Tien except a deserted runway next to a canal, and fifty-five-gallon drums of jet fuel and diesel fuel for us and the boats. Plus, another terrible excuse for mountains in the background. A C-130 would airdrop enough C rations and fresh water to last us while we waited.

Pratt, Campbell, Wallen, and Bagley were the pilots staying with us. McGowan and I were in Pratt's bird. Hunt and Mack were in Wallen's. It was going to be a long, hot, mosquito-infested week. After saying their good-byes, the rest of the Seawolves departed for the Bassac and home. We lifted off and headed for Ha Tien.

It was a short flight across the water to the mainland and our destination. We could see the Cambodian gunboats the whole way. You couldn't help but giggle a little bit at them. After all, if we really wanted to, we could cross over the border anytime, and they couldn't have stopped us. Which of course we did, but that's another story.

As we flew over the short PSP runway, I saw the PBRs tied up alongside where we would be parking our two birds. I've always wondered how the PBRs got there, because I couldn't see how they could take the high seas of the gulf to come around from the Bassac. Maybe they were airlifted in?

Pratt brought us in over the water, flared, and smoothly set us down on the edge of the PSP runway, next to the PBRs. Wallen pulled in on our tail and sat down. We dismounted, tied down the rotor blades, pulled the barrels, and declicked the rocket tubes. All the fuel drums had hand pumps, so we decided to take advantage of the time and top off the tanks. That way we'd be ready for anything. After all, a quick turn-around there would be one hell of a slow turnaround using hand-operated pumps and with no LST sailors to help out. Then we were ready: ammo, guns, rockets, fuel. Everything checked and double-checked. The waiting began.

The airdrop of supplies was scheduled for that afternoon. It was hot and still as we killed time with the PBR guys, smoking cigarettes, telling stories, and killing bugs. There really wasn't anything else to do. Ha Tien itself was far off in the distance, and there was no way to get there other than by walking, and that was too risky. So far as we could tell, we didn't have a perimeter guard. Just half jungle, half desert looking, and half mountain. It actually reminded me somewhat of parts of Texas. Maybe down in the valley.

Lying under the chopper, trying to get a snooze, I heard a strange noise. Like, like a C-130! That's it! The airdrop has arrived!

Sliding out from under my chopper, I covered my eyes to cut the sun's glare and peered into the sky looking for the beautiful bird that was bringing us chow. In case I failed to mention it earlier, we all loved C rations. And we were very thirsty. The C-130 had fresh water for us.

There she was, flying in right on top of us. That thing was low! It was the first time I'd seen a live airdrop. Just as the C-130 got straight above us, several very large bundles cleared her back end and deployed huge parachutes. As soon as the cargo was all clear out the back, the pitch of the engines increased as the big bird made a sharp turn to the left and headed toward Phu Quoc Island.

It took a minute for the scene to register in all of our minds before we came to our senses and broke into a run for the packages that were slowly dropping to the ground around us. They were coming down very close, probably because there wasn't much wind.

About an hour later we had everything unpacked and distributed, including a whole shitload of Budweiser beer. There was only one thing wrong! There was *no fresh water*! We had all the 105-degree beer we could drink for a week! C rations out the ass! But no water? Well, thank you very much, Mr. U.S. Air Force. Where were Harker and his plans when we needed him?

PBRs to the rescue. They were able to purchase, trade, or steal water from villages they stopped at while on patrol. It wasn't much, but it was better than nothing. The diet of Buds and C rats managed to kill anything that was in what little water we drank.

The nights at Ha Tien were still. Cigarette smoke rose straight up until it disappeared from sight. The only waver in the smoke was caused by a passing mosquito's wings as he flew by, carrying one of us home for a midnight snack. We had been issued insect repellent for protection. Right! Well, it worked okay to a point: the bugs came along, landed on me, bit the hell out of me, got himself stuck in that insect repellent, and died right there. So, by morning, I had all these insect corpses stuck all over my body. Made for an interesting cleanup job.

Our job was the usual during these kinds of operations. We were the cavalry that would be called in once contact was made. The PBRs or the SEALs would be doing the calling. Hopefully not both at the same time. I would have been a lot happier if they were working together like the way they usually did. I became very attached to the guys and didn't want to see anything happen to them. All of us felt the same way. However, there was just too much territory to be covered in a short period of time.

The SEALs struck out on their own in an LSSC and transported themselves to a point on the Cambodian border, while the PBRs did the same, but in the other direction, also on the border. The SEALs were doing a combination of setting ambushes and recon. The PBRs were just doing recon. Somewhere, somebody had to turn up something. It was just a matter of time.

But the days kept dragging on. What we wouldn't have given for a nice cool monsoon. No such luck. There was no place we could make ourselves comfortable: we couldn't nap because of the heat and the flies during the day, and at night it was the heat and the mosquitoes. If you weren't a smoker, it was a good time to become one: it helped to kill time, and the cigarette smoke seemed to keep the bugs away.

We talked a lot to make the days and nights go by faster. We had already worn out the usual popular stuff like women, cars, boats, planes, and motorcycles, so conversation graduated to where we were going for R & R. Our choices were Bangkok, Hong Kong, Tokyo, Australia, or Hawaii. The navy paid our way there and back, but we had to spring for the hotel, food, and "entertainment." Other topics discussed were: the first time we saw a girl naked, our first sexual experience, the places we'd all like to see traveling the world over. Of course, that led us into where would we like to live if you could live anywhere? Then it was what kind of job are you going to have? Are you going to stay in the service forever? Becoming a mercenary might be interesting. We had heard from people we met in Binh Thuy that the mercenary money was real good in Africa. Talking about money led us into discussing ideas for all of us getting rich and what that would be like. Then it was what our parents did for a living. How about why we thought the United States was in Vietnam, and the ethnic food we had been eating. What we thought of the Vietnamese people. Our first childhood friends we had and how we met them. The kind of toys we had as little kids, what kind of games we played, and the sports we got involved with. What we received for the very first Christmas we could remember. Our favorite colors, hobbies. By that point, clearly, we were getting desperate.

I'll tell you this, we became a close-knit group as much because of the boring time we spent together as the intensely frightening time.

By our last night at Ha Tien, nothing had happened. It was as if Charlie knew we were coming and just decided to leave. But not on your life; he was hiding, waiting for us to leave. They'd obviously been burned so badly at Square Bay that they were understandably gun-shy. Of course, they had no idea we were leaving the next morning.

It was after dark, as usual. The SEALs had finally gotten lucky and picked the right path to set up on. A column of NVA showed up. *Bam!* The SEALs hit 'em fast, then called us to cover the extraction. We were in the air in a heartbeat, adrenaline flowing, ready for a fight. If nothing else, it was refreshing to be up at one thousand feet where the air was actually moving, and it was somewhat cooler.

Pratt and Wallen had our two birds in formation, Pratt being the fire-team lead, just cruising toward the Cambodian border, zeroing in on the SEALs coordinates. McGowan and I were leaning out our doors looking for tracers streaking across the floor of the black jungle below that would tell us the location right away.

Nothing! No sign of 'em at all. Was the fight already over? I guess their extraction was smooth. Wait a minute! What the hell is that?

I had caught something out the corner of my eye just on the horizon. What was it? Shit! I know what that is! Its tracers flying everywhere like there's no tomorrow! But—but, could we be that far off course?

Pushing my ICS, I said, "Hey, check out the firefight going on like crazy way off in the distance at our nine o'clock! That couldn't be the SEALs, could it?"

Campbell said, "Fuck no! That's just about where the PBRs should be!"

Pratt, throwing us into a sharp turn to the left and taking up a heading straight for the tracers with Wallen's bird right on our butt, hit the radio:

"Snake Eyes. Seawolf One-five. Over."

"Seawolf. Snake Eyes. Go."

"Roger, Snake Eyes. We think the PBRs are in some serious shit. Do you still require our assistance? Over."

The PBRs cut in on our transmission: "Seawolf, Seawolf. Bravo Six, Bravo Six. We need help *now*! Are you in the air? Over!

"Seawolf. Snake Eyes. I copy. You are released. Go get 'em. Over."

"Roger that, Snake Eyes. We're clear. Bravo Six, Seawolf One-five. We are airborne. ETA your location three minutes. Do you copy? Over."

You could hear heavy gunfire in the background as the PBRs came back on the radio: "Seawolf, Bravo Six! I copy! Hurry! We need help fast! Over!"

I'd never heard a PBR sailor on the radio sound like that before. My body started to react, endorphins popping all kinds of circuit breakers in my system. I was getting very pissed. That particular firefight had taken on a personal note for all of us in the choppers. That hadn't ever really happened before, I think. That's probably because of the emotion that was expressed by the PBR guy on the radio and all the time we had spent with those guys this week.

Pratt had the chopper pushed over hard and was going as fast as possible. We all heard him give the ETA of three minutes, and we knew that he was stretching it a lot to give the VC something to think about if they were listening in, and also to try and help those guys in the boats with a little positive input.

It hadn't been two minutes since the last transmission. "Seawolf, Bravo Six. How much longer? Over!"

We still heard all kinds of fire in the background, but it would be another five minutes *at least* before we could get there. Pratt stalled his answer just a little longer.

"Seawolf, Seawolf, Bravo Six, Bravo Six. How much longer? Over!"

The tracers were flying everywhere and were easily visible by then. They were in it all right. We were all leaning forward in the chopper to give it all the body English we could.

Pratt transmitted, "Bravo six, Seawolf One-five. We're rolling in at this time. Over."

Rolling what? There was no way we could be rolling in; we were too far out. Then I remembered that Charlie might have heard us and, because of our reputation, he might back off a little.

"Seawolf, Seawolf. Bravo six! Roger that! Thanks!"

It worked! Almost all the green tracers stopped flying around! Pratt's ruse had bought us a little more time.

As we finally arrived on station, just an occasional tracer was flying around. The PBRs were slowly pulling out and Pratt was getting us set up for a strike, and McGowan and I were noting the locations of all the boats so we didn't hit them with any friendly fire.

Shit! Charlie figured out we were bluffing! They hit 'em again, but this time we could see the white flash of B-40 rockets as they zoomed out of the jungle and into the side of the boats. What they apparently didn't realize was that we were *really* there by then.

Pratt just nosed us over and barked out to Wallen, "Four darts, break right! Over!"

"One-four, roger!"

"Seawolf, Seawolf, Bravo Six. Where the fuck are you! Over!"

"Bravo six, Seawolf One-five. Duck! Over!"

We had Charlie dead cold in our sights. We were in the perfect spot when he opened up on the boats again, because we could see the individual muzzle flashes on the edge of the jungle next to the canal, and we were already facing him. His ass was ours!

Pratt took us in close, right over the tops of the PBRs. I was just saturating the enemy's muzzle flashes with my red tracers and yelling great obscenities as we went in closer and closer. We all were yelling as we went down, guns and rockets ablazing. I always counted the rockets as they went out so I knew when to give myself that little extra brace for the turn at the break. One, two, three, four. Wait a minute! Five, six, seven! What the fuck. Shit! There he goes on the break. I kept shooting. What's going on? As we retreated and I was outside on the pylon shooting back under Wallen's bird, I counted his. One-four put in seven darts, too! What the hell was going on here?

"Sorry, guys," Pratt said over the radio. "That was just too good a target to just use four darts. I couldn't stop."

"Roger that, One-five. One-four did the same," came back over the airwaves.

All the enemy fire had stopped now. Pratt decided to save the other seven darts in case Charlie got ornery again. He just orbited where the B-40s had come out of, and we put in door-gunner fire while the PBRs finished their departure from the area. We had no further trouble out of the VC.

"Bravo Six, Seawolf One-five. Over."

"Seawolf One-five, Bravo Six. Go."

"Bravo Six, Seawolf One-five. What's your status? Over."

A solemn voice came on the radio. "Seawolf, Bravo Six. We have four WIAs and one KIA. We need medevac as soon as we get back. Could you arrange? Over."

"Roger, Bravo Six. We'll take care of it. Over."

Talk about taking the wind out of your sails! That kind of communication does it. Four wounded and one killed. It could have been worse, but that kind of reasoning doesn't help the parents of the one who died.

Pratt called for a medevac right away. We got back to the field before the PBRs and filled up with fuel and rockets in case anything else happened. Once everyone had arrived, not much was said. Things were just taken care of. It was very quiet. The stillness wasn't even disturbed by the air force medevac arriving. They had space only for the four wounded, so the KIA became our responsibility. Or, I should say, we made him our responsibility. The operation was scheduled to end after that night anyway. Once the SEALs returned, we all mounted up and left for Binh Thuy. We took the fallen PBR sailor in our bird. The flight back with our comrade at our feet was very difficult. The poor guy had taken a direct hit by a B-40 rocket, and he never knew what hit him. God bless him; I never did find out his name.

By the time we flew into Binh Thuy, the sun had come up. The hospital had a vehicle there waiting to pick up the body. Again, it was very quiet. I don't know if it was a case of our not knowing what to say or just serious depression that kept the silence so strong.

As the hospital vehicle left, we heard the officers talking about some really good intelligence the SEALs had brought back from their ambush and how it would have a great deal to do with the brass permanently basing a detachment at Ha Tien at a later date. It looked like Zumwalt's idea was paying off.

We took the rest of the day off, got drunk in Can Tho, then got laid.

Chapter 11

The next morning we flew back down to the *Harnett County*. It felt good to get back to the Bassac. It was like home. The LST was smaller, but we liked it all the same.

One of the first things Harker did was have all the pilots practice turning up both choppers on the smaller deck together. He believed we could do the same on the smaller as we had on the bigger LST out in the gulf. They got it down real well. Then we started doing our quick turnarounds at the same time and starting up that way for the scrambles. As far as I know, we were the only team that ever did that. There was only eighteen inches clearance between the rotating rotor blades.

Once we got settled back in, we said our good-byes to Nimmo and Searle. I really hated to see those two leave. Especially Nimmo. He'd been my teacher, the first person who ever had any faith in me. He's also one of the guys we haven't been able to find. I hope after this book comes out, he'll find us.

The first replacement we got was a short fat guy. I have no idea how he ever got that far without having a heart attack. He spent about two weeks with us before he got canned. Never even earned his wings. He thought he was funny. He thought he was good-looking. He thought he was smart. He thought he knew it all. He had absolutely no people skills. To make a short story shorter, nobody wanted him around; he made for bad teamwork. Later, we ran into him at Vung Tau in the line shack, where he was telling lies to the guys he was working

with about how good he'd been out on Det. I didn't have the
heart to say anything. You know, that's funny. Back in 1969
when I came back, as far as many people in this country were
concerned, I was lower than whale shit. Now everybody lies
about being in Vietnam because it's become popular.

We got two more replacements, AMS3 Valladares and
AMH3 Fryburger. They both worked out great, caught on fast,
and made the team easily. Fryburger was a hippie dropout,
about my size, and a lot of fun to have around. Valladares was
another big guy, six feet five or so. Big, big, *big* guy! He was a
team player all the way!

Around ten or so one night, Harker came down to the crew's
quarters looking for two volunteers for a mission that was
probably going to get us in a lot of trouble. News had come via
radio from a Green Beret adviser in a local village that a little
girl had been gored by a water buffalo. They couldn't get anybody to respond to a medevac because it wasn't a military incident. But the little girl would die if she didn't get to the hospital
in Can Tho soon. Adding to the uncomfortable situation, there
was no outpost in the area, and the flight would have to be done
now, at night, with only one gunship, because it would be carried out against orders, and he couldn't justify risking both
birds. Well, I jumped at the chance to fly with Harker on any
mission; besides, his time was short, so I wouldn't have the
opportunity to fly with him much longer. Hunt was the other to
volunteer. They all wanted to go, but we were the first to jump.

All three of us emerged into the redness of the flight deck
from the lit cabin below. Wallen was already in the chopper
making preparations for departure. Great! One of my other
favorite pilots. We'd have the best of the best sitting up front.
This mission had success written all over it! Hunt grabbed his
gear out of the other helicopter and moved it into mine. We did
our thing with the rocket tubes and flex guns, untied the rotor
blade, and made ready for coming hot.

Harker and Wallen set, the rotor blade was pulled from my hands. I ran around to my side, climbed in, pulled on my helmet, slid the barrel into my machine gun, and locked it down. Hunt was giving me thumbs-up. I returned the same, and Harker pulled the collective. The shipboard crewman with the bright yellow vest and flashlights waved us into the night air. Over the edge of the LST we went, into the blackness of Vietnam.

It didn't take long to get to where the village was supposed to be, but it was so dark we couldn't see anything. When there's no moon out in Vietnam, it's like flying in an inkwell. All four of us were straining to see something, anything, a light of some kind to guide us in by. We had no radio communication with the ground because the Green Beret who initially called us was not even at the location; he'd heard of the injury from a very reliable source. Talk about sticking your neck out! For all we knew, the situation could have been a trap. Harker really had a lot of faith in that Green Beret adviser.

Finally, we could see lights. The villagers were waving torches at us, guiding us into the village, but we just couldn't see enough of the ground. Harker had us moving at about sixty knots by then. That's slow. And we were at about one hundred feet. So what to do?

Harker hit his ICS. "Guys, we're going to have to hit the spotlight to find a place to land. What do ya think?"

Hunt said, "We've come this far!"

"Let's go for it," I said.

"Why not?" Wallen said.

"Okay, kids. Keep your eyes peeled and your guns ready, because we're fixing to be the brightest thing in the sky and a Christmas gift of a target for somebody!" Harker said.

Three roger thats came back over the ICS, as we all puckered up and got ready. My M-60 was up, my eyes open and darting around the black night. Harker hit the button. Wow! It was like daylight beneath us. Jungle everywhere. There was absolutely no place to land! This village was built within the jungle.

"Lord have mercy! Do you believe this?" Harker said.

Wallen chimed in, "There's got to be a place to land somewhere."

Hunt and I just kept scanning the night for muzzle flashes. If we were going to get hit, our survival would directly depend on how fast we targeted them.

Wallen said, "Hey, I heard the PBRs come in here all the time. That means there's got to be a canal somewhere."

"And it stands to reason, if they come in here, there's also a dock!" Harker said.

As I was darting my eyes around the darkness out my door, I caught a glimpse of something below on the edge of the spotlight's illumination. It was the outline of a canal weaving under us.

I hit my ICS. "There's a canal right under us!"

"And I think I see a dock on my side!" Hunt piped in.

Harker said, "You're right. There it is. It's awful small, though. You guys think we can land on that? And the next question is, do you think it will hold us?"

Hunt and I looked at each other, shrugged our shoulders, as if to say who knows, and said, "Sure. No problem!"

We were thinking, After all, we've come this far. Let's go for it! I've come to the conclusion that's the best way to tackle life! One step at a time. We've come this far, let's keep going. That's the only way you can become a winner. If it's a wrong decision, then change to another direction and keep going. At least you're still moving forward. Those that don't always end up on Loser Street.

Harker started his descent to the dock while Hunt and I continued to scan the banks. We were also keeping our eyes on the rotor blades to make sure they were clearing the trees around our rickety landing pad. These were very close quarters. As he eased us just a few feet off the canal the water spray coming down through the rotor cooled us off real nice. Ever so slowly, we slid over onto the top of the dock as the skids of the chopper lightly caressed it. Harker lowered the collective gradually, and we heard the popping and creaking of the wood under us as the skids spread out under the weight of the gunship. We were down. The old dock was holding.

A little group came out on the dock with the injured girl. Hunt's side was facing them, while I was faced with dark jungle. Fighting to keep my concentration on my side and not look at what was going on with the people on Hunt's side, I kept scanning the never-ending blackness out my door for muzzle flashes or B-40 rockets at any moment. Remember, I'd met Marcinko's Mr. Murphy once, and I was damned if I was going to meet him again!

After just a few moments of popping and creaking of old wood, I felt the chopper lift off the dock. Out over the canal, past the misty spray of the water coming through the rotors, and up into the safety of the darkness as the spotlight was extinguished. I was finally starting to feel somewhat safe. Especially when we broke through one thousand feet on a course for Can Tho.

Relaxing and placing my M-60 on my lap, I turned and tried to see the passengers sitting on the floor between Hunt and me. The red lights from the instruments just barely showed the outline of a person lying on the floor and someone leaning over her; both were being blasted by the wind howling through both sides of the chopper. Long hair was flying in all directions, and their clothes flapped madly in the gale.

Harker brought us into Can Tho to a Vietnamese hospital landing pad, and we sat down smoothly. Doctors and nurses were waiting. Once we were on the deck, I could see our passengers clearly by the landing pad lights. The injured girl was very young and in some serious pain. Her mother had tears streaming down her face, holding on to that little girl as if to keep her soul from escaping her body. Blood was everywhere.

I broke into my usual Our Fathers and Hail Marys. I hadn't liked those nuns at Catholic school, but the things they taught me were sure paying off over here. When I didn't know what else to do and was at an emotional low, those prayers always helped. I didn't give that little girl much of a chance, though.

Once the medical entourage cleared away from the chopper, Harker had us airborne and on our way back to the LST. Would you believe it, that's when we all started to get nervous. We're in for it now. I wonder what they'll do to us for disobeying an order. I'd never done that before!

It was still dark when we returned to the LST, and all of us went straight to bed. Hunt and I didn't get up till past noon. We got away with that because everyone was told to let us sleep since Harker had to fly up to Binh Thuy for a meeting about what we'd done the night before. As it turned out, the little girl was the granddaughter of the district chief, and the rescue made us a lot of brownie points. Especially since she survived, and the doctors at the hospital said that if it hadn't been for us, she would have surely died.

On another positive note, the PBRs ventured into the area where we'd gone that night and paid said village a visit to follow up with some more PR. But one of the boats brushed against the dock we'd landed on, and it collapsed into the canal. All the wood was rotted totally through.

The more time I spent in Vietnam, the more I became a believer. Few knew that since I came on board with the Det, our little team alone had made over forty medevacs of civilian and military injured. And we weren't supposed to be a med-evac team, just a combat team.

Back to the usual grind. We heard that the SEALs were in the area doing some ops north of us. Then the LST moved upriver quite a ways and anchored. Rumor from the wardroom had it that the latest intelligence said that there was to be a big buildup of VC in the area that the LST had moved to. And it was supposed to be the same group we had tangled with last year, when I accidentally shot us in the hydraulics and we had to skid-land at Vinh Long. I'd love to get another shot at them.

Det 7 would normally have covered that operation because of how far north it was, but they had been moved to Ha Tien for a week to take their turn at those monkeys we left behind.

Both choppers were on deck, rotor blades untied because there was no wind, and we were inside the choppers waiting for a call from the SEALs. Eventually it got too hot, so we adjourned to the lower cabin and our stereo equipment and good old Coke! Some of us had received care packages from home, mine had summer sausage and pepperoni, with sardines, sharp cheddar cheese, and saltine crackers. Time for a feast and some tunes! There just ain't nothin' like a sardine, cheese, pepperoni, summer sausage, cracker sandwich, with a Coke chaser.

We were really enjoying ourselves in the air-conditioning, eating and listening to some serious rock and roll when the alarm sounded.

Bong! Bong! Bong! "Scramble the helos! Scramble the helos! Scramble One!"

I was surprised we got called so soon. The operation hadn't been going on very long. Unless it had started earlier than we thought. That was always possible. Anyway, when we hit the flight deck in a run for the choppers, it was dark out. I never could get over how neat the deck looked when lit up at night with the red lights. Sliding around my chopper, I hit the contacts down on the rockets, threw the barrels into the flex guns, and mounted up while McGowan was doing the same on his side.

Harker was already in his seat and yelling, "Coming hot!"

"Roger! We're clear!" I answered.

Wallen was in the other bird and was also starting to turn up. Our first double scramble. We'd been practicing the maneuver for a while. It would put us en route to the target in half the time. There were two LST guys on deck with yellow vests and flashlights to direct us and give us the go-ahead to take off together. Wallen would turn downriver and Harker would turn upriver as soon as both went over the side. That way, we didn't get any closer. Both choppers pulled up for hover check at the same time, just like in practice. Our LST friends in front of us gave the go-ahead, and it was over the side, once again into the darkness, both slipping in opposite directions. I kept my eyes on the red lights of the instruments, to make sure our rate of climb was correct. We could hardly make out any horizon line because it was so dark, and we didn't want any surprises like flying into the water at night. Harker brought us around and placed us on the heading for the SEALs while Wallen went around the other side of the LST and came up on our six o'clock. Once we leveled off at one thousand feet, Harker tried to get as much speed out of the Huey as possible.

Along the way, we were briefed on what was going on. Evidently the SEALs were trying to extract to or on their LSSC but were receiving heavy resistance. We had to give them cover fire so they could get out of the area. We weren't sure if they were back on their boat or not, but we'd be finding out soon enough. It sounded as if they were pinned down.

You could tell when we were close by all the tracers lighting up the night sky. Green, red, and white flashes were everywhere. It was all concentrated on one spot, and that's where the SEALs were. The adrenaline hit hard! Endorphins on an all-time high! How does that saying go? It's time to kick ass and chew bubble gum, and I'm all out of bubble gum!

The closer we got to the fight, the closer the fight looked. I mean, seriously close-quarters firefight! This wasn't going to be easy. I know we were designed for close air support, but this looked ridiculous.

"Shadow One. Seawolf One-six. Over."

"Seawolf, this is Shadow One. Use tracers as marker and strike as close as possible, ASAP. Over!"

"Roger, Shadow One! Seawolf is rolling in at this time. Out!"

"One-four, One-six. Five darts, break right. You copy?"

"Roger that, One-six. One-four is on your tail."

Harker hit the ICS. "Get your machine guns as close as you can get, but be careful! I'm putting the darts along the backside of the tracers."

"Will do!" McGowan answered back.

"No problem!" I said.

Harker nosed us over and down we went, aimed straight at the bundle of tracers exploding into the night like a very expensive fireworks show. I kept my tracers centered in the middle of the green ones. So did McGowan. The flex guns were following suit. *Swoosh*, there goes the first rocket. Then the next one and the next. The first one out hit right where it needed to be. Several green tracer streams stopped. Then the other darts started to reach the target. Huge explosions lit the night with great flashes of light, going off like huge flashbulbs. All five darts found their marks as we broke off the attack, with Wallen coming in right underneath us. *Boom!* Five more rockets smashed into the edge of the green tracers as I stood out on the skid shooting backward, protecting One-four's break.

"Seawolf, Seawolf. Shadow One! They're right on top of us! Can you get any closer? Over!"

Shit, these rockets went by Kentucky windage, not laser sighting or fly-by-wire. A gust of wind in the wrong direction and we'd have some seriously dead SEALs on our hands.

Harker glanced over his shoulder and hit his ICS. "Kelly, see how close you can get with your M-60. The rockets are just too risky, and these guys need some kind of cover fast."

"Okay, bring them around to my side as close as you can," I said. Instantly, I started praying, God, don't let me screw this up! Guide those tracers to the right spot.

Harker did a perfect job lining me up. As the target came around, I took aim with the machine gun. The sight before me was frightening. All I could see was black jungle below. Tracers, red and green, streaking across each other below me. I couldn't make out a canal to focus on, some kind of landmark, anything! Just a mass of tracers, some coming up at us now!

Over the radio I heard a calm monotone voice saying, "Seawolf, we need that cover anytime now!"

With that, I had to make my best guess, started saying the Catholic old reliable Our Fathers and Hail Marys, one right after the other, and squeezed the trigger. My tracers walked themselves very slowly right through the middle of all the colors that looked totally out of control from our vantage point. As I kept firing, the other gunners were concentrating their machine guns on the rear area of the battle. Talk about focus; I had put about six hundred or so rounds in on the target before I realized there was communication going on the radio that I had been missing. The green tracers had all but stopped as I let up because we were too far off from the target for me to maintain accuracy. Harker was going to have to come around for another pass and line me up again.

McGowan said, "Did you hear that shit?"

Harker and Bagley were laughing. I said, "Hear what?"

McGowan said, "I don't think I've ever heard a SEAL sound like that on the radio before. Damn, he was excited."

Hitting my ICS, I said, "What the fuck did he say?"

"You didn't hear that?" McGowan answered back.

I looked at him with a look that said, I'm going to tear off your head and shit down your neck if you don't tell me what I missed!

"He said, 'Son of a bitch, Seawolf. Nice fucking shooting! We're out of here! Roger?' "

"No shit?" I said.

Now it was McGowan's turn to give me my look back.

Harker still brought us around for another strike. Just to make sure all bases were covered. Five more darts, and that was it. He wanted to save the others in case the SEALs had more problems on their further extraction. We just kept orbiting over the general area until they called us and let us know they were in the clear.

Surprisingly enough, we didn't take any more fire after the SEALs had left.

After we returned to the LST and the SEALs got back aboard, I found out what had actually taken place on the ground. They were getting overrun when we arrived, and with all their firepower, they couldn't kill the NVA fast enough to keep up with the numbers that were coming out of the jungle. They were so busy killing that they didn't even have time to get the boat out and escape. It was that close a battle. The rockets slowed things down enough for the SEALs to reach the LSSC, but then the VC caught up again. When I cut loose with the M-60 and a prayer from about five hundred feet above, the rounds walked straight down the bank, and by the hand of God, took out a whole string of Victor Charlies. Between that and what the SEALs were firing from the boat, they got just enough breathing time to get the boat away. I got many pats on the back from SEALs that night. My self-image went up another notch. That fantasy self and reality were getting closer all the time. A very wise man once told me that if you pretend to be something long enough, you'll become that which you pretend to be. Maybe so.

Chapter 12

I was off the next day and decided to use the time to accompany the PBRs on patrol. They were going to make a sweep of the area where the big buildup was occurring, where the SEALs had been chased out a few nights earlier. I put on my tiger-striped fatigues and bush hat, grabbed my M-16 and bandolier of extra magazines, put on the shoulder holster with my trusty Colt .45, and over the side I went, down the metal ladder, and into a PBR.

I picked a spot up front with the boat captain, an old chief petty officer (i.e., God), tough as nails. The kind of guy I liked hanging around. His face reflected a lot of experience. Tough looking. He took a liking to me right away, thank goodness.

As I recall, four PBRs were on that sweep. The chief barked out instructions to everyone at the same time as he started up the two diesel motors. The two big Jacuzzi jet pumps came alive, shooting two streams of water out back. The crew untied us from the LST, and we slowly drifted away from the ship. Once we all got in line, the throttles were pushed up to cruising speed, and the PBR slowly came up on step, cutting through the brown water of the Bassac. We headed upriver, me in the first boat, and went close into the bank, hoping that Charlie would give his position away by shooting at us. We had about a twenty-minute ride to the spot that really interested us, but why waste good shoreline. We might stumble onto something else en route. The two guys on the .50s kept their barrels pointed at the bank. We were cruising fast, just watching and waiting.

As we approached the canal the SEALs had used, I felt the adrenaline slowly start on an upward swing. I inched my way over to the near side of the boat and chambered a round in my M-16, eyes fixed on the jungle not thirty feet away. Steadily, all four boats passed the ambush site. Nothing! Nobody's going to shoot at us! It always seems to happen that way. When you expect it, nothing!

We continued up the Bassac for about a klick, made a slow turn out toward the middle of the river, and then back down for another pass. I moved over to the other side, getting close to the bank again. My M-16 was up and ready as we started the second run. Pucker factor was *way* up. My eyes darted from one palm tree to another. From one bush to another, trying to get a glimpse of something. Once again, we cruised right on past without a hitch.

Another klick down, we started our turn back. I was relaxing, dangling my hand in the spray being thrown up and out by the bow of the boat, thinking again about being back in Texas on Lake Travis.

Hello, Mr. Murphy! Relax, and he bites you in the ass. My heart stopped, I swear. The most terrifying noise I'd ever heard in my life went right by me, and a B-40 rocket exploded in the river about fifty yards on the other side of our PBR. Then I heard the sound of incoming heavy automatic-weapons fire. I knew that sound well. Snapping my hand up out of the water, I grabbed the front of my gun. I already had my other hand on the pistol grip with my trigger finger resting alongside, slid it into place, and pulled. The sound of my M-16 running through the first clip on full automatic was drowned out by the sound of twelve .50-caliber machine guns and four M-60s tearing the hell out of the jungle on the bank. Another B-40 rocket whizzed by two boats back. The river water was shooting up everywhere as the enemy's AK-47s were trying to find their mark. They were just slicing through that fiberglass boat. The chief was already on the radio to the LST, getting the Sea-wolves scrambled. To give Charlie a harder target, all four boats were running wide open.

Harder target my ass. I wanted to just get the fuck out of there. Even at full throttle these boats could be hit by kids on the bank throwing rocks, let alone rockets. My hat was off to those guys in the PBRs. But I'd rather have been back in my helicopter.

By then, we had completed the third pass going upriver. They had hit us in the middle of our turn after going downriver on the second pass. Now the chief was taking us back down on another one. Jesus, come on, Seawolves! Where in the hell are you guys at? Well, I'd wanted to see all that I could see of that war, and I was doing just that.

I was wearing out my M-16. Not too many magazines left. It wasn't like my M-60, where I had a seemingly endless belt of two thousand rounds. Plus, if the M-16 broke, I had no spare parts. Despite my fears, I just kept shooting.

Finally, I thought I could hear the chief talking to Harker on the radio. For what seemed like forever, I waited to hear the familiar sound of those rotor blades popping in the air as they rolled in on target. That's a loud sound. If you ever hear it, you won't forget it.

Another empty magazine fell to the floor of the boat as I hit the release button. I grabbed my bandolier, pulled out another, and slammed it into the gun. Pushing the bolt release button and hitting the plunger, to make sure it was in place, I con-tinued to fire. The .50s were really rocking the shoreline, but we were still taking fire. Then I heard it. Oh yes! There was Mad Man Harker and the boys!

The sound of a 2.75-inch rocket coming in over your head is almost enough to make you wet your pants. I had thought the .50s were tearing up the jungle! Man oh man! Up-close rocket explosions—now, that's an experience! We could feel the shock wave from the blast! One rocket after another crashed into the jungle. The lead bird broke off his run right above us, and the trail bird came right in behind them. All of a sudden it started raining brass all over us. That was a shock.

I looked over at the guy who was shooting the aft .50. Yelling, I said, "Is this normal? Do we always give you guys a shower like this?"

He yelled back, "Hell yes!"

Well, I'll be damned. I'd never thought about that. I guess there's no way we can catch all of it. I just kept on shooting.

The helicopters weren't having any luck suppressing the enemy fire, and we were running out of ammo, or at least I was. The chief was called on the radio by one of the other boats. Evidently someone, or ones, had been hit. The choppers were putting in one strike after another. It was just like the time I shot us in the hydraulics the year before. Nothing seemed to work then either.

Both sides still exchanging fire, the casualty report came back. We had one wounded, a bad one, and if we didn't get him to a hospital fast, he wouldn't make it. I guess a couple of AKs found their mark. He needed medevac right away!

"What in the hell are we going to do? It'll take us twenty minutes to get back to the LST, and then there's the chopper ride up to Binh Thuy," the chief said.

"Hey, call Seawolf One-six. Harker's our idea man. He's always got a plan," I said.

I knew Harker wouldn't let us down. He had an idea all right: he'd just fly down and land on the back of the PBR and pick up the wounded sailor! There ain't no way he can do that; it's like a Chihuahua mounting a Great Dane, I thought to myself. But far be it from me to offer negative input; I just kept my thought to myself.

I looked up into the sky at Harker's chopper flying in orbit around us while we maneuvered out to the middle of the river and out of range of the VC. We were still taking some fire, though.

He made his approach to the boat behind us, the one with the wounded man. Soto was flying the trail bird and gave us cover with door-gunner fire. Harker came closer and closer. Slower and slower. Then, in a hover, water spraying everywhere, he slid the chopper's left skid onto the back of the PBR and rested it there, hovering. Hunt stepped out on the skid and helped lift the WIA into the chopper. All the while, the .50s on the other boats were still shooting at the distant shoreline to counteract the small-arms fire we were still taking. It seemed like forever till Harker pulled away from the boat and headed across the river to get transitional lift, then slowly moved upward to one thousand feet cruising altitude and on to Binh Thuy Army Evac Hospital. As far as I know, a helicopter landing on a PBR to rescue a sailor had never been attempted before and hasn't been since. The wounded sailor recovered nicely.

Once the choppers were clear, we departed the area and headed back to the LST to regroup, lick our wounds, and come up with another plan to break the enemy's back.

When Harker and Soto returned from dropping off the wounded sailor at Binh Thuy's evac hospital, they joined our brainstorming session. Evidently the NVA were dug in pretty well, so it would probably take some heavy firepower to get them out. We decided to move the LST to that location and hit them with the 40mm guns on the ship, using one of our helicopters as spotter. We would keep that up for most of a day, then follow up with a B-52 strike the day after. Once *that* was completed, army slicks would bring in an ARVN group with a Green Beret adviser and sweep the area while we provided close air support once again.

It was a restless night on the ship. Everybody looked forward to the next day's action upriver. We would move the LST early in the morning, going to battle stations just before arriving at the target. Meanwhile, we worked out the logistics of using one gunship to spot, and the other to relieve him when he was low on fuel. That way, we'd have a gunship in the air the whole time. I had been in on a mission like that once before the previous year, so I knew we were in for quite a ride. From above, watching those 40mms explode in the jungle was something. It was about this time that we got word the PBR sailor was going to be all right. Nothing like turning into our bunks for the night on a high note.

The night passed quickly, and we got up to the sound of the anchor being lifted from the murky bottom of the Bassac. As the LST was preparing to move upriver, we climbed out of our racks and headed for the shower. That's the only thing I hated about living on board the ship: taking a shower was a pain in the butt. We had to conserve the water, so we'd get all wet, turn the water off, lather up, turn the water back on, then rinse quickly. Oh well, at least we had hot water. When we operated on land, all the water was cold.

Once back in the compartment, I slipped on my tiger stripes and headed up to the flight deck. The morning sun was just coming up, and reds and blues were beautiful across the sky. The slight breeze moving across the river made coming up on deck feel like we were in Hawaii. It was going to be a beautiful day for a battle.

I walked across the deck, past the choppers, and aft to the chow hall. The cooks were in a good mood, laughing and joking while I went through the chow line to grab a cup of coffee. I said my hellos and strolled back on out by the birds. Lighting up a cigarette and taking a sip of my coffee, I rested my ass on the nose of my helicopter and looked out across the brown river at the jungle moving slowly by as the ship steamed upriver. I was thinking about that young kid at Reagan High School in Austin, Texas, the shy guy with no self-confidence, the one who was convinced that he was stupid. I was wondering what all *his* friends were doing right about then. They would have graduated in the class of '68. Well, he'd be famous someday even though he wouldn't be able to attend that high-school reunion because he hadn't graduated. That's the only regret he had; he had come a long way, the little skinny kid, in two short years. The fantasy self and the real self were getting closer and closer. Prayers were getting answered.

Hunt's popping me on the head yanked me back through the time-and-space warp from Reagan High School to Vietnam. He had just joined me with his cup of coffee.

"What were you thinking about? Looked like you were in some serious deep thought," Hunt asked with a little laugh.

"My old high-school days and how I really hated it there because of who I was."

Our conversation was interrupted by the LST's going to general quarters: what a ruckus that was! Guys running everywhere with life vests and helmets on. You'd think Pearl Harbor was getting attacked again and we were in the middle of it all. Hunt and I just drank our coffee, watching the action take place. We wouldn't be lifting off first anyway—well, *I* wouldn't be; Hunt's bird was going up first. And they wouldn't be taking off for ten minutes or so. Fryburger showed up on deck and joined us.

"Hey, if you're going to get a cup of coffee, you better do it quick. We're first up," Hunt told Fryburger.

Fryburger replied in his usual relaxed way, "Cool, man. No problem."

I swear, I could have dropped a grenade down his pants, and he wouldn't have gotten rattled. I don't think he knew the meaning of the word panic. Just the kind of guy I wanted on my side.

Hunt and I looked at each other, then looked at Fryburger's back as he disappeared aft for his coffee, strolling calmly the whole time. Then I helped Hunt preflight his aircraft. While he inspected the jet engine, I looked over the tail boom, drive-shaft, and tail rotor. Then we both inspected the main rotor head. All was good to go. As we were refitting the cowling, Fryburger strolled out.

"Hey, man, I would've helped you do that. We had time," Fryburger said.

"No sweat, dude, I already had my coffee," I said.

Hunt was probably going to say something humorous, because he was already chuckling, but he was cut short by Soto. "Are we all ready to lift off, boys?"

Our favorite Cuban pilot, all ready to go, maps in hand, was standing right behind Fryburger, who slowly turned as he sipped his coffee and said, "Yup." A man of few words, Fryburger.

Hunt and I were all finished, so I picked up our cups and took them back to the kitchen. When I returned, Soto, Bagley, and Hunt were already loaded up, and Fryburger was holding the rotor blade in front. As Soto yelled out his side, "Coming hot!" the jet engine screamed to life, steadily building up power and torque, finally pulling the rotor blade from Fryburger's hands and whirling it around and around, faster and faster. I stood there watching as they completed the hover check and were given the go-ahead to take off. Then our first-shift spotter was en route to a one-thousand-foot orbit around the target area.

I walked back across the flight deck to take up a good position to watch the big guns work out. Those 40mms were loud, but not nearly as loud as the 81mm mortars we were firing as well. I had a great spot up forward between the mortar tube and the cannon to watch the show. Soon Valladares and Mack came up and joined me. McGowan was still asleep. I wondered how long that could last.

It took a few minutes of communication between the helicopter and the gunners before they got on target, but I could tell real quick when they hit the right spot because the sporadic spotter rounds were suddenly followed by *boom! boom! boom!* And the cannon went like crazy, the cacophony interrupted briefly by a much larger *kaboom!* from the 81mm mortar tube.

They were giving someone all kinds of hell out there in the jungle. The continuous blasting of these guns and mortars was going right through me to the bone. It's a wonder I didn't get a headache. But we never heard a thing from McGowan. That guy could sleep through anything.

Then it was time for Valladares and me to preflight our aircraft. Getting up from our Fourth of July, picnic-type atmosphere, we made our way down to the flight deck. Amid the bone-shattering blasts from the guns and mortar, we worked around the chopper, making it ready to relieve Soto and his band.

Once we'd finished with the inspection, we got into our gear in preparation for liftoff. Then, Campbell by his side, Harker came strolling across the deck, maps in hand, smile on his face, and ready to go. Campbell had on his sunglasses and was looking his usual stunning Hollywood self. We all mounted up, and Valladares stood out front holding the rotor blade.

"Coming hot!" Harker yelled out, and the jet engine climbed to a high pitch and pulled the rotor blade from Valladares. We were all ready to head upstairs and relieve Soto.

Harker slowly pulled up on the collective, and the rotor blades started popping louder as the pitch on them increased and they took a bigger and bigger bite out of the air. I looked down at the skids and watched them come closer together as the weight of the helicopter was decreased by the progressive lift of us pulling into a hover. One, two, three feet off the deck we hovered. Just a little farther up, and the hover check was complete. Harker nodded at the deck officer out in front, the yellow vest on and flags in hand, that he was ready for departure. He waved us all clear for takeoff.

Immediately, something went *pop! pop! pop!* followed by a very loud crash from behind, and we started spinning in circles, gaining speed as we went. Shit! We lost our tail rotor! Then the deck officer dove into the river to keep from getting hit by the out-of-control helicopter. Everything was going by the front of my eyeballs fast, but it had to stop quickly or we'd be history. We didn't even have time to pucker, it all happened so fast.

Thinking quickly, Harker dropped the collective, and we pancacked onto the flight deck, sliding to a spinning stop but facing back where we'd started from. Campbell cut the power and hung all over the main-rotor-blade brake to get things shut down as fast as he could. We all scrambled out of the chopper to see what damage had been done while the LST was running the man overboard drill for real.

Well, there was no tail rotor. And wherever it went, it took the whole gearbox with it! Our helicopter wasn't going anywhere! We couldn't fix that. It was time to call the army Chinook in for a sick helicopter pickup. We stood around in amazement, looking at our injured aircraft. Evidently a sniper had hit it while we were doing our hover check. A lucky shot. Actually it was probably more than one if those pops were rifle fire.

Campbell said, "I guess that qualifies as getting shot down, doesn't it?"

We all laughed, and Valladares said, "Hell yes!"

"Well, if you're going to get shot down, it might as well be over the flight deck," I said.

Walking up behind us was a soaking-wet deck officer, who'd been picked up by one of the PBRs.

"How'd you like your swim?" Harker said.

"Scared the shit out of me! I just knew I was dead!" he said. He was still shaking.

So much for the LST's guns having an effect on the bad guys. It was time to have the big ones come in and do their thing. Good old mother B-52. Meanwhile, we needed another chopper.

After we recovered Soto's chopper, the LST moved farther upriver and away from the target area. There we would wait for the army to come out and pick up our bird.

Much later in the afternoon, Soto was instructed to take off with his chopper to make room for an army slick with the hookup team for the Chinook. We all came up on deck and got comfortable to watch the show. Seemed like the whole ship's crew eventually turned out for it.

The army slick came in and landed on deck. The hookup crew was out with their gear in an instant, and the chopper lifted off. These guys were good! Like ants swarming over a chocolate cake, they were on our chopper, hooking up straps and cables. They were quickly done, and the Chinook arrived, its two huge rotor blades popping in the wind, and the hookup team was on top of our chopper ready to rig a line that was being lowered from the Chinook as it came to a hover over the flight deck. The prop wash from the big machine was awesome. I don't think it took the team more than a minute before the chopper was being lifted into the sky. Now, that was impressive! The wind from the Chinook hadn't even settled down when the army slick returned to pick up the team. In and out. We didn't even get a chance to meet any of them.

But we still needed another chopper so we could deal with our little problem. That meant a trip into Vung Tau. Hunt, McGowan, and I were chosen for the trip in. Harker and Campbell were to be the pilots and we were leaving right away. Hunt and I would be the copilots coming back with the new bird.

The ship's crew topped off the tanks in our remaining bird, and I laid myself out on the floor in the back while Hunt and McGowan took the door seats. It was going to be a great flight, because I could sleep the whole way. All I remember was the liftoff and our going over the side of the ship.

It was dark when I was awakened by the change in temperature as we descended into Vung Tau. Big difference between one thousand feet and three hundred feet; it got a lot warmer. Harker flared the chopper and pulled up to a stop. Slowly moving sideways, he parked us in a revetment next to the runway where all the other HAL-3 helicopters were parked.

Time to go to work again. We secured the aircraft and went into the hangar with Harker and Campbell to find out which of the birds was ours. That's where I ran into Abbott and Welch and when I found out from Welch that Abbott was about to start training for a combat team.

"Are you kidding?" I asked.

Abbott said, "Nope."

"Well, I'll be damned. Say, when we get finished here, let's meet over at the EM club and have a few. We're not leaving till early in the morning," I said.

We had a good time that night, and I was glad things worked out the way they did, because that was the last time I saw Welch. Some time later, two members of his immediate family died, and he was sent home. God bless him!

The next morning, we were up early and out pulling the preflights on the aircraft. Harker and Campbell showed up just as we finished. Campbell took the new bird with Hunt in the copilot seat and the back all closed up. McGowan took the door seat in ours and I piled into the copilot's seat. From the line shack, Welch and one of his buddies held our rotor blades as we turned up. Both birds good to go, we pulled up into our hover checks.

"Vung Tau tower. Seawolf One-six and One-two. Hover check complete. Request clearance for eastern departure. Over."

"Seawolf One-six and One-two. Vung Tau tower. You are clear for eastern departure, altimeter three zero point two one, wind west at one zero knots. Have a nice day. Over."

"Vung Tau tower. Seawolf One-six and One-two. Roger."

We in the lead, Harker nosed us over, and we smoothly started forward motion, picking up speed and gaining altitude as we passed over the fence at the end of the metal runway. We climbed out to one thousand feet and turned for home. Bassac, here we come.

The weather was incredible: blue sky spotted with little

white puffy clouds. When one happened to fall right into our path, Harker would say, "Get ready to log IFR flight time." And when we hit the cloud, we'd cover our eyes as we flew through it. What a nut.

It wasn't long before we were turning on final to the LST. Home once again. After the birds were shut down and secured, we discovered a big buzz about the ship: the B-52s. They were due "anytime," and the ship was moving back downriver to the target area so we could all get a good view of the strike. Picture it: all the sailors lining the LST with chairs, carrying drinks and munchies from home, getting ready for the show. As I stood on top of the new helicopter giving the head a once-over, I looked down at everybody lining up on the flight deck. What's wrong with this picture? Who knows how many people were about to be vaporized by the attack, and you'd think we were going to a USO show or a drive-in movie.

As I looked back to the job at hand and away from the audience, something bothered me. I couldn't put my finger on it. It was almost like I could hear something. The faint sound of leaves rustling in the wind, except there weren't any leaves around. I looked up into the blue sky. Nothing! I couldn't see anything at all, so I assumed that the B-52s hadn't arrived yet.

That thought was blown away literally, and my body was overwhelmed by a series of concussions that were so ear- and earth-shattering that I thought my skin would come off before my eyes. The power of the explosions was the most incredible thing I had ever experienced. Looking in the direction of the shoreline, I was shaking like a leaf while standing up on top of the helicopter. I saw a sight that few have seen and lived to tell about. It was like God Almighty himself had taken a giant shovel and just turned the jungle over. Whole palm trees, roots and all, were tossed hundreds of feet into the air along with all the other greenery. The dirt was close behind. I couldn't take my eyes off the spectacle. I was completely awestruck. And the blasts just kept on. I slowly was driven to my knees and then my butt as shock wave after shock wave surged through my body and past me. The whole ship, including my new helicopter, vibrated as the shock waves drove past us upon each and every explosion. My God, I thought, nothing could live through that! Finally it stopped. Then it took a minute for all the dirt, trees, and general green stuff that had been tossed skyward to settle back to Mother Earth.

I glanced back down at the flight deck, looking over the audience. A lot of sailors were still just sitting there, stunned. Then, slowly, the *wows* and *oohs* and *aahs* started making their way through the crowd, punctuated by the occasional "Mother*fucker*! Did you see that shit?"

I never did see the B-52s. Not even a vapor trail. How did they do that? Sure was glad they were on our side. It took a while for my nerves to settle down.

Chapter 13

After the dust had cleared, it was time to move on to the next phase of our operation, which would take place the very next day. The Mike force, advised by Green Berets, would be airlifted in by army slicks. They would start at the northernmost point of the area of operations and sweep the entire AO, looking for remains of the VC and anything else they might find. Then, coming out on the southern end of the target area, they would make their way to the river to be extracted by boats.

A good night's sleep under our belts, we were ready to go. Both birds loaded for bear, we would make occasional orbits of the area, keeping an eye on the Mike force troops for a bit, and then back to the LST, top off on fuel, and wait.

Pratt was the fire-team lead on this mission, with Bagley as his copilot. McGowan and I in the back. Wallen and Campbell were in the trail bird with Hunt and Mack in the back.

We first lifted off close to lunchtime and made the rounds of the target area, watching our guys on the ground as they forced their way through mangled trees and undergrowth of all kinds. The going was tough and very slow. The huge bomb craters exposed many tunnels. Exploring what they could, but hindered by collapsed tunnels, the body count the ARVNs were accumulating just wasn't near what we had expected. A few weapons were turned up. Some B-40 rockets, a few AKs, nothing of the size we had found in the Zigzag. A lot of expense in bombs and not much tangible to show for it so far.

Flying over the newly desolate area was just a little overwhelming. As we flew circles above, I watched the ARVNs working through the rubble, ant-size people in olive-drab fatigues against a backdrop of reddish-brown dirt broken up by an occasional green bush. They were moving slowly so as not to miss anything, and some of the weapons and bodies they stumbled on were half buried under the dirt. The bomb damage assessment (BDA) was going to take all day.

We were going back to the LST. We had seen enough. It was time to wait. Both birds turned on final together, approaching the ship simultaneously. Two guys in yellow vests and carrying flags were on the flight deck, one standing in front of each parking place, directing us in. I looked out to my nine o'clock position; Wallen was just a little back from our lead so as to give a little more clearance between rotor blades. Pratt brought us in with his usual perfect flare and smoothly set us down. Wallen touched down next to us just a few seconds later. What a sight. Wallen and Pratt always impressed me with their flying skills.

Securing the aircraft, we topped off the tanks, then went below to cool off. Those guys out in the bush would have given anything to be in our shoes just then. I sat there for a minute, but I couldn't relax. I was too wound up. I mentioned that to Mack, McGowan, and Hunt, who said that they were having the same problem. We decided to put on our SEAL trunks and go below, where the weights were, to work off a little bit of that excess energy. There was a pretty nice gym set up on the cargo deck where we could get pumped up pretty good. So that's where we spent the next hour, pumping iron and waiting to hear from the Mike force. After that, we retired to our compartment. We didn't have any more problems relaxing.

The patrol the Mike force made was long, hot, and rigorous, and it took them most of the day to sift through the rubble and come up with nothing (in comparison to the time and money spent). As the day drew to a close, the Mike force found itself at the end of the sweep but still a ways away from where the PBRs were to be picking them up on the river. The operation had taken a lot longer than anticipated. Even traveling as the crow flies, making straight for the waiting PBRs, they would have had to cross a huge area of rice paddies to reach the pickup area before the sun went down. And making that crossing would expose them to the enemy. A jungle route that gave them more concealment could have been followed—which was the original plan—but it would be way after dark before they came to the bank of the Bassac. The ARVNs did not like that idea at all; they didn't like being out after dark with Charlie in the area. The Green Beret adviser tried to convince them to take the longer, safer route, with no success. He was upset that they hadn't made any contact and thought that patrolling through the jungle might rectify that. But in either case, nobody was really worried because of the lack of evidence that there were any VC within miles.

It was just after dinner, and I was down below catching a nap, when bells went off and a familiar sound echoed through the compartment: "Scramble the helos, scramble the helos!" I was on my feet and on the ladder to the deck in a heartbeat! Adrenaline immediately started pumping into overload, the way it always did when we got a scramble. Pratt was sitting in the chopper reading when he heard the bells, so he was already turning up the jet engine. McGowan and I were both caught napping. By the time we got to the flight deck, the engine was coming up to speed. Running to the back of the helicopter, I got the main rotor blade unhooked from the tail boom just in time for the torque of the jet engine to tear it from my hands. McGowan went straight to his side of the gunship and was clicking down the rocket caps and putting the barrels in the flex guns for the copilot. Bagley came running across the flight deck from the other side with the mission maps in his hand. He dove into his seat and strapped in. Mack and Hunt were doing their thing while Wallen and Campbell were turning up the other bird. Running around to my side, I clicked the rocket caps down, slammed the flex barrels in, swung my Mae West and armor plating on, pulled the helmet onto my head, and jumped in my seat. McGowan had already cleared his side.

Pushing the ICS button, I said, "Clear left!" Upon hearing me, Pratt instantly pulled us into a hover.

Pratt said, "Seawolf One-five is off at this time!"

We went up and over the side of the LST. As I was pushing the barrel into my M-60, I looked back at Wallen's bird. He was coming up right behind us. We started upriver and climbing.

Sure enough, it was the Mike force. They had gone about halfway across the rice paddies toward the river, when they were hit and were pinned down by what I heard the Green Beret adviser describe as a "plenitude" of automatic-weapons fire.

"Plenitude! What the hell is that?" I asked on my ICS.

Pratt said, "It means 'a lot.' "

"Oh, we gotta get this guy out. Anybody cool enough to be humorous in the middle of a firefight needs to be saved. Besides, I'm going to ask him how to spell it," I said. Nothing like a well-educated professional killer.

Climbing to one thousand feet, we approached the coordinates where they were reported to have been pinned down. Now I really understood the meaning of that phrase. Tracers were coming out of the jungle on three different sides, converging on a bunch of black dots up against the dikes in the middle of the rice paddies. Shit, those guys weren't going anywhere through that wall of tracers.

"Seawolf, Seawolf. Big Bear. Over."

"Big Bear, Seawolf One-five. On station. Over."

"Seawolf. Big Bear. Roger. There on the edge of the jungle. Just pick a tree line. Over."

"Roger that, Big Bear. When we hit, you move. You copy?"

"I copy, Seawolf. Big Bear out."

Big Bear didn't have to tell us where to put in our strike. The targets were obvious. Pratt lined us up to hit each one of the three tree lines the fire was coming from. As we rolled in on the middle one, McGowan and I would concentrate our machine guns on the other two. Bagley shot the flex guns at the one Pratt was going to put the rockets on. We were headed straight down the middle of the ambush site with a tree line on my side, one on McGowan's side, and the one we were putting the strike on right in front of us.

I remember thinking of that poem, "The Charge of the Light Brigade." You know, about charging into the valley of Death, guns to the left of me and guns to the right of me. Leaning outside and into that 120-mile-per-hour gale, my left foot on the top of the rocket pod, M-60 pointed forward and off to the left, I squeezed the trigger. My machine gun came alive, eight hundred rounds a minute, a tracer every four rounds, headed toward the tree line on my left. Like a giant stream of water, the tracers wove back and forth, up and down, reaching from one muzzle flash to the next. The tracers stopped momentarily and then started again, but this time they were all coming up at us. I didn't ease up, and neither did they. And there were a lot of them.

The black ants, our guys on the ground, were beginning to move, I saw as we kept shooting. Then *swoosh!* Sparks everywhere. Pratt was punching off his rockets at the target. It was like the Fourth of July, and we were flying through the middle of the fireworks display. The second rocket out of the tube glued a cap on my shinbone. I felt the sting, but kept spraying down the tree line on my left while trying to subdue the enemy fire. It was futile. I thought back to the previous year when we were in the rainstorm and we couldn't suppress the fire coming up at us then. That was when I shot us in the hydraulics; there was no way I would repeat that mistake this time. I guess getting haunted by mistakes keeps us from repeating them.

Every once in a while, I heard a round hit us, the familiar ring of metal getting a hole punched through it. We got lower and lower, closer and closer to the middle tree line in front of us as Pratt sent three more rockets into the center of the enemy gunfire. At five hundred feet, we broke off to the right, and I covered our exit. My foot still on top of the rocket pod, I was standing up outside the helicopter, twisted around, shooting over the top of the flex guns and back behind us under the tail boom. Wallen timed his strike perfectly, and Seawolf One-four's five rockets exploded into the jungle beneath us as we broke off the attack run.

Coming around ninety degrees off our last strike path, we placed the second rocket run on both adjacent tree lines at the same time, hoping that it would give the guys on the ground opportunity to move closer to the river. Over the radio, Pratt barked out to place three darts on the near tree line and then three darts on the far tree line, with a left-hand break. That meant the door gunners on the right would be concentrating their fire on the third tree line, the one that connected the other two, while everyone else would be hitting the near and far targets. We came around to our right and lined up the two tree lines with our guys in the middle. Taking my usual position outside, I started firing forward as Bagley opened up with the flex guns. McGowan was working over the third on his side, and tracers were coming at us from all of them. Sparks flying back into the cockpit, three rockets were on their way to the first target. Breaking through six hundred feet as I worked over the jungle below with the M-60, I saw the guys on the ground were moving to a dike closer to the river. We were almost over the top of the first target when Pratt punched off the other three rockets at the second target. As he broke left, out toward the river, two rounds crashed up through the floor of the chopper. Those kinds of hits are always really loud. I *hated* it when that happened; always made me jump and interfered with my concentration.

We were down to five hundred feet before we started climbing out, and I could almost feel the blast of Wallen's rockets as they hit the first target. Once Seawolf One-four was clear of his run, we started lining up for our third and final rocket attack because we only had three rockets left each.

Over the ICS, Pratt said, "This is bullshit! These guys aren't letting up a bit." That's when he put a call in to the LST to request some Cobras out of Binh Thuy or a couple F-4s out of Saigon. Spooky would be nice, too.

Our last strike would be the opposite of our very first run. One-four would space his rockets out on the left, and we would do the same on the right. Getting the most coverage for our buck. Changing our barrels, I was ready for the last blast before a pit stop.

It took us a few minutes to get in place, because the run had to be started clear around the other side of the ambush. Rolling in, I concentrated my fire on the jungle to my left as Pratt slowly picked out three spots that looked to be the best for our last few rockets. All six M-60s might as well have been slingshots, because they didn't seem to make any difference at all in the number of tracers that were coming back at us. At least we were good decoys so the troops could once again get moving. By then, we had covered them sufficiently that they had all moved two dikes closer to the river. But that left ten or so to go, and we were all out of rockets.

Then Big Bear notified us he had three Vietnamese WIAs.

It was going to take a medevac chopper pilot with balls that clanked to make a pickup there. But Pratt made the call, and Binh Thuy quickly had one en route to our location.

"Big Bear, Seawolf One-five. Over."

"Go, Seawolf."

"Big Bear, Seawolf One-five. Medevac is en route. We're going to rotate our gunships to reload on rockets. We will give you continuous door-gunner fire while we complete rocket reload. Keep your head down. Over."

"Roger, keeping head down, Seawolf. Thanks. Over."

Wallen stayed on station and orbited the area, putting in door-gunner fire while waiting for us to get back from the quick turnaround. Seawolf One-four staying on station would keep Charlie from advancing on our guys while we were gone. We hoped.

On our way back to the LST, I pushed the ICS. "Where'd all these guys come from, and where in hell are they getting all their ammo?"

Bagley just shook his head.

"Did that B-52 strike miss them entirely?" McGowan said.

Pratt said, "Who knows, but there must be a lot of them down there!"

The LST moved so that we could land into the wind. The deck crew was ready and waiting to help us reload and refuel as soon as we touched down. Pratt brought us in quick with a very short final approach, flared, and put us on the deck with the perfection we'd grown used to. While he communicated with the ship on the radio, McGowan and I jumped out and got busy with the work at hand. McGowan began refueling the bird while I cleaned out all the expended brass from the inside of the chopper. The deck crew was shoving new rockets into the tubes while other sailors brought us door boxes full of 7.62 ammo for the M-60s. Once I got the bulk of the brass out of the way, I reloaded the flex-gun trays. By the time McGowan was done, new door boxes were in place, and I was getting settled in my seat.

"Clear left," I said.

"Clear right," McGowan echoed.

On the radio Pratt said, "Seawolf One-five is off at this time."

Fuck hover check—he pulled straight up on the collective, and we were moving forward and over the side, turning upriver. The LST had weighed anchor and was moving closer to the battle so we would have an easier time making quick turnarounds. Once up to speed and altitude, we learned from the ship that our request for additional air support had been denied because none was available till the next day. That was probably because the sun was going down. I guess they hated planning missions so late in the day. And it was a fact that ARVNs weren't very high on the priority list. So it was up to us to get the guys out. It was going to be a long evening, and there wasn't much daylight left.

As soon as we had Seawolf One-four in sight, Pratt told him to head for the LST. Then we put in more door-gunner fire as we stayed in a tight circle over the troops on the ground. It seemed to be working. We were sufficient intimidation to keep the VC at bay. No rockets would be expended until Seawolf One-four returned, and then we could put in a series of strikes to cover the medevac chopper.

But Charlie kept the automatic-weapons fire going constantly, so the ARVNs still couldn't move. It was stalemate until we got the wounded out and put in more rocket runs so the Mike force could start jumping once again from dike to dike. The VC must have had truckloads of ammo down there. All of the barrels in my cooling rack were hot. It was a choice of which barrel was the least hot.

Seawolf One-four came back about the same time we heard from the medevac chopper. Pratt had us put in three strikes, one on each tree line, and the sky lit up again with thousands of tracers. We took a few more rounds through the floor and the tail boom. Some of them were hitting us at one thousand feet. Those guys were not run-of-the-mill, farm-boy VC.

The medevac went down to pick up the wounded, but that poor army pilot didn't break four hundred feet before he was pulling out because he had taken so many hits, and one of his crew had been shot up pretty badly. So much for the medevac. The rocket runs would just keep the bad guys' heads down for a moment, and then they were right back at it again. My shoulder was killing me from holding that M-60 up so long shooting, and a couple of times, I had to break off the ammo going into the gun because the receiver had become so hot, rounds were cooking off.

We called in another medevac chopper from Binh Thuy, then took turns reloading and covering the troops. Once the medevac chopper was on station, it was time to try again. Pratt and Wallen put in two more strikes on all three positions, with us wearing out our M-60s. The ARVNs hadn't been able to move since they'd gotten the three wounded. Down went the second medevac. He made it through four hundred feet, down to two hundred feet, then pulled out. Nobody was wounded, but his instruments were lighting up like a Christmas tree because he had taken so many hits. He said the LZ was too hot and he would be lucky to make it back to Binh Thuy.

Pratt told Seawolf One-four to escort the medevac back home in case he couldn't make it. We stayed and kept Charlie neutralized so he couldn't move on our guys. By the time Wallen returned, the sun had gone down, and it was twilight. Big Bear said that the ARVNs were going to have to leave the wounded behind if any of them was going to have a chance to get out. By then it was too late to call for another medevac, and everyone knew that if the three were left behind, they would be tortured to death.

Pratt turned to me and said, "What do ya think, Kelly? Feel up to going for another medal?"

Without hesitation I said, "Sure, might as well. Can't dance."

My *choice*. Shit for brains, but my choice. I needed a serious reality check, which I was fixing to get, the hard way.

"What about you, McGowan?" Pratt asked.

"Let's do it!" he answered with exuberance. McGowan always liked making a big show.

"Well, Bagley?" Pratt said.

"Fine with me," he answered.

"Okay, boys. Let's do it! Big Bear, Seawolf One-five."

"Go ahead, Seawolf."

"Big Bear, Seawolf One-five. We're coming down to pick up your three wounded. Give us as much cover fire as you can. Over."

"Seawolf, Big Bear. Are you crazy?"

"Big Bear, Seawolf One-five. Roger. One-four, One-five. Give us all the cover you can. Over."

"Roger that, One-five. One-four is on you."

"Here we go, boys!" Pratt said on the ICS.

We started down. All our rockets were gone. All we had were the M-60s. The plan was to have Wallen keep circling and putting his door-gunner fire on the enemy while we kept shooting all the way down. As soon as Pratt dropped the collective my finger glued itself to the trigger of my machine gun. Bagley was wearing out the flex guns, and McGowan was burning up his M-60. We broke through seven hundred feet and were taking rounds through the floor, which was beginning to look like a giant cheese grater. By then the main rotor blade was whistling, it had so many holes in it. It was really starting to get dark and the tracers looked like basketballs as they flashed through the cabin and out the other side. Muzzle flashes were visible everywhere. The jungle looked like a strobe photo session at a Jimi Hendrix rock concert. At two hundred feet, the tail boom was sounding like the New York Yankees were using it for batting practice. We slowed, flared, and dropped into the rice paddy.

Still shooting into the tree line, I noticed that we weren't getting any cover fire from the ARVNs. They were just lying against the dike in the rice paddy with their hands over their heads. Figures! Anyway, I quickly forgot about that when something else got my attention. Out, just beyond the last of the light left, at the edge of the jungle where darkness began, I saw something that I definitely didn't want to see. Viet Cong!

Hundreds of them. All in a dead run straight at us. My trigger finger and shoulder were screaming with pain under the pressure of firing for so long without stopping.

Hitting my ICS foot button, I yelled, "McGowan! Take the wounded in on your side! I got all the fuckers in the world coming at us over here!"

"Roger that!" he blurted back.

Black-pajama-clad individuals were coming out of the jungle into the rice paddies like a river. Wave after wave. Where in the fuck were they all coming from? There must have been a little yellow-man factory under the ground stamping them out. I couldn't kill them fast enough. They were closing fast because they weren't stopping to shoot. Bagley couldn't do anything but sit there, because the flex guns wouldn't turn that far in my direction and were mounted too low to fire over the dike.

A Green Beret worked his way around to my side firing his M-16 at the bunch charging us as he moved. He was a very large man. If that was Big Bear, I knew how he got his name. He was yelling in Vietnamese at the ARVNs on the dike, telling them to get the hell out of there and run for the river. At the same time he'd grab each one he passed by the back of the fatigues, lifting him clear off the ground with one hand and throwing him in the direction he wanted him to go. After all the ARVNs had split, this guy kept shooting, dropping empty magazines, reloading and continuing to fire on full automatic, as he worked his way back around to the other side where the wounded were getting into the chopper.

I was beginning to feel like I was the only gun between us and getting out alive. Seawolf One-four probably couldn't see them from where he was because of how dark it had gotten. And we were still taking fire from the other tree lines. I couldn't think about them, though; I had to stay focused on the problem at hand. The VC were almost on us when I felt a nudge from behind. Turning quickly, I saw it was the three wounded Vietnamese squeezing in. Glancing back again where I was shooting, I saw one had stopped and raised his AK to fire while the others were still running at us. I wasn't quick enough; he got off several shots at me before I could get on him. I felt it, too. It was like someone hitting me with a hammer on the left hand. I was spun around, and I dropped the M-60. But I managed to pick it up, tucked it under my right arm, the way Nimmo had taught me, and held my injured hand up behind me where I couldn't see it, so I wouldn't go into shock. Opening fire once again, I nailed the bastard who got me, and kept shooting.

Another round came from somewhere and put my gun out of commission. By then we were pulling into a hover, and the VC had dropped their weapons and were trying to climb onto the chopper, trying to weight us down so we couldn't take off. Capture was definitely on their minds. The only things that were on my mind were don't look at the hand and get these little motherfuckers off the aircraft!

By then all the ARVNs and the Green Beret had hit the road out the other side and were running for the river because Charlie had stopped shooting at them while trying to get at us. I was kicking and punching like a frenzied madman, trying to get them off the chopper. By then, so was McGowan. The little guys were clawing, pulling, and tugging at me, trying to get me out of the chopper. It was like fighting one hundred fifth-graders on crystal meth, and they all wanted a piece of us. Most of them had uniforms, too. That meant NVA. We had really stumbled on something big, but I sure wished we'd stumbled someplace else. One of them found his way into my lap and was grabbing for my hand, the one that had been shot. That little yellow bastard had to go. Two more were hanging on to my left leg, four or five were on the skids, and two were between the pussy pole and the back of the copilot. I threw my head as far back as it would go, then launched it forward as hard as I could. The front of the flight helmet found the forehead of that Chink in my lap, and split it wide open, driving him backward, off my lap and into his pals behind. They all fell off the skid and plummeted into the water in the rice paddy about two feet below, into a pile of bodies. Grabbing the pussy pole with my right hand and using it as leverage, I brought my right leg around in a swing kick, catching both VC in the chest, driving them back into their friends behind them and off the skids into the rice paddy below. Then I turned my attention to the two clawing at my other leg. Bringing my left leg straight up, I caught one in the chin with my knee and bloodied his mouth. These guys must have been convinced they were going to capture us because the ARVNs were gone, and the other chopper was concentrating on the two tree lines fire was coming from. That left us fair game. The NVA behind those trying to grab our chopper still had their guns and were closing in fast. I guess that's why the closest ones had dropped theirs; they thought they were covered. Now they were hanging on to the skids and trying to climb up again. About eight of them. Plus, the one with the bloodied mouth and his buddy, still clawing at my leg, were hanging on to the flex-gun pylon. Pratt had us moving forward trying to get up enough speed to make transitional lift and get us out of there. But we were already heavy with the wounded on board. I was afraid of what the second group of NVA would do if they thought that we were going to get away, because they were all around us. If they all opened up at close range, we'd be dead meat.

Then, somehow, Hunt and Mack had found us with their M-60s; .308s came crashing down the side of our gunship, just outside the rotation of our blades, splashing rice paddy water eight feet in the air, dismembering enemy bodies as it went. Black pajamas and NVA uniforms were falling lifeless everywhere in the hail of red tracers. With my right hand I grabbed an M-60 barrel from the cooling rack and buried it in the head of the guy with the bloody mouth. He went limp, then fell between the rocket pod and the pylon. The other guy was hanging on for dear life to the top of the pylon. Behind them, their buddies' guns had been neutralized. The charge was stalled just long enough to give us time to move out of reach. Long enough to get transitional lift and get airborne. It happened so fast you should have seen the surprised look on their faces as we started gaining altitude. By then I was sitting on the floor, kicking at NVA who were hanging on to the skids. I kicked the last one off when we were one hundred feet in the air. Turning back to my seat, I noticed that idiot was still on top of the pylon, his face all distorted by the one-hundred-mile-per-hour wind. I got back in my seat. Got comfortable. Looked out at the piece-of-shit NVA on the pylon. Slowly took my smoke grenade out of the can on the pussy pole and held it outside right in his face and let it go off. Nice pretty red smoke trail. What do you know? He's gone! I wonder where he went.

As we climbed up through one thousand feet, our rotor blades were whistling from the bullet holes. We'd made it! It was by the power of God we made it. I was the only one who'd been hit, and that was just in the hand. No way you can tell me there's no God. We were too big a target.

Time to take care of my hand. McGowan was busy with our passengers, so I was on my own. A first-aid kit was attached inside just behind the copilot seat. I reached for it with my one good hand and pulled it off the snaps that attached it to the bulkhead. Of course, the inside of a helicopter gunship was very, very, windy because there were no doors, and I was operating with just one good hand. Well, I fumbled with the bag, but I opened it and proceeded to search for an appropriate bandage. Of course, the wind caught everything in the bag and blew it out the door while I grabbed at empty air for anything. So I kept my hand up behind my head. I'd let the corpsman on the LST worry about it.

It wasn't long before we were turning on final approach to the ship. Once aboard, the Vietnamese were looked over by the navy corpsman and placed on stretchers on the flight deck to await another medevac. In an emergency, they would come downriver to the LST after dark but not into a hot LZ. Down below, the corpsman bandaged my hand and gave me something for the pain. While I was getting worked on, Hunt and the others were looking over the choppers. Then they all came down below together and presented me with an AK round they had dug out of the side of the chopper. They said that it had to be either the one that hit me in the hand or the one that struck the gun, because it was the only one they could find. All the others had gone clear through. Something had to have slowed that one down or it wouldn't have lodged itself in the other side. They sure were a thoughtful bunch! I still wear that bullet around my neck to remind me of that reality check.

My bird was downed because of all the hits we took, so Wallen had to take his up to make room for the incoming medevac. I was escorted up to the flight deck by the gang. The army chopper had just landed, and they were loading up the VN wounded. Harker ran out at the last minute and told me that the PBRs had successfully picked up the ARVNs and Big Bear, and that was great news! As I was helped into the medevac chopper and settled into a seat, the army corpsman made me lie on a stretcher. Then Harker said, "Job well done." And he gave me a salute. I returned same.

Reclined on the stretcher like a good boy, I felt the helicopter lift into the night air and off into the dark sky headed for Binh Thuy Army Evac Hospital. As I stared off into space, it dawned on me that a lieutenant commander had just saluted *me*! That had to be a first. Sure made me feel good.

Chapter 14

The ride to the Army Evac Hospital in Binh Thuy was a quick one. When we landed, the Vietnamese were taken to their hospital, and my stretcher was taken into our emergency room.

Nurses! Real live round-eye nurses, and good-looking! My lucky day. There's a silver lining to every dark cloud. I hope all those female nurses know what a ray of sunshine they brought into that ugly place. The doctor was a real nice guy with a great sense of humor.

"Well, let's see what we got here. A gunshot wound to the hand, huh. I'd say you were one lucky son of a bitch," the doc said with a laugh.

"What do ya mean, Doc?" I asked as I lay there on the emergency room operating table.

"We got the word about you Seawolves from our last customer. An army medic was just in here and had been shot up pretty bad. He said you folks didn't have a snowball's chance in hell getting those guys out. I guess you make some pretty tough snowballs." He chuckled as he kept examining my hand.

He gave me a local and joked around the whole time he was working on me. I never did look at the hand. All I did was stare at the nurses. The doc told me there was a hole through the middle of my hand he could drop a fifty-cent piece through, the wrist was broken, and three knuckles were shattered. Three of the main bones in my hand were broken in three places with some pieces missing; plus the end of my little finger had been shot off. Doc told me that it would be a miracle if I ever regained the full use of the hand. He thought I'd bought myself a one-way ticket home and out of the service, but I told him there was no way I'd be getting out.

Painkillers finally put me to sleep, and I woke up the next morning on a ward with a bunch of other wounded. The hand was in a cast that only came up to the elbow, so I could still move the arm around. The doctor came by later that morning to check on everybody.

Stopping at my bed, he looked over my chart and said, "We're going to keep you here for two weeks, then release you to outpatient status for another couple weeks before taking the cast off and removing the wire stitches. The other stitches we have in there will dissolve on their own. Shortly after that they'll send you home for discharge from the navy because you won't be able to pass your flight physical. That's the good news. The bad news is, I don't think you'll ever regain use of that hand."

Talk about negative input! I remembered him telling me pretty much the same thing in the operating room. Once was enough, thank you!

"Doc, you don't seem to understand. I will regain full use of my hand, and I will pass my flight physical, and I will be back. You see, I have friends in high places," I said with a typical Irish smirk on my face.

"Well, that's what it's going to take," he said. "And, somehow, I think you will."

"By the way, what's the news on our three wounded we brought in?" I asked.

"Oh, those guys did okay, thanks to you crazy bastards. What I've heard, you guys did the impossible. You're the buzz of the medevac teams here. Two of the three will probably see action again, but the third won't. He'll be all right, but like you, he won't be able to pass any physical for combat. Unless, of course, he has the same friends you do."

"You never know, Doc," I said.

"Oh, one more thing," the doc said. "Do you want your next of kin notified of your injury?"

"Hell no! You'll scare the shit out of them. What they don't know won't hurt them!"

With that, the doc went on to his next patient, and I lay back for one of the many naps to come over the next two weeks I spent in bed.

That time wasn't totally boring, however. There were a few high points. For example, air force general Jimmy Stewart and his wife visited all the patients. He stopped and talked with me for a few seconds. A time I will never forget. Especially the fact that the famous actor had no hair. Otherwise, he still looked great. Oh, and his wife was a total babe. He asked the usual questions: how I was injured; where I was from; how much longer until I got to go home. Then it was on to the next bed. They both were so sweet.

The next thing that happened was a real eye-opener. I was fast asleep one night when we were awakened by sirens going off in unison with the sound of incoming mortars. That wasn't so unusual, but it was accompanied by the sound of a lot of running feet on the concrete floors in the hospital. What the hell was the deal there? Was the hospital staff jumping ship, or what? I couldn't see very well because all the lights were out except the ones around the nurses' station at the end of the ward. Then, all of a sudden, around the corner a whole bunch of people ran down through the middle of the ward. I'm talking a dead run here. Whoever they were, they obviously had just one thing on their mind, and that was how fast they could get to the other end and out of the hospital.

As they went tearing by my bed, I suddenly recognized that they were VC! I couldn't believe it! There were Viet Cong running past my bed! What the fuck was going on? By the time all of us on the ward figured out what was happening, they had exited the building. Just then, we heard another bunch of feet running around the corner, right on the heels of the VC. All of us in the ward froze for a moment, waiting to see who this was. This time it was the 9th Infantry in combat gear, hot on the trail of the retreating Varmint Cong. By then, we were all sufficiently awake to realize what was going on and cheering our boys as they passed through. None of us got any more sleep that night.

After my two weeks were up, the doc released me to outpatient care. But instead of staying in Binh Thuy, I chose to rejoin my team on the Bassac and spend the final two weeks of treatment with them. Harker, Wallen, Hunt, and Mack flew up to get me at Det 7's pad. When they arrived, I was anxiously waiting for them on the PSP out by the trailer. The sound of that chopper coming in, and the sight of it starting to flare as it made that familiar popping noise, and that blast of wind hitting me in the face while I stood grinning from ear to ear, just sent a thunderbolt of excitement right up my spine. They pulled into a hover, sat down, and I climbed aboard. Harker pulled us back up into a hover as Hunt helped me put the helmet that they'd brought along on my head and plugged me into the ICS.

"Welcome aboard, son," Harker said.

"Welcome back, Dumbo," Hunt piped in.

"It's good to be back!" I answered.

Mack just slapped me on the back while giving me that big Seattle McAlester smile.

With that, Harker tipped the chopper forward and up, up, and away we went, over Binh Thuy and turning left, headed to the LST. I couldn't believe how much I had missed the team. Flying along in the gunship caused a feeling to well up in me that I couldn't describe. It was as if I had been dead and I was coming alive again.

On the way downriver, Harker said that he had talked to my doctor, and it looked like they were going to have to cut orders to send me home early. I told him that I had already signed up for another tour with Hunt and I fully intended to complete that commitment. He said that because of the injury, they didn't expect me to be able to pass the flight physical, or any other physical, and that I'd probably get retired out of the navy.

I couldn't believe that was happening! I couldn't go out that way. I was becoming "somebody" over there. The guys needed me. Volunteers for the team were way down. My self-image was finally being repaired, and I couldn't let anyone get in its way. Call it selfish. Call it whatever you want. It was the first time in my life that I felt I'd been successful about anything. People noticed and gave me pats on the back. Maybe I was the kind of person the military looks for to fight the wars? I don't know about all that deep stuff, but I knew then that I wasn't finished in Vietnam.

I asked Harker if he could just get my orders cut for the thirty-day leave that was due me for extending my tour in Vietnam. That way I could go home and work on rehabilitating my hand. Then come back, do the flight physical, and if I failed it then, I would go quietly. My *choice*! He agreed. Matter of fact, he arranged it so Hunt and I could go together because Hunt was due his leave as well.

The next thing to happen was a changing of the guard, as it were. It was time for Harker to be pulled into the squadron for preparation to go home. That was still a couple of months off, but for some reason, they called the pilots in early. Getting to know his replacement would have to wait till my return. Then we lost Pratt to another team. I was going to miss Pratt, but Harker was the tough one. The day of his departure, just before he lifted off the deck, he popped me another smart salute, and I returned it, fighting back a tear in my eye.

After Harker's departure, two new pilots came on board and joined our family. Both of them would become very close to me later. Two really great guys and excellent pilots, Lt.(jg) Bob Shore and Lt.(jg) Rick Saddler.

The next two weeks I spent just watching instead of participating. I hated that, but it couldn't be helped. Before the waiting period for our departure was up, we had a group picture taken at my request because we didn't know what the future would bring. I was upset that I hadn't thought of it before Harker had left.

The big day eventually arrived. With all our stuff packed, Hunt and I boarded one of the PBRs and headed upriver to Binh Thuy; we would catch a C-123 to Saigon and then the old Freedom Bird home. It was a long ride up the Bassac, but a calm one. We stretched out on our duffel bags and snoozed in the sun. I dreamed of parades welcoming me home and of seeing all my friends from school. That one was interrupted by the boat rubbing against the dock. Naps always make trips go faster.

Up and off the PBR, Hunt and I made for the evac hospital across the base. Arriving on my old ward, on time, wringing wet with sweat, we asked for my doctor.

Coming out of an office behind the nurses' station, he said, "Hey, Kelly, how's that hand doing?"

"Itches like a bitch, Doc! Can't wait to get this cast off."

"Well, we'll take care of that right now. Follow me."

"Hey, Doc. Can Hunt come?" I said.

"Sure."

He led us into a little room that had cast-making equipment and supplies everywhere. The place looked like shop class in school. Strange-looking tools were scattered all over. Anyway, he cut the cast off with a little saw, then checked out my hand. Then he grabbed something that looked like pliers or wire cutters. I knew that couldn't be good, because I had all those wire stitches in my hand.

"Hold still now, Kelly. You won't feel a thing."

Bullshit. Then why was sweat running down my forehead when he was done? And it was air-conditioned there.

"That's healed up remarkably well. Take care of it while

you're gone and try working with a rubber ball. We'll see you back here in thirty days and see how you've done. Okay?"

We said our good-byes and headed for the air force side of the base. Time to catch that C-123 for Saigon. Checking in with operations, we learned that it would be another thirty minutes or so before we would board the aircraft. Great! Everything was working out perfectly. I'd rather be early than late. We soon found ourselves strapped in and lifting off.

When you're used to traveling around in a helicopter gunship, a C-123 is like a supersonic jet. In no time at all we were landing at Tan Son Nhut Air Base. Waiting for us as we disembarked was the old familiar gray navy bus to the Meyer Cord Hotel. Much to my disappointment, though, we had a different driver. He wasn't nearly as colorful as the previous one. Of course, that had been almost a year earlier. The other guy was long gone, back home in the World. We were at the hotel in no time, and we needed to be because our Freedom Bird was departing soon.

It took Hunt and me no time at all to take a cold shower and put on our dress blues. Funny, by then the presence of the Vietnamese cleaning ladies in the latrines didn't bother me at all. Anyway, standing there, looking at myself in the mirror in the bath area, I was admiring all the ribbons on my uniform. I'd had only one ribbon when I arrived the year before. Now I had a whole bunch, and I was wearing gold wings and my new rank.

"You pleased with yourself?" Hunt asked.

He'd caught me, damn it. "Hell yes! Why not?" I said.

"That's the spirit! Now, when you're done admiring yourself, we have a plane to catch."

We grabbed our duffels and ran downstairs. Jumping on the waiting bus, we told the driver to hurry up and get us there before we built up too much sweat in these uniforms. He took off and the race was on. Down and around, through and over, honking and yelling, all the way to the main gate and up to the terminal where all the Boeing 707s were standing. The good news was that the engines were already running and the air-conditioning was going. The bad news was that we had to wait in line to get our duffels inspected for contraband. Things like pictures of dead bodies, automatic weapons, drugs. Nothing of any importance. So, by the time we got to the plane, we were a mess again. We didn't spend a whole lot of time worrying about it, though. Probably all of ten seconds passed before Hunt and I, sitting next to each other in our Freedom Bird, were fast asleep. A twenty-four-hour sleep, because that's about how long the flight was. We were two tired puppies.

The plane flew into Travis Air Force Base on a beautiful day. Once we'd disembarked, we were glad we had the dress blues; it was in the middle of winter in the United States. We retrieved our duffels and went straight to the bus stop for a ride off base and into San Francisco to the airport. There we made our way past the hippie protesters and to my gate for a nonstop flight on American Airlines home to Austin, Texas. Damn, that had a nice ring to it. Hunt said good-bye there because he was headed for a flight home to Florida. We'd see each other again in thirty days.

Showing my boarding pass, I went and found the best window seat I could find, and made myself comfortable. The stewardess told me that would be okay because it was going to be an almost empty flight to Austin. Sitting there, my seat belt fastened, I peered out the window at the Good Ol' USA. I couldn't help thinking how complacent we were as a people. Slowly I stared down at the injured hand that I could barely move, the long ugly scar on both sides and the end of my little finger, what was left of it, sewn shut. I was zoned, in a daze. Sometimes I think the mind processes things without us consciously knowing it. I think that's part of the reason I had the mind-set I had on the plane. I knew what to expect at the airport, and it wouldn't be a hero's welcome. After all, I had seen it when I left to go over to Vietnam a year before. The Bible says with knowledge comes sorrow. Well, I knew things about Vietnam that the hippies didn't know. Hell, I knew things that Congress didn't know and, furthermore, probably didn't care about. They just looked at the "big picture." It's always the same. Managing from the top down instead of the bottom up. The war was about the villages and what was happening there. Not the economy in the country. If we'd fixed the lifestyle in the villages, everything else would have taken care of itself. This war had become personal, not just for me but for the little kid in that village who had all his fingers cut off by the VC because his dad refused to fight with the Communists. One of the many visions I would not forget.

My thoughts drifted to my '56 Pontiac I had in high school because the pain and disappointment was getting too great. The times Bob Liarakos and I took the muffler off so we could hear what it sounded like. The party we had at my parents' house when they were vacationing in California. The first close slow dance I had with a gorgeous blonde back at Pearce Junior High School. She didn't even know I was alive, but I thought she was really something. The first teacher I had a crush on, Mrs. Roden, had had her elementary school class write me letters while I was in Vietnam. Then my train of thought switched to how I had quit the Civil Air Patrol; how I had quit band; how I had quit high school. If I had it to do all over again, quitting high school's the one thing I wouldn't have done. I'll never have a high-school reunion I can go to. All those years invested in all those friendships, gone with the class of '68. It seemed like my whole life was a waste. But not so! They were all my *choices*! No one else's! The navy was not a waste! So far I had accomplished something most couldn't, and that also had been my *choice*! There was no way I was going to be a failure at the navy, even if my own country wanted to reject me! I was not going to quit! *I had to get my hand working again!*

I was interrupted when a very beautiful stewardess bent over me with a cold beer in her hand and a big smile on her face. She handed me the drink, which was against the law because we were still on the ground, and I was just twenty years old.

She said, "Here, it looks like you could use it!"

I thanked her, and she sat with me, and waited on me the rest of the flight. She asked me what had happened to my hand, and I told her the story. She was a saving angel. I'll never forget her.

We landed in Austin, and my mom, stepdad, and little brother Sam met me at the airport. No band. No parade. Just my family and I walking down the long corridor toward the luggage-claim area, no one even giving me a second glance. I was so glad to see Mom and my stepdad, but the thing that really brought bright sunshine into my heart was seeing my little brother again. That little three-year-old kid really made me feel good. We had a lot of fun playing together. I've been accused, more than once, of being twelve years old with gusts up to sixteen.

I never did see most of my school friends while I was home. I did spend time with Jimmy Strawser and Robert Griffith. Jimmy was the little brother of Bill Strawser, the guy I'd met in San Diego who was going to nuclear submarines. And Robert and I go way back to elementary school. He was a great friend. Then there was the Strawsers' sister, Kathy. What a babe! So I did get with some of the crowd after all.

Mom and my stepdad took me out partying at some of the local nightspots a couple of times. Then I hooked up with my dad and stepmom and partied with them a little. In between, I just slept a lot, when I wasn't playing with my little brother. And I constantly worked my hand with a rubber ball I purchased at a local toy store. That took up a couple of weeks.

After that, I got together with my dad and stepmom, and we drove up to Iowa to visit my big brother, John, who was going to college. I played in the snow, got drunk, and generally wasted a lot of time with my brother and all my cousins, of whom there were about a dozen. Besides the special time I spent with John, the only other thing that stands out about my leave time is a poem that my cousin Lori wrote for us while we were visiting at Grandma and Grandpa's house. It was an assignment she was writing for a high-school speech class, and it touched on veterans. It really touched my heart. The memory probably stands out because I was so hungry for recognition.

But eventually, it was back to Texas for me and time to gear up for the trip back to Vietnam.

Once we returned to Austin, I had only a few days left. That was spent really hitting the rubber ball exercises with my hand and playing with my little brother. The last night home I spent with my childhood friend, Kathy Strawser, pondering my return to the war zone. She was a real godsend. She provided the understanding female companionship that I so desperately needed at that time in my life. Don't get me wrong; we didn't "do" anything, of course; I just needed a hug that I hadn't gotten from my country before I returned to Vietnam. Thank you, Kathy. I'll never forget you.

The month had gone by quickly, and going to the airport was tough. The two big reasons for that were big brother John and little brother Sam. I was really going to miss them. But the rubber ball and Jesus had done the trick; my hand was back to normal. I was ready. Vietnam or bust.

Austin to San Francisco, past the hippies, and out to Travis Air Force Base, where I hooked up with Hunt again. Something seemed different this time. The building was the same, and it was cold again, and all the soldiers looked the same. We were getting on the plane during the daylight hours, but that wasn't it.

After Hunt and I had exchanged stories about our month-long leave while waiting in line, we loaded up on the plane, strapped ourselves in, and relaxed, both in a quiet, tranquil mood, staring off into nothingness. I noticed how tense and excited everyone else was as they bounced around the compartment getting settled in. Then it hit me. There were a few other guys on the plane, like us, just sitting there in a daze. Then I remembered noticing similar guys on my first trip over. It was their second tour they were making, just like us. I was one of *those* guys! I understood why they looked the way they had; they'd changed. So had I!

Chapter 15

This time, our trip to Vietnam was by way of Hawaii, where we spent one hour filling up with fuel, and then it was on to Vietnam and Saigon. After we had passed Guam, we saw a squadron of B-52s flying home after a bombing run. Those big things, with their superlong wings and long vapor trails behind against that dark blue, almost black sky above, were an awesome sight. That was the high point of the trip back.

Upon arriving in Saigon, it was the same old thing. Customs inspection, gray navy bus to the Meyer Cord Hotel, change clothes and then, well, it was our lucky day. There just happened to be an army UH-34 pulling a mail run out close to the Bassac River where the LST was. The pilot said that he would make a minor detour to drop us off on the ship.

That flight was an experience. I had never been on one of those old things before. The UH-34 was powered by a great big Korean War–era radial, internal combustion engine. One army aircrewman was in the back with an M-60 mounted in the door. I guess all they ever used that antique for was running mail. Hunt and I just curled up with the mailbags and took a nap.

On arrival at the LST, we had a big reunion with the guys. Stories flowed freely for several hours about our trip home and back, and everything that we had missed there in the Nam. We discovered that our squadron had moved from Vung Tau to Binh Thuy, which was a big surprise. Also, we got the low-down on our new fire team officer in charge, "Pizza Man." He didn't hang out much with the crews. Kind of kept to himself. Word had it also that he was a heavy drinker. And the scariest part was, he couldn't fly for shit. No one could figure out how the guy had slipped through the system. Oh well. Hopefully his incompetence will be noticed, and he'll be replaced soon! Eventually, the guys got around to mentioning that the latest intel said we had tangled with four regiments of NVA the night I got shot. I guess we were truly blessed that evening.

At the top of my priority list was getting up to Doc Spence, our flight surgeon in Binh Thuy, and taking a flight physical. As I hadn't been dubbed flightworthy yet, I had to ride middle seat between McGowan and Fryburger. Wallen was flying in the pilots' seat with Saddler as copilot. The whole team went, making a vacation out of it. They hadn't had a beer in a long time, and it was as good a time as any. Besides, it was Sunday. (Of course, that made no difference in a war zone.)

The LST was already quite a ways upriver, so the flight didn't take long. I hadn't had the privilege of formally meeting our new Seawolf One-six yet, and after listening to the others, it sounded like he was a big step down from Harker. He was flying lead. Good ol' Seawolf One-four, Wallen had us bringing up the rear.

As we came in over Binh Thuy, I noticed there had been a lot of construction going on. A whole new runway had been built: barracks, hangar, everything was new. Coming in over the river, we turned on final approach. I also noticed off to our right a line of new revetments with strange-looking green planes. They reminded me of twin-boom P-38s from World War II on steroids. As I was taking note of all the changes, especially the strange-looking planes, Seawolf One-six overshot the turnoff. That put Wallen in position to turn left into the revetment area first. As he hovered along past all the new stuff, I was looking everywhere at once, taking everything in. New hangars for the strange green planes. New hangars for us. New everything everywhere. Boy, the navy Seabees had been busy!

As Wallen kept us headed for our parking spot, I hit the ICS. "What's with all these green planes?"

McGowan said, "That's a new outfit that just moved in to give us heavier air support. VAL-4 Black Ponies."

"What kind of planes are those?" I asked.

"They're OV-10 Broncos. Wait till you see them fly. They're really cool!" McGowan said.

I thought the added support was probably part of the result of Admiral Zumwalt's visit in Ca Mau. I wondered what else he was planning for us.

We turned left again, between two rows of Huey gunships parked in revetments pointing away from the runway. The two spots we were headed for were closest to the hangar. We moved down to our parking place, came to a hover, made a right turn in place, and slowly moved forward into the revetment.

About then, Seawolf One-six transmitted something, but to this day none of us can remember what it was he was saying or trying to say, because as soon as he keyed his mike "the freak thing" happened that everyone thought couldn't "really" happen. One of the earliest parts of my helicopter training stressed the importance of lifting the contacts off the back of the rockets as soon as you land so that the transmission of a radio wouldn't set off a rocket. Well, one of our rockets launched.

We all held our breath as it sailed out of its tube, across the open field in front of us, through a fence, and into our laundry. It exploded, hurling sheets and pillowcases everywhere. We sat down in a panic, wondering how many of our guys we had just killed. One of the linemen, recognizing the frightened looks on our faces, ran to let us know that the laundry was closed because it was Sunday. No injuries at all except maybe a little pride. Welcome home!

After securing the aircraft, we went straight over to see Doc Spence while the officers dealt with the laundry incident. Doc was glad to see me and surprised. He had been in touch with the army surgeon who had patched me up, so he knew what the odds were with my hand.

He gave me my physical while the guys waited outside. All the working out with the rubber ball had paid off. My hand was back to normal. Doc was amazed. "I would have bet my profession that you wouldn't ever get full use of that hand back." He walked out with me and announced the good news. Time to celebrate. We all went in to Can Tho, got blasted, and met some friendly women.

The next morning came way too soon. But it was business as usual. We flew back to the LST and started patrols as normal, but this time we had a new kind of fun awaiting us. The place where I got shot, the same place the SEALs had been hit, and the same place the B-52s put in their strike was still a hot area and had been declared a free-fire zone. We had standing orders to kill anyone that we saw. Anything! People, water buffalo, pigs, chickens, anything! While I was at Binh Thuy getting my physical, the team had acquired a new toy that the squadron wanted us to try out to help judge its feasibility for future use. This "toy" was a belt-feed 40mm grenade-launching machine gun operated with a crank like the old-fashioned Gatling gun. We mounted it in the door. An ammo can was attached to the side of it, swivel mount. I couldn't help but laugh when I first saw it. I didn't think much of it, but it did look like it would be a lot of fun to play with.

Mack and I mounted the thing on Wallen's bird and got ready to go have fun in the new free-fire zone. Campbell and Shore would fly cover for us, with Hunt and McGowan in the back. It was going to be Mack's farewell flight, because it was time for him to go back to the World.

We loaded four ammo cans in the chopper, untied the rotor, and got her turned up. Seawolf One-two on our tail, we lifted off and headed directly for the target as soon as we got to one thousand feet. The test gun was mounted on my side, so I got first turn at it.

Looking out at the jungle and the huge potholes below, near where I had gotten shot, gave me a strange feeling. Shaking it off, I made sure the grenades were loaded properly, got comfortable, and away I went. Cranking out those 40mm grenades as fast as I could, it didn't take long to empty the ammo can. It was an odd sensation, because I could see them all going through the air as they left the gun, and before the first one even hit the ground, I had already emptied the can. Leaning out my door, with Mack at my side, we waited for them to start impacting the ground. Wow! We both, including Saddler in the copilot's seat, started laughing. The explosions looked like a tiny B-52 strike, all real close together, walking a line through the jungle. Laughing, we fed another can into the gun, and Mack took his turn.

Saddler said on the ICS, "This sucks! I want a turn at that thing, too."

We had a real great time with the new weapon, but there was no way I'd have it in my door for a real mission. It just took up too much room. And anything that decreased my maneuverability with the M-60 had to go. I wanted the freedom to be able to shoot anywhere I needed in order to cover us and our team.

"Well, that was fun. All the grenades are gone. I guess we can head for home," I said on the ICS.

"Not quite yet," Mack said.

I turned to look over at Mack. He had something strange-looking in his hands.

"What are those things?" I asked.

"These are bombs from World War I that Harker and I found a while back. I've been saving them for a special occasion. This being my last flight, I figured now's the time," Mack answered.

There were two of them. One for him and one for me. They were about the diameter of a softball, a foot long, with fins on the back end. We located some thatched huts in the jungle below and had Wallen line us up.

Wallen banked the chopper around hard because he wanted to see what the "strike" looked like. I was surprised how big the blast was. Even so, I missed the hut.

"Okay, let's see if you can get it any closer than that, Mack."

"This is in the bag," he said confidently.

Giving directions to Wallen, he got the target lined up and dropped. Again, Wallen whipped the bird around so we could all see the hut. Damn, that thing took its time getting to the ground.

The hut was vaporized in the explosion. Ah yes! Another day in the life and times of the Southeast Asia Police Action.

Back at the LST, we all said good-bye to Mack, who boarded a PBR and went upriver to Binh Thuy. A good man and good friend. We planned to build an A-frame in the mountains and chase women together once we were both back in the World. I was going to miss him.

Later that night, we pulled a patrol downriver. It was a beautiful clear night with a full moon. My first day back and already at work. The plan was to just fly downriver, at about eight hundred feet, over one bank and back up the other one, with our running lights on to see if anybody would shoot at us.

Soto and Beem were flying, and it was me and McGowan in the back. Wallen was the pilot of the trail bird flying with Saddler; Hunt and Valladares were the gunners. While we were flying along, McGowan was briefing me, using the ICS, on what had been happening while I was gone. One of the stranger things was when we flew over one *South* Vietnamese outpost on the river, at night, they would shoot a stream of tracers up at the bird.

I said, "You're kidding."

"I wish I was," McGowan answered.

"And nobody has done anything about it?"

Beem said, "Like what?"

Soto said, "There isn't anything you can do. That's all Vietnamese government stuff in Saigon."

"And they shoot at you every time you go over," I said.

"Only at night," McGowan said.

"I'll point the outpost out to you just before we get there, and you can see for yourself," Soto said.

We continued on with the mission, flying downriver, over the top of Dung Island and up the other side.

"We're almost there. About a half a klick further," Soto said.

Sure enough, when we got over the outpost, up came the tracers, a bunch of them. Came pretty damn close. Our individual M-16s, which we kept as backup in case we were shot down, were loaded just with tracer rounds so that when we fired them it would look like a minigun going off. It was quite a spectacle. I don't know what came over me, but I grabbed up the M-16, placed it on full automatic, leaned out my door, pointed it down where the tracers had just come from, and pulled the trigger. I ran the whole clip out of it right down into the middle of that outpost. Soto about shit! I thought McGowan was going to fall out of the chopper laughing. All Beem could do was say, "Son of a bitch!"

"Nobody saw that!" Soto said.

"Saw what?" Beem answered.

McGowan couldn't talk. He was too busy laughing.

They never shot at us again. We never got in trouble for it, either. I had changed considerably since my first tour. No way I would have done that before.

Chapter 16

The last major mission we had on the Bassac was a big strike on Dung Island that was set up by the SEALs. They had intel that said that there was going to be a big meeting at a pagoda on the island. All the people from the VC's high command for that area were supposed to be there. The SEALs were to go in at night and set up around the spot before morning, then keep watch to make sure that everyone targeted had arrived. The SEALs would call us when the time was right. We would assault low-level while the meeting was under way, and hit it with everything we had. The SEALs would polish off survivors and clean up. It should be seriously demoralizing for the enemy, not to mention it would screw up their communications for a while.

It was about midnight when the SEAL team slipped over the side of the LST and into the LSSC. We watched as they started those big 427s, bringing the Jacuzzi jet pumps into action, then quietly streaked downriver into the darkness. Then it was back to the old waiting game. Jesus, I hated that part. Retiring to our compartment, we attempted to get some sleep. The plan called for us to be up and ready to go just before sunrise. That meant if we were going to get any rest at all, we'd better sleep quick.

Lying there in my bunk, I was trying to go to sleep, but I ended up staring at the red lights in the compartment, wondering what time it was and thinking about how tired I was getting. Finally, my eyes got so heavy, I passed out. *Damn it! Leave me alone, will ya!* What? It's time to get up? I just now closed my eyes!

Hunt was hitting me in the shoulder. "Get the fuck up, Dumbo. We got VC to kill."

So it was get your body in gear and get with the program. It was up and out of the rack, into the tiger stripes, and up on deck to preflight. Then coffee and cigarettes. Then wait in the chopper for our guys to call in the hell from above.

The sun coming up over the jungle was always so beautiful. Sitting there, sipping on my coffee, smoking a cigarette, looking at the jungle on the bank, always brought me back to that same old thought of what a great resort place this could be. War sure had a way of fucking up a good dream.

Soto came running across the flight deck, followed close behind by Shore, Saddler, and Wallen. Hunt and Valladares were flying with Wallen and Saddler.

"Turn 'em up, kids! It's time to go," Soto hollered out.

We went into action. Two minutes later both choppers were turning up full speed.

"Seawolf One-five. Hover check complete, and we're off at this time."

Over the edge of the deck we went, staying low-level and circling the LST once while waiting for One-four to fall in behind us. Then, turning downriver, we hugged the water at about three feet as we made our way to the northern tip of the island. I always loved that kind of mission. It was so exhilarating to come up on the jungle at one hundred knots right on the water, watching the land get closer and closer, then, at the last minute, popping up just enough to clear the tops of the trees, then down the other side, to follow the terrain as closely as possible. Many times that meant getting leaves stuck in the skids. What a rush.

All guns at the ready, rocket sight pulled down in front of Soto's watchful eye, we approached the objective. Leaning way outside, with my foot in its usual spot on top of the rocket pod, I pointed the M-60 forward while straining to get the first glimpse of the pagoda. Wallen right on our tail, we were two gunships screaming along, bobbing up and down with the changing elevation of the jungle canopy, weaving in and out around some of the taller trees, trying to stay hidden as much as possible, with four gunners stretched outside, copilots peering through their flex-gun sights, and pilots ready with fingers on the rocket-launch button, the rocket systems set for salvo. We charged toward the prize!

There it is! I squeezed my trigger at the same instant Shore and McGowan opened up, sending a wave of tracers down on the pagoda. Soto hit the rocket button, and all fourteen rockets blasted out of their tubes, sending a deluge of sparks in our faces as they sped at the VC gathering below. My God, what a huge devastating series of explosions! The pagoda was almost totally destroyed as pieces of wall and roof erupted skyward. Breaking off to the right, Shore stopped firing the flex guns because they wouldn't turn to the left any farther. I kept my machine gun on the pagoda, tearing up the fragments of walls, doors, and windows that were left as we exited the location. Then One-four's strike hit! I felt the concussion as all those rockets exploded.

After both gunships had cleared the target, we orbited off a ways to wait for word from the SEAL team. I don't think we received a single shot from the enemy below. That meant just one thing. We caught them totally by surprise. So far, the mission had come off like clockwork. I just loved it when that happened. Then we heard from the SEALs on the ground. I held my breath as I waited to hear what they had to say.

"Seawolf One-five, Shadow. Nice shooting. All present and accounted for. Over."

All right! Thank you, Jesus! Time to go home and celebrate. When the SEALs returned, they told us we had a body count of forty-eight. We got 'em all! That should give Charlie something to think about.

After that, the Bassac and Dung Island became pretty docile. Not much going on. An occasional potshot taken at us, but that was about it. So I guess it was time to move on to better ground. And good old Admiral Zumwalt was ready!

Mr. Zumy had put together a big operation down in Ca Mau. This was the result of our round-robin strikes on Square Bay to Ha Tien. We would be assisting the UDT (underwater demolition teams, later absorbed into SEALs), SEALs, Swift boats, Coast Guard, and the Vietnamese Marines in placing an outpost in Ca Mau. It was to be located on a barge on one of the big rivers and would be positioned by the Swift boats. From there, we would run operations all over the peninsula. The location was to be called Seafloat. In the meantime, we would be stationed on the LST *Windham County* in the Gulf of Siam while getting Seafloat positioned and operational.

During and after the move, several new people joined our family. The pilots were Bud Barnes, Marty Chamberlain, and Mack Thomas. The gunners were Andy, Jasmann, Olby, Marcus, and Christenson, but their arrivals were spread out over several months, so we were definitely doing double duty at times.

Bud Barnes was a Naval Academy graduate, always prim and proper. Marty Chamberlain was a skinny little guy, like most of the rest of us, and kind of quiet. Then there was Mack Thomas, a crazy guy. All three were a lot of fun and spent time with us enlisted pukes. They were great leaders and always set a fine example for us to follow. Outstanding pilots, too.

Andy was my student and gunner. Jesus, was he another big one. Tall and lanky. Shaved his head and grew a Fu Manchu. He'd have scared me silly if I'd run into him in a dark alley. But he had a great heart. Jasmann was a typical West Coast Mr. Cool, a wizard when it came to sound equipment, and very athletic. Also very good-looking. Olby was another ladies' man. He was also one hell of a shot. He and Jasmann were always in competition with each other. Marcus was as likable as air and very conscientious. Christenson was a born ass-kicker. He always had that look, the one that said please give me some shit so I can kick your ass. He couldn't get enough combat. He was a supernice guy—and we all were very tight—just as long as you were part of the team. I loved all of these guys. We became very close.

Once we were settled in on the *Windham County*, we were ready to start preparations for the installation of Seafloat. The first order of the day, as far as the officers were concerned, was where to put it. That would depend on the intel the SEALs gathered, the reports from the Swift boats that ran the canals daily, and the Seawolf pilots identifying where the heaviest fire came from. We wanted a central location so we didn't have to go far to hit any given point.

I got assigned to fly with Pizza Man. I learned firsthand, finally, what the guys had been talking about. He was enough to make you give up flying. He had no idea about how to properly fly that gunship, and he came damn near getting us killed on several occasions. One of the gunners was accidentally thrown from the chopper because Pizza Man didn't know how to turn the thing on a break. Luckily the gunner had his pussy belt on so he could climb back in. Another time, while covering a SEAL recon—fortunately, I was in the trail bird for once—we put in a strike, and he called a break left but broke right!

Wallen said, "Where the fuck is he going?" Since we were pretty tight, I could get away with things an enlisted puke normally wouldn't dare do.

I reached up and clicked the ICS over to transmit outside the chopper, keyed the mike, and said, "Which way did he go, George? Which way did he go?"

Pissed, Pizza Man came on the air instantly and said, "Who said that?"

There was silence over the airwaves; I looked up at Wallen, who was about to fall out of the chopper, he was laughing so hard! Pizza Man didn't recognize my voice over the airwaves because I had made it sound like that Warner Brothers cartoon character.

Upon returning to the LST, everybody, including the pilots, adjourned to the enlisted men's quarters for a serious laugh session. But our laughter was cut short when Barnes brought us news that Det 3 had lost a chopper up at Ha Tien. Rick Abbott was one of the crew that went down. My longtime friend. My big brother away from home. That really hurt. Later, we got word that Rick had survived. He was permanently disabled, but he had survived. Things were definitely heating up down here.

The SEALs performed several recons, and when they had narrowed down the many possible locations, they brought in UDT-13 guys to sweep the canals in the area they were thinking about. We acted as UDT's taxi service to the drop-off location. Wallen was the pilot on that hop, Chamberlain the copilot. Rick Saddler and Barnes, with gunners Hunt and Jasmann, were in the trail bird that was going to cover us. How the pilots kept Pizza Man from taking part, I have no idea, but that was a good thing because I doubt he could hover long enough for the UDT to jump out.

It was an overcast day when we took off with our two passengers in the back. Sitting on the floor of the gunship, with all the scuba gear and their SEAL trunks on, they looked like two Mike Nelsons from the old TV show "Sea Hunt." We went low-level all the way in from the LST out in the gulf to the mouth of the river and on upstream. The divers told us where to stop. While we hovered to let them out, Saddler orbited the area, keeping us covered. Wallen slowly worked us into the center of the river and kept us about five feet off the water, then the divers got out on the skids, one on either side, and jumped. They disappeared into the murky brown water below, and we hovered downstream, watching their bubbles as we went. That was very stressful, because we were sitting ducks as we nearly hovered, trying to keep an eye on the divers' location and staying alert with our M-60s pointed at the jungle on both banks. The pucker factor was off the scale!

Hovering along at about twenty feet, the mist from the water coming down through the rotor blades, squinting at the jungle for any bad sign at all, my eyes darting down to the water and focusing on bubbles, then back again to the jungle, was giving me a splitting headache. Following the light brown water to the dark brown mudbank and then the green jungle from tree to tree to bush to bush and back to dark brown mudbank, I began to notice things I hadn't ever seen before. Creatures crawling in the mud, strange little things that looked to be half frog, half fish. And some of them were large—well, as big as a bullfrog, anyway. They were camouflaged well, too, the same color as the mud around them. It's amazing what you'll notice when your life depends on it. I just hoped I'd see Charlie that well.

Finally we got to the mouth of the river, and our two divers surfaced. Wallen put us right down on the water, dipping the skids ever so slightly in the river as the UDT personnel crawled aboard, one on either side, while Andy and I pulled them up and in. We had to let our M-60s down for that, which I hated, but we got them on board and moved on to the next river. It was a very long day!

A few days later, Andy and I were on again, but this time it was our turn to fly with Pizza Man; Hunt rotated everybody so no one person had to fly with him all the time. The SEALs had gone in the jungle on a recon at night and were to stay out till the next night. They were checking out another location for our new base. It was about midday when we got scrambled. Taking off, our chopper wobbling like a wounded duck, which was usual when Pizza Man was flying, we headed for the SEAL team.

"Outlaw, Seawolf One-six. Over."

"Roger, Seawolf. This is Outlaw. Over."

"Outlaw, Seawolf One-six is at your location at, ah, right now. Ah, where do you want us to strike? Over."

"Seawolf, Outlaw is popping red smoke. Target is two hundred yards east of red smoke. Do you copy?"

"Ah, two hundred yards east of red smoke. I understand. Over."

Barnes piped in on ICS, "That jungle is really deep down there, and we have a pretty heavy wind blowing that smoke. We better move that target out a little farther, don't you think?"

"No, it's fine," Pizza Man answered.

I looked over at Andy, and he was looking back at me, a disgusted look on his face. We could see that the wind was blowing pretty quickly and the smoke drifting like crazy as it broke through the tops of the trees. Everybody could see that except Pizza Man.

The trees there were exceptionally tall, with several elevations of jungle growth between the tops of the trees and the ground. In most places, if you were on the ground, it could be broad daylight, but it would seem like it was night because of the thickness of the canopy.

Totally ignoring the obvious drift of the smoke, Pizza Man rolled in.

Holding my M-60 up and leaning outside ready to open fire, I pushed the floor button with my foot, "Sir, that smoke is drifting really bad down there. We need to shoot further east."

Totally ignoring me as well, he punched off the first of three rockets. Andy and I opened up but aimed our fire where it was supposed to go, and as we did, we were screaming great obscenities at Pizza Man. So did Barnes with the flex guns. All three rockets dropped way short and exploded under the jungle canopy.

"Seawolf, Seawolf! What the fuck are you doing? Cease fire, cease fire!"

With that, Pizza Man took us straight over the real target in a panic before he broke off at two hundred feet, getting the shit shot out of us by Charlie in the process. What saved us were beautiful timing and shooting by Wallen. *Kaboom!* Three large explosions as Seawolf One-four put three rockets right under our ass, on the correct target. The helicopter shook from the explosions. Exiting the target, Pizza Man took us up to one thousand feet and orbited the area, putting in door-gunner fire only. As it turned out, the SEALs were okay because they were in the middle of a mud bog that absorbed the rocket shrapnel and kept much of it from doing any damage. They did have extensive ringing in their ears for a while, though. That was basically the end of that mission, because the SEALs didn't want us putting in any more rockets. They cleared out of the area and went back to Hai Yen to regroup. Pizza Man didn't have a whole lot to say, because the SEALs had him for breakfast, lunch, and dinner on the radio before they left. Oh, special note, where the VC were, there was no mud! Wallen's three rockets and our door-gunner fire did the job. I sure was glad Wallen knew the meaning of close air support.

As I sat staring a hole in the back of Pizza Man's head, I got angrier and angrier. How in hell did that guy slip through the system? I guess there aren't any perfect systems. Some foul balls are always going to slip through. But why there? Why then? Why in the fuck did it have to be there with *me*? Oh well! Shit happens! It's all in what you choose to do with it.

Then our radio erupted with "Mayday, Mayday, Mayday! Seawolf Three-six is going down! Map Long Xuyen! Scale one to two-fifty! Coordinates four five, five zero! Mayday, Mayday! Oh my God!" and then silence.

That was Schaffernocker and Page! We gotta get to 'em!

As he took out a map, Barnes said, "We got to go help them!"

Pizza Man said, "How far is it?"

A long pause, and then Barnes said, "It's too far! We don't have enough fuel. Besides, it would take us forever to get there."

We wanted to go so bad, but there was no way! They were

just too far out of reach. I was already pissed, and this just made things worse! It was the most painful experience of my life, listening to them holler "Mayday" on the radio and us looking at our fuel and being almost out of ammo. They were just too far away, and we were just about out of everything. We felt so helpless.

When we got back to the LST, I was pissed. Getting out of the helicopter, I threw my stuff on the deck instead of putting it in my seat. Threw my M-60 on the floor of the helicopter in the back, and went straight to Hunt and told him I was through.

"I'm not flying anymore with that unprofessional idiot. He's going to get people killed, and that fat fuck will probably get out without a scratch!" I yelled.

Remember, Seawolves was strictly a volunteer outfit. You could quit at any time. Besides I wanted to get back to Binh Thuy and see Harker before he left country to see if he could do anything about Pizza Man. Somebody had to know what that fat tub of goo was doing out there. My *choice*.

Hunt said okay and it was just a matter of waiting for a hop back to Binh Thuy. I packed all my stuff and sat back, smoldering about what had been going on and what had happened to Page and Schaffernocker. Valladares was pissed at me for quitting because he'd have to fly more turns with the Pizza Man.

Valladares was a very nice guy and great gunner. I miss him a lot, and we've lost track of him. He was fun to party with, another guy who had a great sense of humor. Seawolves was a good-humored outfit. When we weren't fighting, we were laughing. We had to in order to cope with the lifestyle. A great team. Anyway, I knew where he was coming from when he got mad about my quitting, but I had been flying Seawolf missions for thirteen months with professionals. He had just been doing it for perhaps three months. I had five more months to go. Besides, there was a chance that I could make a difference back in Binh Thuy where I couldn't on the *Windham County*.

The next day, the guys got scrambled into a serious shit

storm. A battle that would go down in history as the battle of the 43 Boat. I listened on the radio to what was going on, and it just made me sick. It was a classic cluster fuck. Eight Swift boats were running a sweep up the Duong Keo River. The last Swift had UDT-13 Detachment Golf on it, along with over eight hundred pounds of high explosives to blow bunkers located upriver. The 43 Boat got left behind because of its heavy load and was going full throttle to catch up when the ambush hit.

The 43 got hit by B-40 rockets, went out of control and hit the bank, still at full throttle, pushing itself up the bank and into the jungle before it came to a stop. Nobody knew where they were. We could hear the UDT lieutenant on the radio calling for help, but his signal kept breaking up because the radios were shot to hell. The operation turned into mass confusion, and everybody was talking on the radio at the same time. When the Seawolves got on location, Seawolf One-four, Wallen, got on the radio and told everybody to just calm down and let one person talk at a time. It took the Seawolves a minute, but they found 43 and passed the location on to the rest. Then he helped guide the rescue boats back down to the 43.

When it was all over, the bravery of countless individuals shone brightly. The success of the rescue was due to a lot of brave individual effort. When they started bringing the wounded aboard the LST to be medevacked to other locations, I mingled with them, trying to cheer them up. One of the UDT members who had been hit in the face told me that after he was wounded, all he could do was throw grenades. We lost two good men that night. Barnes lost an old academy friend, one of the "66 Raiders" (after the Naval Academy graduating class of 1966). A small group of his classmates had ended up in the Ca Mau: a Seawolf pilot, captains of Swift boats, and a SEAL. The captain of the 43 Boat, Don Droz, one of the 66 Raiders, was killed in that battle. Along with him was CPO Robert Worthington of UDT-13 Detachment Golf. They are—and will be—remembered and missed.

Chapter 17

The next day, I rode into Binh Thuy with army medevac choppers. It was a long way back to the home of the Sea-wolves. I hated to go, but I just couldn't sit by and watch what was happening. Once we got back, I got myself checked in, and they put me on the line inspecting helicopters. Before checking in at work, I looked up Bill Harker and told him about Pizza Man and the incident that had made me come in. I asked him if there was anything he could do. He said he was already working on it. It seemed clear to me that he already knew something, but he wasn't talking.

The next several weeks I spent moving aircraft in and out of the hangar and pulling inspections. The routine was very laid-back in comparison to what I had become used to, like a regular nine-to-five job, the kind that comes with weekends off. And we all know where off-time was spent! Either in bed or at the EM club getting drunk. Well, that's not totally true; I did keep lifting weights and exercising to stay in shape. I never knew when I might need that extra edge. Remember Mr. Murphy?

A week later I heard that Pizza Man had been relieved of command by a great guy by the name of Habicht. Harker was gone by then. I hope he knew the good news before he left, and I hope that I had a helping hand getting rid of that bad-news pilot. Wallen had also checked out for home. I'd miss him, too;

he took some of the greatest Super-8 film out the front of the helicopter that I ever saw.

The monsoon season was going great guns by this time, and things were unseasonably cool. I loved pulling inspections out in the rain and moving choppers in and out of the hangar. The precipitation falling from the sky really felt good. I loved the season until it stopped raining—then Binh Thuy became a steam room.

I was over at the EM club one evening, as usual, leaning over a cold beer after a long shift at work, when out of nowhere, a hand appeared in front of my face holding a Polaroid picture of McGowan on a stretcher, smiling, holding up a hand that was all bandaged up. I looked up. Jasmann and Marcus were standing in front of me, all dirty. They were still in their flying gear.

"What the fuck is this?" I said excitedly.

Jasmann said, "McGowan got shot!"

"Earned himself a Purple Heart!" Marcus said.

"Is he okay?" I asked as I sat back, still startled.

Laughing, Jasmann said, "Are you kidding? He's already tried to pick up two nurses over at the evac hospital!"

"You finished taking your vacation yet?" Marcus asked.

"What do ya mean?" I asked.

Jasmann said, "We need you, man! We need you back bad!"

"Besides, Hunt misses you!" Marcus said.

"Well, you interested?" Jasmann asked.

"Does a fat baby fart? You bet your ass I'm interested! When we headed back?" My *choice*. This one would definitely send me down a different road! We never know from one choice to the next how little or great that choice will affect the rest of our lives. Just always remember, you made that choice! Nobody else!

"Right now!" Marcus said.

"Shit! We gotta get hold of the chief and get me some orders cut, fast!" I said.

With that, the three of us were out the door of the EM club

and headed on a search mission for the chief. He wasn't at the chiefs' club. That left his bed. It was around midnight when we pulled his ass out of a sound sleep. He approved the transfer and said that he would take care of all the paperwork in the morning.

We raced to the barracks and packed my gear. The next stop was to visit McGowan and see how he was doing. The hustler was out of surgery already and making himself known to the rest of the nurses. He'd be fine! We said good-bye and headed back south to Ca Mau in the choppers. That's the last I saw of him. McGowan's another one we haven't been able to find. A great guy. We miss him. He's probably basking in the Florida sun, chasing women.

When we got to the LST, Hunt was waiting for me. I got out of the chopper, we walked up to each other and shook hands, and he said, "Welcome home!"

I was back!

Hunt introduced me to our new CO, Lieutenant Commander Habicht. He was a big man. Not fat, just tall and solid. A natural leader, excellent pilot, good people person with a good sense of humor. Wrapped tight as a banjo string, always ready to go, Lieutenant Commander Habicht had the good sense to listen to those who had been around for a while. He was blessed with wisdom and was very well liked by everyone.

As I got settled in down below, Hunt filled me in on what had been going on while I was away. Sea Float had been put in place. The Swift boats had been running patrols from it, and the SEALs had been doing parakeet hops, body-snatch (kidnapping) missions, and ambushes, gathering more intelligence to try and nail down that POW camp we had heard about. The intelligence reports confirmed that American pilots were brought down to Ca Mau from up north, through Laos and Cambodia, just as we'd thought. To cause even more trouble for Charlie, Habicht had come up with an idea that would make our choppers more effective than they had ever been before.

We had been given, on loan, an army pilot and his crew chief with a Hughes 500, OH 6A Cayuse, to be used as bait and recon for our two gunships that would orbit above it. The big plan was to use the Cayuse to rattle Charlie's cage until he made a mistake and exposed himself enough so we could get a solid line on the POW camp.

Early up, Andy, my gunner again, and I were flying with Habicht and Saddler. The trail bird pilots were Shore and Chamberlain, and its gunners were Marcus and Olby. Jasmann was flying backseat in the Hughes 500 with army captain Brocheux as the pilot.

Brocheux had balls of iron, and bigger than the chopper he was flying. So did the crew chief who flew as copilot. They would zip in and out of the jungle, blowing things up with grenades and shooting things up with Jasmann's M-60 in the backseat, trying to piss Charlie off so that he would give away his position. Then the gunships would roll in with their twenty-eight rockets and twelve thousand rounds of 7.62 M-60 gunfire. During low-level flight, the prop wash of that Hughes 500 would blow jungle undergrowth back, exposing all kinds of enemy hootches and sampans for them to destroy.

We stayed up around one thousand feet and just generally flew around, keeping our distance from the movement of the little army helicopter so as not to attract attention to ourselves; we wanted Charlie to think that the Hughes 500 was an easy target operating on its own—which of course it was until *we* pounced. Once they drew fire, then the crew chief would drop a smoke grenade to mark the location, and we rolled in.

I could just barely make out that little thing as it disappeared below the trees and then popped up again in another location as an explosion occurred where it had been. Then an occasional M-60 burning off some rounds as Jasmann was probably sinking a sampan or two. The Hughes 500 had no doors on it, just like our Hueys, and Jasmann had a two-thousand-round door box of M-60 ammunition on the floor between his legs. A case of fragmentation grenades and a case of white phosphorus grenades were sitting next to him.

Everything was going well. We kept flying around, not straying too far from the army chopper, waiting for something to pop. It was a beautiful day. The temperature at one thousand feet was perfect as I sat there in my door seat, smoking a cigarette, M-60 in my lap, and watching the bumblebeelike moves of the Hughes 500 down in the jungle. It felt good to be back in the saddle again. I had almost forgotten how much I loved the work. It was such a rush to be up there on the edge, knowing that you could be in an incredible life-threatening shit storm at any second. What in the hell am I saying? That is nuts! I think I need help!

My God! I do need help! Flak, right out of World War II, just like in the TV show "Twelve O'clock High." What the hell was this? An airburst shell went off right between us and our trail bird! Then another in front of us and another below us! The sound it made and the shock wave that hit us turned my blood to ice!

Habicht immediately got on the radio and said, "Break off, break off. Get down on the deck and head for home." He didn't even use a call sign!

Dumping the collective, we dropped out of the sky like a rock. Myself, Andy, Olby, and Marcus had instinctively tossed our smoke grenades out the doors at the same time, marking the spot where the antiaircraft gunfire had come from. The jungle came up rapidly as we autorotated down and out of range for the antiaircraft guns that were shooting at us. For a moment it looked like we were going to beat the smoke grenades to the ground. As we descended toward safety, Habicht called Captain Brocheux and told him what had happened, then instructed him to head for Seafloat as well.

"Jesus Christ, let's not do that again!" Saddler said.

"You got my vote!" I answered.

Habicht said, "Oh, we're going back, all right! But this time it'll be with one hundred percent flechette rockets! We've got some stashed on Seafloat that we got from the Air America boys." Flechette rockets exploded above the ground, sending out thousands of little darts that would just about disintegrate anything in their way.

As we wove in and out of the tops of the trees, making our way back to Seafloat, Habicht said, "Hey, Kelly, I heard from Harker just before he left that they used to call you Magnet Ass. I guess that's true, huh?"

Andy looked over at me with his usual funky expression and said, "No shit?"

I didn't even honor that with a response. I just kept my eyes on the jungle passing rapidly under us, my M-60 at the ready. I knew everyone was laughing. Slowly, I started to giggle.

"Munster, Seawolf One-six. Over."

"Seawolf One-six, Munster. Over."

"Roger, Munster. I need that special package brought to the flight deck—the one that was left for us by our Air America friends. Over."

"Roger that, Seawolf. It will be waiting. Munster out."

Once we got on the deck at Seafloat, Habicht had us load up the flechette rockets in both birds and, knowing where the fire had to come from, set up a plan to hit it immediately. We were in the air in minutes.

The plan was to approach the target at treetop level, staying low all the way in, flying abreast of each other. Just before we got to the target, we'd pop up to two hundred feet, salvo with both birds next to each other and firing at the same time, then break off in separate directions getting back down among the trees. Circling back around toward Seafloat, we would meet up again and stay low the rest of the way home. It seemed like a good plan, and we hoped that it would work well.

Shore and Habicht knew the route back, and off in the distance, red smoke was still drifting up. Seawolf One-four was on my side. As I looked out across the top of the jungle trees at Shore flying next to us. I could see Olby half standing outside with his M-60 pointed forward at the ready. I glanced over at the instruments between Habicht and Saddler. All was as it should be. I looked over at Andy. He was also outside, pointing his machine gun at the target out in front of us. Everyone was ready! Turning my focus ahead toward the target, I felt the saliva being blown out of the side of my mouth as the 120-mile-per-hour wind caressed my face. I should have been tense, with a dry mouth, but I wasn't. For some reason, I was totally relaxed. This mission was going to go okay. Hoping not to let Mr. Murphy jump in to spoil the mission, I stayed alert and kept my M-60 on the target. It was time!

"Seawolf One-four, One-six. Over."

"One-six, One-four. Go."

"On my mark. Three, two, one. Mark!"

With that, Habicht pulled up on the collective fast. We climbed hard, the G forces pushing us all down. Twelve M-60s rang out across the jungle as we increased our altitude to two hundred feet. As we reached the top, Habicht nosed us over and hit the salvo trigger. We became almost weightless from the negative G forces as the helicopter came over the top and launched fourteen flechette rockets, filling the cabin with sparks. All twelve M-60s stayed on target as the darts exploded above the trees hurling hundreds of thousands of death needles below. As planned, we broke in opposite directions, got low, and regrouped, making our way back to Seafloat. We never took a single enemy round on that run. Must have really taken them by surprise. Still, I was glad that was over. Slow-moving helicopters are no match for antiaircraft artillery designed to shoot down jets.

That evening the SEALs went in to check out the target area.

They said that the flechettes had made such a mess it was hard to get an accurate body count, but we wouldn't be taking anymore antiaircraft fire out of there. Later, Habicht told us that as far as he knew until that point in the war, no helicopter gunships had laid a strike on an antiaircraft site. How about that. We made history.

Chapter 18

The next day we were playing the old waiting game, both birds sitting on Seafloat, with us stretched out beneath them, trying to hide from the heat. It must have been another record-breaking 130 degrees. Not a breeze within miles. Not a cloud. The river was like glass, hardly moving. It was the dry season once again. The place was so desolate. Nothing but jungle all around, and no friendlies at all. SEAL Team 1, Kilo Platoon, had gone downriver with a Swift boat a couple of klicks and disembarked, going in on foot to a very large defoliated area. They were looking for a VC who had been bringing recruits into the Nam Cam Forest and transporting large sums of money for the cause. So we were at the ready.

Trying to kill the boredom, Andy and I were lying under our chopper, the only shade on Seafloat, talking about the cars we were going to buy when we got back to the World, and Hunt was telling Christenson about the Corvette he had in storage waiting for his return. Thomas and Brocheux had a better way to overcome boredom: they took the Hughes 500 up to do some exploring. I wasn't sure that was a good idea, but what did I know? I wasn't an officer.

As I was saying to Andy, "I can't decide between a new GTO or an Oldsmobile 442," a pair of boots with feet in them that disappeared into a flight suit showed up next to my head.

Habicht said, "We've got to go, guys," as he dropped a rope on the deck by my side.

"What's this?" I said as I rolled out from under the helicopter to preflight it. Hunt and Christenson were coming alive on their side of the deck, as pilots Barnes and Shore were climbing into their seats up front. Andy instinctively started pulling the rocket caps down and sticking in the flex-gun barrels. Habicht said that the SEALs had called for help but no enemy contact was involved.

"So what's the rope for?" I asked.

Evidently one of the team had stepped on a punji stick or something and was slowing the rest of the platoon down. They wanted to get him out so they could proceed with their search, but there wasn't an LZ within two klicks, and they were smack in the middle of a thick forest of dead trees in that defoliated area. Habicht thought that if we could lower a rope to them, they could tie the guy on, and we could pull him up clear of the trees to bring him home. Sounded good to me.

I had already gotten my rocket caps down and put the flex-gun barrels in. Andy had untied the rotor blade from the tail boom and was ready to come hot. Climbing into my seat, pulling my helmet on, and laying my M-60 in my lap, I slid its barrel into place, clicking the lock down. Leaning back, I was enjoying the nice breeze the rotor blades were causing as they accelerated. Andy got settled in, and we cleared both sides for hover check. There was no wind, so it made no difference which way we took off. Both birds ready to go, Habicht pulled up on the collective and slowly slid us skyward as we moved down the river toward the team's insertion point.

Leaning out into the one-hundred-plus-mile-per-hour wind, I looked back. Seawolf One-three was moving into formation on our tail. We were at three hundred feet and still climbing when Habicht made a right turn coming up past the riverbank and over the jungle for a more direct route to the SEALs. I was in my usual position, my right butt cheek on my seat, left butt cheek hanging off, my left leg outside with my foot on top of the rocket pod and my right leg hooked around the pussy pole. Holding my

M-60 at the ready position, resting it on my right leg, I scanned the jungle below, always with the intent to get the jump on anything that was down there. He who shoots first wins!

I hit my ICS. "By the way, who hurt his foot?"

"Hudak!" Chamberlain answered.

"No shit?" Andy said. "Very bad?"

"He'll be okay," Habicht said. "As long as we get him out."

The transition to the defoliated area was like turning the page of a book—beautiful green to ugly gray instantly. No matter how many times I saw it, it was still a surprise. I could see how high the jungle really was when it was stripped clean. The trees were so tall, they seemed impossible. Otherwise, it was like the surface of the moon. Dust, gray dust, everywhere. Like the aftermath of a great forest fire in which nothing had burned. Such devastation.

"Shark One, Seawolf One-six. What is your location? Over."

"Seawolf, Seawolf. Shark One is at your eleven o'clock. Take it slow. You're almost on top of us. Over."

They had to talk us in because they were so well camouflaged, we couldn't see them, even though the area was completely defoliated and I knew their coordinates. Habicht pulled us into a very slow hover as the SEALs talked us in. Meanwhile Seawolf One-three was making a large circle around us at treetop level, keeping us covered.

"You're right straight above us, Seawolf."

I hit my ICS. "I see 'em! Stop! We're right on top of them," I blurted out.

"Roger that, Kelly!" Habicht pulled up to a stop.

Slowly guiding Habicht, I had us directly above them. If they hadn't been moving, I never would have noticed them. Those guys were good at disappearing.

As I tied the rope off on my pussy pole, Seawolf One-three was at treetop level covering us, guns at the ready, whizzing past my side as they orbited. We were just a little conspicuous, as usual.

Waving at Crane and Bryant on the ground with the rest, I signaled that I was dropping the rope to them. When I kicked the rope out my door, we were as low as we could get without clipping the tops of the dead trees. It unraveled as it fell toward the SEALs, down past all that dead wood. Finally, Crane grabbed for it as the wash from our rotor blades blew it around. He caught it. The rope came to a rest in his outstretched hand, above his head. Shit! The rope was too short! Now what?

"The rope won't reach! It's five or six feet too short, maybe less," I told Habicht.

"Roger."

He kept his hover as I looked below at Hudak, Crane, Joseph, Bryant, and the others, and the depressed looks on their faces. I gave them the old open-hand sign as if to say, don't worry. Just hang on. We'll come up with something.

Punching the ICS, I said, "Now what the fuck are we going to do?"

There was a long pause. Nobody was saying anything. I kept looking down at the guys, giving them positive signs. Why, I had no idea. They were fucked. I looked up at the back of Habicht's head. He was still motionless. Just hovering. He was thinking. I knew that silence well. He'd come up with something, just the way Harker always did.

All of a sudden, he said, "Hey, Kelly, do you think these trees are dead enough and our rotor blades strong enough to chop the tops of the trees off?"

"Are you kidding?" I replied.

"No," Habicht answered abruptly.

I looked out at the trees. The tops weren't that big around. They looked pretty dead to me. Maybe we could. I'd seen those rotor blades take a lot of bullet holes and keep flying.

Finally I said, "Sure, I think they can take it if you don't go down too far. I'd get a second opinion from Hunt in One-three first, though."

Habicht got on the radio to Hunt. I couldn't help but laugh a little, because of the long silence that followed.

"Seawolf One-three? Did you copy? Over."

Static. Finally, we heard, "One-six, One-three. He said that it just might work. Over."

I wondered what was going through the SEALs' minds by then.

Habicht said, "Okay, boys, here we go! Kelly, keep a close eye on that rope, and tell me when we're down far enough!"

That was the least of his worries. I didn't want to end up in a big pile of helicopter and SEALs hash.

As we started down, things got real messy, real fast. Dust and dead wood chips flew everywhere—in the chopper, down at the guys, *everywhere,* one hell of a mess. And the SEALs, the look on their faces when we started down was sheer terror. But they pulled on the rope to get Hudak enough slack to tie him on as soon as possible. Meanwhile, down we kept going, lower and lower, ever so slowly. Great! We got him!

"That's it! We got him! Pull him up! Pull him up!" I yelled in the ICS.

Habicht stopped his descent instantly and hovered, watching, listening, *feeling,* all senses attuned to the performance of the helicopter. Everything seemed to be normal. No unusual shaking or vibration.

"I think we're okay, sir!" I told Habicht. "Bell sure knows how to make one tough son of a bitch, don't they!"

"Roger that!" Habicht replied.

Very slowly, we started up. Chamberlain was watching the instruments closely, looking for signs of disaster. Andy had his M-60 up, poised to shoot, just in case. Remember, Charlie was very good at camouflage, as well. I kept my eyes glued to our passenger, making sure he was clear of the trees as we gained altitude going straight up. If the UH-1B had been one of the older models, the kind we flew when I first came to Nam, we would not have had enough torque to pull off that stunt. The models we had by this mission had more powerful engines.

When Hudak was clear of the treetops, I told Habicht. We started forward motion in order to gain transitional lift. As Habicht pushed forward on the cyclic and pulled up further on the collective, the helicopter left its hover, leaned forward, and gained speed as it increased altitude. Seawolf One-three kept circling us, knowing that we couldn't move very fast with the cargo we had dangling below, and that our slow speed made us very good targets. Habicht steered us straight for the river. Getting over to the river was going to be out of our way, but we wanted to get Hudak over water. If the rope broke or he slipped off, it would be easy to hover down on the water and pick him up.

Once we came out over the river, Habicht decreased altitude so that if anything happened, our passenger would have a very short drop into the water. Banking into an easy turn to the right, we headed upriver to Seafloat, our passenger, I thought, safely hanging under us. I looked down.

Oh shit! Hudak was skipping on the river like a flat rock you'd skip across the creek back home. I jumped on the ICS. "We're dragging him in the river! We're dragging him in the river! Go up fast! Go up fast!"

Habicht yanked Hudak out of the water so quickly he almost got whiplash. Soaked from head to toe, Hudak was still attached. After shaking his head as if to clear his brains of that rattling experience, he looked up at me with a big smile on his face and took one hand off the rope, momentarily, to wave the bird at me, as if to say, "Thanks for the dip, I needed that, and I'll kill you later!" That mishap nearly scared me to death. After all we went through to extract the guy, we almost ended up killing him ourselves by trolling him in the river at sixty miles per hour.

Habicht slowed back into a hover as we approached the landing deck at Seafloat. He eased us up and over the deck, per my instructions, and ever so slowly brought the chopper down far enough for the guys on deck to grab Hudak, unfasten the rope, and help him to sick bay. I told Habicht when Hudak had cleared and we were safe to depart. Slowly the chopper nosed over as he brought us back up to speed in order to come around and make our approach to land.

The deck was cleared of our injured SEAL, and Seawolf One-three was on final to the landing pad as we circled around at about five hundred feet, moving downriver to turn on final ourselves. Banking to the right and lining up with Seafloat, we started down on our final approach to landing. I was still at the ready with my M-60, because our newly built floating outpost was smack in the middle of enemy territory that had never been ventured into until our arrival. To make the area seem a little safer, both sides of the river where Seafloat was anchored had been defoliated so we could see Charlie coming. It was our kill zone. Seawolf One-three was on the deck and its rotor blade was winding down slowly. Christenson was already outside and taking off his gear, but the pilots were still in place waiting for the rotor blade to come to a complete stop. Turning my attention back to the jungle onshore, I continued to scan the one hundred yards of defoliated bank for any sign of movement.

Our approach was shattered by the panicked voice of Brocheux on the radio calling us for help. I knew the Cayuse shouldn't have gone out alone.

"One-six, Trouble Maker. We need some assistance. Over."

Habicht nosed the chopper forward, gaining speed and aborting our landing approach. He said, "Trouble Maker, One-six. We're en route. What's up? Over."

"One-six, Trouble Maker. Thomas is stuck in the mud. Over."

Habicht answered, "Trouble Maker, One-six. Say again. Over."

"One-six, Trouble Maker. He's stuck in the mud, and we're

trying to pull him out. There's movement to the east of us, and I think we may need some cover. Over."

Habicht pulled on the power and climbed out. Alongside One-three, below, Christenson was putting his gear back on while climbing back into his seat. Seawolf One-three's rotor blade started gaining speed again as they prepared to lift off. Habicht got the coordinates from Brocheux, and we made a sharp turn to the left, heading out over the jungle. Climbing up to one thousand feet, we set our course as Seawolf One-three followed. Once Shore fell into formation behind us, we increased our speed.

Andy hit the ICS. "I sure wish we had time to check the rotor blades out before doing this!"

I answered, "No shit! Not to mention the jet engine intake!"

Habicht and Chamberlain didn't say anything. They just looked at each other, but I knew what they were thinking: Don't say anything, because it might jinx us.

It took us just a few minutes to reach Brocheux. Andy was the first to see them.

"I got 'em! Down here at our two o'clock. There on the bank of this little canal."

"I see them!" Habicht said.

As Habicht started bringing us around and down to low level past their location, I asked Andy, "What the hell are they doing?"

Andy said, "I have no idea! The chopper is just hovering there just a few feet over the mudbank of the canal."

We dropped off altitude as we went down the edge of the canal about half a klick, turned 180 degrees, and came back up at about three feet, following the winding creek through the jungle, working our way back to where the Cayuse was hovering. Guns all at the ready, we rounded the last curve, and there on our left was the army chopper, hovering down next to the mudbank. Thomas was chest-deep in the mud, arms wrapped around the skid of Brocheux's chopper as it was trying to pull him out. We couldn't help but laugh. What in the hell had they been doing?

The laughing stopped abruptly, when we heard *pop, pop, pop* coming from the jungle as a tracer ricocheted off the water alongside the Hughes 500.

Fuck me! Hitting the ICS, I yelled, "Receiving fire!"

I tossed my smoke grenade out on the bank as Habicht got us even lower and faster down that winding canal, Seawolf One-three on our heels. Raising the M-60 off my leg, I cut loose, sending a deluge of red tracers back into the jungle. Andy, Christenson, and Hunt had all tossed out smoke grenades as well, so we had the target area well marked. Brocheux came on the radio and told us he had finally pulled Thomas out, but they were catching all kinds of fire as they beat feet out of the area low and fast.

As we cleared the battle site and Habicht felt that it was safe to gain altitude and get into position to put in a strike, he pulled us up to one thousand feet again and brought us around facing where we had just been. Oh, that was a pretty sight, red smoke from the smoke grenades hanging against a green jungle backdrop! The target was marked, and we were going in.

Brocheux called the all clear as Habicht nosed us over, and we started down. Nine hundred feet, eight hundred, we opened up with our flex guns and door guns, seven hundred feet, Habicht squeezed off the first rocket, sparks spiraling around as the rocket engine cleared the tube. Down toward the target it raced. The glowing tail of the rocket disappeared into the jungle, right where the fire was coming from, and exploded, throwing dirt, mud, and pieces of trees high into the sky.

Swoosh. Another rocket left the tube, but that one looked funny somehow. Then the warhead on the front of the rocket came unscrewed and parted from the rocket. Silently, all eyes stuck on that lone warhead in front of us as it drifted back toward us, flipped end over end, then went up and over the chopper and disappeared behind, not to be seen again. Still firing all our guns forward, we were in a momentary daze, shocked by what had happened. All four of us about shit!

Habicht didn't launch any more rockets, because he had already assigned the strike as a two-dart strike and didn't want to be out of balance with number thirteen left. We broke off, and Seawolf One-three came in under us and fired its two rockets with no problem. They impacted the target area as I sprayed .308s backward, under our tail boom, covering One-three's break.

Both gunships got clear of the strike zone, and we started to set up the next run.

Chamberlain said, "What in the hell was with that rocket? Habicht, you ever see that before?"

He said, "Never, and I hope I don't again!"

"Yeah," I said, "I can just see the mission report now. Seawolf One-six blows self up."

"You're a fine one to talk," Habicht said. "I heard last year you almost shot yourself down!" He laughed.

"Oh! You heard about that, did you?" I said.

I looked over at Andy, and he was laughing so hard I thought he was going to fall out his door. We had obviously recovered from the frightening experience. It was time to put in the next strike.

Turning attention back to my door, I leaned out into the wind and braced myself as Habicht rolled in on target again. Down we went, tracers darting back at us once more. We answered them with four rockets, four flex guns, and two M-60s spitting out .308s. We broke left this time as our trail bird hit them again. Clearing the target, we circled and placed one final strike, using the rest of our rockets in salvo mode. Eight rockets, all launched at once, made a mess of the jungle below. When One-three broke off its attack, they said that they weren't receiving fire anymore. Just before we salvoed, I had noticed that there were a lot fewer tracers coming back up at us.

As we headed for Seafloat, Andy and I sat back and lit up.

There wasn't much said as we came down from our adrenaline high. We were all just glad that our rotor blades stayed in one piece. The order of the moment, be cool!

As we turned onto final approach, we flicked our cigarettes out the doors and got set with our guns again. The Hughes 500 was already sitting on the deck, shut down. Brocheux and his crew chief, Dickson, were standing next to it, talking to a really messy Thomas. The closer to the deck we got, the better I could see Thomas. Jesus, what had he been up to? He was wearing his tiger-stripe fatigues, jungle boots, all painted up like a SEAL. Mud from head to toe.

Upon landing and shutting everything down, I had two things on my mind: (1) let's get a look at that rotor blade to see if it needs changing; (2) what the hell had Thomas, Brocheux, and Dickson been up to?

The main rotor blade circled slower and slower as Habicht pulled on the rotor blade brake to stop it quicker. The rest of us stood around our chopper, eyes fixed on the leading edge to get first glance at any damage.

"Oh my God! Do you believe that shit?" Hunt said.

As the leading edge became visible, it was clear that it was a mess, destroyed. There were gashes all over it.

Habicht, looking at Brocheux and Thomas, said, "Sure am glad we didn't stop and look before we went to help you guys out. You'd have been up shit creek."

"I can't believe we didn't feel any vibration from that," Chamberlain said.

I just stood there thinking, Thank you, Jesus! Once again, you came through.

Well, now what? We needed an airworthy gunship fast.

Habicht turned to Hunt and asked, "Can you change main rotor blades out here if I get you one?"

Hunt stood for a minute looking at Habicht and then looking at me, Andy, and Christenson. He paused, scratching his head.

"Sure! We can do it. No problem." I was flabbergasted, but I kept my mouth shut; we were a can-do organization!

Habicht got on the horn to Binh Thuy instantly to have an army Chinook deliver new rotor blades and the tools for us to do the job. We were in a very volatile situation here, so we had to do this fast. We just hoped Crane, Bryant, and the other SEALs wouldn't stumble onto anything until we were ready. Although, if push came to shove, we still had one gunship and Brocheux's Cayuse.

After about twenty minutes of silence as we inspected our helicopter and waited on Habicht to emerge from the radio shack, he walked out onto the flight deck with a smile on his face. A Chinook would be there within the hour carrying all we needed to change out the blades. Oh! And one other thing. They were bringing us out a surprise in addition to the parts—the navy gunships were finally getting their first miniguns! Army choppers had been equipped with them for quite some time by then. So we had two big jobs to do. Install the main rotor blade and the new miniguns in the middle of unfriendly territory while the SEALs were on patrol.

That ate up the rest of the day: a lot of backbreaking, sauna-sweaty work. Down to the last torquing of the Jesus Nut that held the rotor head on. I hoped it would be a long time before we chopped down any more trees. Of course, with the miniguns we could chop them down before we got there—they could fire six thousand rounds of .308s a minute.

All right! We were back in business.

Then it was time to find out what had been going on with Brocheux and Thomas. The officers retreated to a private compartment to debrief them on their activities. Evidently Thomas had wanted to explore on foot while Brocheux and his crew chief followed above for cover. Dickson had an M-16 and a case of grenades for backup. Thomas got out of the chopper with M-16 and ammo bandolier, then struck out to see what he could get into. After about forty-five minutes, he stumbled on some VC. They didn't see him because they were too distracted by Brocheux and the helicopter. Thomas slowly backed out of the area and, in the process, discovered some interesting bunkers. After taking note of their location, he worked his way over to the canal and waved Brocheux down to pick him up. But as he worked his way to the edge of the water, he found himself sinking in the mud. Before he knew it, he was up to his waist and getting *very* nervous. They all knew that the VC were probably tracking the Cayuse to see what it was up to, so that meant the VC could be right on top of them at any time. That's when Brocheux called us for help.

So all was well that ended well. Besides, Thomas had stumbled onto a pretty important target in those bunkers. Way to go, Thomas!

We adjourned to see how Hudak was doing. I thought he'd be mad at us for dragging him in the river, but he wasn't. Quite the opposite, actually. And flying him upriver made for some great pictures. Unfortunately the photos were later lost in a fire.

The sun was starting to go down by the time that a Swift boat pulled up alongside with the SEAL platoon on board. As they disembarked the Swift, we mingled with them on the deck, tipping a cool one or two and enjoying a nice smoke. The gist of their conversation was that we were the craziest son of a bitches they knew, but they really appreciated our extraction, no matter how suicidal it might have appeared.

After the little reunion on the deck, the SEALs debriefed with Habicht and Thomas. They had a big planning session, and then broke up the meeting. Then we loaded up our choppers and headed out to the LST in the Gulf of Siam to spend the night. On the way out, Habicht told me that the next morning it was my turn to fly the Hughes 500. Brocheux, Dickson, and I had been assigned to go back to those bunkers and blow them. My adrenaline started to pump, and we hadn't even returned to the LST.

We all slept fast and hard because of the previous day's activities, changing rotor blades, mounting miniguns in place of the flex guns, pulling Hudak out, and saving Thomas's and Brocheux's butts. It had been a big day, so the quiet night aboard the LST—no scrambles—was a true comfort. Then getting up to the usual sunshiny day of the dry season was perfect. It was like vacationing in the Bahamas. Putting on my tiger-stripe fatigues and going up on deck, I started loading my equipment into the back of the army chopper. One two-thousand-round door box of belted ammunition for the M-60, one case of high-explosive grenades, and one case of white-phosphorus grenades. I placed the M-60 on top of the large ammo box that would be between my legs, and set my flight helmet in my seat, with my front body armor and Mae West. I was ready to go!

Dickson, the army crew chief, was going over his chopper, doing the preflight inspection for this morning's mission. The rest of the guys were giving the two gunships the once-over. I pitched in with ours, to get things done faster, then we all went to breakfast. Taking advantage of our usual head-of-the-line privileges, we loaded up on powdered eggs, sausages, and pancakes. I would live to regret that breakfast.

After the chow break, we converged over by the edge of the flight deck, smoking cigarettes and looking out over the beautiful blue water of the gulf. The topic of the conversation was still about the previous day's activities and also what the day would bring. Jasmann was telling me that I was in for the ride of a lifetime in the Cayuse. He had already flown several missions backseat, blowing sampans and tunnels. He kept telling me how fast and maneuverable it was. He said it with a strange grin. Well, we'd see.

Time to go. Brocheux and Dickson came out and climbed into the cockpit. I quickly strapped on my .45, threw on my Mae West, fastened my armor chest plate in place, climbed in right behind the pilot, pulled my helmet on, plugged into the ICS, and gave them a "Roger, I'm ready!"

The engine revolutions per minute increased as the jet-engine whine got louder and louder. Brocheux got everything up to speed for takeoff. All my guys were ready to go, standing by their birds, just waiting for us to lift off so they could bring their rotor blades around and start to turn up. There just wasn't enough room for all three to do it at the same time.

Just about up to speed now, I looked at my guys once again as if to say, well here I go, and they all waved. Wow! Did we ever lift off. It was like a ride at the carnival!

Brocheux said, "Hover check," and shot straight up like we'd been shot out of a cannon. He didn't even wait for the flight-deck official to give us the all clear to lift off. By the time he said, "Hover check complete," we were at five hundred feet and headed for the coast of Vietnam. We're flying army style!

By the time we reached one thousand feet, I was sticking the barrel in the M-60 and locking it down. I adjusted the box so I was comfortable, then shifted the position of the two cases of grenades next to me so that they were as convenient as possible. Then the coast was coming up, and the headset in my helmet said, "Seawolf One-four is off at this time. Seawolf One-six is off at this time."

As the coast got closer, the adrenaline pumped harder. We had good backup, and the mission was going to be fun. It was such a rush going in, it's hard to describe. As we crossed over the coast, it was time to get down to business. Shifting in my seat a little more to make sure I was comfortable, I brought the M-60 to the ready, resting on my right leg, pointed down. I was leaning out the right side of the chopper, eyes scanning the jungle below for any sign, any sign at all. Going over everything in my mind, double- and triple-checking: ammo belt in feed tray properly; HE grenades in case on right; WP grenades in case on left; don't worry about smoke grenades because the crew chief will take care of that; settle down, focus, do the job! Finger on the trigger I was ready.

The air at one thousand feet was cool and fresh as I sat there looking over the jungle below. Then, all of a sudden, Brocheux went down like a rock. Nothing I'm not used to, but that little bumblebee of a chopper went down a lot faster than a UH-1B. My gosh!! The jungle came up fast, and so did the temperature and humidity. It was like going from the Iowa farmlands to Amazon jungle in seconds. Brocheux was like an artist with that bumblebee. We'd come up on a tree and be just high enough to clear it with our skids and then down the other side, below the tops of the trees down to the next level of the jungle. Weaving in and out of undergrowth, actually flying under trees at some points, working our way over to the canal Thomas had been mired in. My eyes darted here and there, and my gun was up off my leg and ready to fire as we broke into the clear out over the creek. Brocheux had us on the water as we banked a hard left and followed the path of the muddy water, winding back and forth. His turns were so sharp, I'd be looking at the ground most of the time when I looked out the doors. The jungle was the kind of thing you'd expect to see in a Tarzan movie. Jungle was everywhere. A stream about twenty feet across wound its way down to the bigger rivers and out to the gulf.

Brocheux came over the ICS: "If you see anything, anything at all, sampans, hootches, and especially bunkers or tunnels, it's open game. You let me know. Okay?"

Keying in, I said, "Roger that!"

Of course, he was going so fast it was hard to see much of anything. I was strapped into my seat, but the harness would allow me halfway outside the helicopter as he maneuvered up the canal, taking heart-slamming turns to the right and then to the left, heading to where we'd been the day before. I'd be looking at the edge of the jungle one second, scanning it with my eyes and gun, then the next second, I'd be looking at blue sky, then the second after that, the water in the canal. Jesus Christ!!

"Here we are, Kelly," Brocheux said.

"Roger." I looked into the jungle intently.

I heard the high-pitched whine of the little jet engine on the other side of the wall I was leaning against, and the smooth hum of the four rotor blades whirling above us. Everything was still except right at the edge of the jungle, where our prop wash was thrashing the many kinds of growth that lined the sides of the canal. Brocheux started moving slowly in over the jungle, letting the strong wind created by our rotor blades clear a path in the undergrowth below us. First he went straight in from the mudbank, then we drifted to the right, then back left, zigzagging through the jungle. Because of the possibility of booby traps or snipers, I found myself having to look *up* into the trees as we moved along in some spots. Charlie had been known to string traps for helicopters between trees. We scanned the area as sweat started dripping off the end of my nose. It was so hot and humid down there that the wash from the rotor blades couldn't even evaporate the sweat. After a few minutes of the dance through the jungle, Brocheux pulled power and wham! Up to one thousand feet again, so he could get his bearings. Man, that was fast. I loved that helicopter! Back down we went, faster than we'd come up. Hot and humid, up to cool, and back down to hot and humid, weaving in and out, brushing back the jungle with our rotor wash.

"I got one!" Dickson said on the ICS.

"Where?" Brocheux said.

"My ten o'clock."

Brocheux snapped the chopper around 180 degrees and brought me right up on top of a bunker. Sure enough, there it was. Looked like something a beaver back home would have built. I could just make out the entrance down through all the undergrowth.

"Keep your eyes peeled while I blow it!" I said.

The gunner was really hanging his ass out at a time like that, because the hovering chopper was not only a sitting duck, but the gunner had to set his M-60 in his lap to get a grenade, pull the pin, and drop it in the hole to the bunker. It was pucker time. Setting my gun gently down, I grabbed an HE grenade, pulling the pin but holding the spoon down so the timer didn't start. Then I held the grenade out the door at arm's length. Looking down at the opening to the bunker, I told Brocheux which way to move the chopper so that I was in the perfect spot to say bombs away and drop it in the hole.

"Easy, easy, a little more to the left. Perfect. Grenade away!" I said.

Brocheux banked us hard to the left and accelerated away from the bunker, staying low, right on the tops of the trees. Three seconds later, bang! One bunker down.

He circled around, coming back to the bunker, and hovered over it again. Slowly, we started to search from that point, systematically crossing the area so as not to miss anything. We knew there were more bunkers there somewhere. There had to be. Brocheux did it again; pulling power, up we went to one thousand feet in the nice cool air. It was like the wildest roller-coaster ride I'd ever been on. And on a full stomach. Jasmann tried to tell me. Brocheux got his bearings, and down we went again. Hot and humid, up to cool and not so wonderful, back down to hot and humid, and it was getting worse. A cold sweat popped out on my forehead, and I started to get the shakes. Shit! Me, getting airsick? What's that over there? I thought to myself as I weaved dizzily around.

Sure enough! "Bingo!" I struggled to say. "Here's another at our four o'clock!"

As we drifted back and to our right, I directed Brocheux over the top of another bunker, leaned out to look down, my hand outstretched with the grenade, ready to release it. And promptly threw up all over the top of the bunker!

Hitting my ICS as I spit vomit from my mouth, I said, "Grenade away!"

Breaking left once again, we ducked and ran. Bang! Scratch one more bunker. I felt much better.

Brocheux came on the ICS. "Was that vomit that landed all over the top of that bunker back there, Kelly?"

"Are you kidding, sir? Not hardly!" I said, keeping my fingers crossed. Dickson looked back over his shoulder long enough for me to see him laughing at me. I knew I had been caught. Shit!

Continuing the hunt, we found another, and another, then another. *Bang! Bang! Bang!* We were kicking ass. The place was saturated with bunkers, and I was surprised we had gone unmolested so long. Where were they? I remember thinking of what happened at Ha Tien. Days of operations, causing trouble for Charlie, and him not retaliating at all. Then, when we were about to give up and leave, the shit hit the fan. Now was not the time to let down. Don't get relaxed. I had to stay alert and keep my focus.

Continuing on, we discovered a hootch, then another one just a few feet away. Then a whole group of them popped up, and a canal that we hadn't seen from the air passed right through the middle of them. Most important, we saw very large sampans docked by the largest hootch. Things were getting very interesting.

Brocheux told me to take care of the sampans, which I did in quick order with the M-60. Watching what a .308 can do at close range is very impressive. Pumping eight hundred rounds a minute into those sampans, it didn't take long to sink 'em. The bottom just exploded into wood chips, with water shooting way up in the air as the bullets ripped through and into the canal below. Just for good measure, I tossed a WP grenade onto the remains of the sampans that were floating on the surface. As we left, a nice fire was burning.

Following the newfound canal, we moved on. By the way, you couldn't see any of this from up in the air where our two gunships were circling.

"Pay dirt!" Dickson hollered out.

"What?" Brocheux said as he pulled us up into a stop.

"Check this one out at my ten o'clock," Dickson said.

As the chopper swung around to our side so we could get my gun on it and Brocheux could get a better look, a beautiful sight came into view, a huge bunker that looked like it was made of concrete.

"The grand prize!" I said.

We circled around the bunker, trying to find someplace to toss in the HE grenade. But we couldn't find an entrance to the thing anywhere, just a breathing hole right on top, just off center, and I didn't think we could get a grenade down the thing. Of course, it was worth a try!

Taking the HE grenade out and pulling the pin, I held it out the door at arm's length and directed Brocheux down as close to the opening as possible. Hitting my ICS, I said, "A little to the left. Hold it. Just a little more. Hold it. Back to the right. Hold it. Now forward just a bit. Down just a little more. Hold it right there."

I crossed the fingers on my left hand and let the grenade drop from my right. The spoon flipped off into space as the grenade left the safety of my hand and fell earthward, down, dead center on the tube. It disappeared into the darkness of the bunker.

It made it! I don't believe it! It made it in! Oh shit! I forgot to say "Grenade away"! And we're still here!!

Stomping my ICS with my foot, I yelled, "Grenade away, grenade away!!"

Brocheux hit the road, breaking off to the left, fast and low, but not low and fast enough. *Kaboom! Bang!* The blast was enormous as it blew past the chopper, shaking us to the bone, rattling every nut and bolt in the Cayuse and scaring the shit out of us. I could see Dickson and Brocheux were checking the instruments, making sure that we were okay. Minus some sheet metal on the back of the chopper, but still flying, we were thinking, That couldn't be just the grenade. Something other than dead air space had been in that bunker.

After pulling a complete inventory on the instruments and having me look outside at the back of the chopper as best I could without falling out, we decided that we could continue the mission, but that I'd have a lot of holes to patch once we got back to the LST.

On our way back to the big bunker, Brocheux flared and pulled up short because he thought he saw something move underneath us. He stabilized his hover, and the wash blew a mass of tall grass flat, exposing a woman and a little girl, probably her daughter, huddling under the jungle trying to stay invisible to our searching eyes. Brocheux kept his hover steady as I covered them with the M-60, not knowing what was going to happen next. I couldn't see a weapon, but that didn't mean they didn't have one. Holding my machine gun steady, I hit the ICS with my foot.

"What do you think?"

"I don't know," Brocheux answered back.

Dickson said, "They couldn't be out here by themselves."

About then, something caught my eye. Looking up slowly, with my gun still trained on the other two, I saw a black-pajamaed figure just on the edge of the jungle that our rotor blade wash was clearing and everything went into slow motion. He had a gun!! I instantly started up with my M-60 as I saw him bringing up an AK-47. I yelled out in the ICS, "Receiving fire!" And we both pulled our respective triggers at the same time. Dickson popped a red smoke grenade out his side to mark the spot for our guy upstairs. My .308s tore up the jungle as I walked them through the tall grass toward the Victor Charlie as he was punching holes in the side of the Cayuse, trying desperately to get me before I got him. I hit him once in the leg, again in the chest, and a third time in the head, watching it explode like a ripe watermelon.

By the time his head came apart, Brocheux had us rolling over and exiting stage left, in a rapid fashion, because at that moment the whole damn jungle came alive with VC. Muzzle flashes out the butt. The chopper was getting riddled with bullet holes.

"Seawolf One-six, Trouble Maker. We are receiving fire. Over."

"Trouble Maker, Seawolf One-six. Roger. We are rolling in on red smoke. Over."

Great! Come on, boys, go get 'em! Follow that red smoke right on down here. As we rolled out of the neighborhood, I was still shooting back in the direction of the guy I'd greased. Didn't think about that little girl and mom. Didn't have time to. War's hell!

Once clear of the strike zone, I leaned out to check the damage on the chopper. Right by my head was a hole that could have been made by a softball. Thank you, Jesus!

The gunships blasted the jungle with rockets and machine-gun fire, and tracers continued to fly back at them without letting up. That was surprising, too, because the miniguns had just been installed. Six thousand rounds a minute times two, plus rockets and door-gunner fire. That's a tough rain to live through. We were orbiting at about one thousand feet, watching the show, and every time the Seawolves rolled in and cut loose with the miniguns, the jungle parted. It was like a giant weed whacker. Those .308s would cut trees in half, just mowing the jungle down.

After two quick turnarounds on Seafloat, and no sign of Charlie letting up, Habicht decided to pull back, reevaluate, regroup, and call for an air strike. We had been looking for that big POW camp since day one, and with all the obvious defenses we'd stumbled across, we might be getting very close. And there had always been news of an in-country R & R location for the VC somewhere around the POW camp. Could we have found it?

We landed at Seafloat and waited for a response to our request. It didn't take long. Habicht came out from the communications room and told us that the air force would have three F-100s on site first thing in the morning to bomb the hell out of the VC. We were going to fly spotter for the strike. We would mark the exact location of the target with WP (white phosphorus) rockets and then back off to watch the show.

Well, we'd had enough action for one day. It was time to return to the LST and have everybody make fun of me while I patched the holes in the Cayuse. That would take the rest of the day. Of course, word got out about my getting sick. How would I tell my kids someday about that mission: I almost shot us down; I almost blew us up; I got airsick; I puked on the enemy? Some navy special forces story it was turning out to be.

Chapter 19

The next day, we took off to meet the F-100s. Another beautiful day for flying. Blue sky with a smattering of little white puffy clouds. Saddler was the fire-team leader that day, with Thomas as copilot. The trail bird was Shore and Chamberlain, with Olby and Jasmann as gunners. Andy and I were covering One-four's back. All of us were watching for the air force's arrival.

"Seawolf, Seawolf. This is air force Super Sabre Flight Lead. Over."

"Super Sabre Flight Lead, Seawolf One-four. Go."

"Seawolf, Sabre Flight Lead. Where do you want the package? Over."

"Sabre Flight Lead, Seawolf One-four. We will mark target with Whiskey Papa. Over."

We rolled in and Saddler, in his usual precise manner, placed the WP rockets right on target, the whole time taking heavy fire from the ground. Still the miniguns didn't have any apparent effect. The explosions of our rockets marked the target very clearly with a huge amount of white smoke that couldn't be missed. Shore came in right on our ass and did just as well. I was glad to put some distance between us and the VC down below and let the air force take over. We were taking heavy fire.

Those guys put on an air show to end all air shows. Napalm is the most devastating, most spectacular sight imaginable. Saddler had us orbiting off to the side of the strike zone but as close as safely possible. Unfortunately, none of us had a camera to take pictures that morning.

I was leaning outside and stretching my neck to follow the actions. Holy smokes, there they were, coming straight down, one behind the other, from way up there. Boy, were they starting up high. Of course, in all our time in Vietnam, we'd seen only helicopters do this, so that's all we were used to.

"Here they come, guys! Check this out!" I said.

"Oh man, doesn't anybody have a camera?" Saddler said.

"Jesus, this is incredible!" chimed in Chamberlain.

Andy just sat there with his mouth open.

The jets came almost straight down, pulled up, dropped their loads, hit their afterburners, and—with an explosion—they'd be headed back, way, *way* up into the sky!

"Seawolf, Super Sabre Flight Lead. We are receiving heavy ground fire from the target area. Do you have any suggestions? Over."

What the fuck does that mean? That's why we called on these guys.

"What does he mean by that?" Andy asked.

Saddler said, "I have no idea."

Silence fell over the airwaves for a moment. Saddler was the first to break the long pause. "Super Sabre Fight Lead, Seawolf One-four. We will orbit the target and put in door-gunner fire on your break. Come down inside our circle and break outside the circle. Do you copy? Over."

"Seawolf, Sabre Flight Lead. Roger we run inside your circle and break outside your circle. Over."

"Sabre Flight Lead, Seawolf One-four. Give us a minute to get into position. Over."

"Seawolf, Sabre Flight Lead. Give us a go when you're ready. Over."

"Sabre Flight Lead, Seawolf One-four. You have a go! Roger."

"Seawolf, Sabre Flight Lead. We have a go. We are commencing our run. Over."

"Roger, Sabre Flight. We copy."

I watched as the first bird came in and dropped his load. As soon as he hit his afterburners, I opened up with my M-60. You could tell that Charlie on the ground was confused. He couldn't decide whether to shoot at us or the jets. We were both in range. The jets were a bigger, more spectacular target, but we were easier to hit. I guess it was rather puzzling for them. In any event, the F-100s did their thing very well and without incident. The ground fire finally disappeared, and the show was over. That could have meant a lot of different things: they ran out of ammo; we killed them all; they got tired and left via tunnels; or they took a dinner break. I don't know which.

"Seawolf, Super Sabre Flight Lead. Package delivered. Thanks for the cover. Over."

"Super Sabre Flight Lead, Seawolf One-four. The navy thanks you for your assistance. Over."

"This is air force Super Sabre Flight. Our pleasure, navy. Have a nice day."

When we got back to Seafloat, Habicht decided that we had earned a break, and we flew out to the LST to spend the rest of the day and the night.

The next morning at sunrise, we put on our tiger stripes, strapped on our guns, and loaded up in the two gunships. But we didn't head inland as we would have if we'd being going to Seafloat; we headed out to sea instead. Habicht had a surprise for us. We rendezvoused with a navy supply ship way out at sea in the Gulf of Siam. It was as big a ship as I had ever seen, with a big helicopter landing deck aft. After circling twice, Habicht approached and landed under the direction of the shipboard sailor's flags. Once on the deck, we jumped out and tied her down to make room for the trail bird. When both birds were on the deck and secured, we started wandering. We looked our usual ragged selves, and everyone gave us a wide berth. The deck officer had no idea what to make of us and the look on his face was one of half shock and half fright. And the other sailors had never seen navy personnel dressed like us before. Like a flock of kids hitting the mall for the first time in ten years, we hit the ship's store and bought a lot of stuff. Wristwatches were the big thing on our list. We went up on the bridge, looked into the officers' wardroom. We did the whole tour, and nobody said a word to us. They just moved away. It was really funny.

Then Habicht loaded us back up, and back we went to the LST. Andy and I were off duty by then, and Olby and Jasmann took over our spot. Another operation was planned for the army Cayuse again. This time it was Hunt's turn to fly in the backseat. They were going back to where the F-100s had put in their strike to see what, if any, results we had obtained from all that expended ordnance.

Meanwhile, Andy and I were busy being lazy and enjoying every minute of it. Listening to a little rock and roll, sipping a Coke, and dreaming of the World and a hero's welcome—the kind you see in the movies. The day just slipped by, way too fast. We really needed the rest.

Our rest belowdecks was interrupted when Thomas hurried down the ladder into the crew's quarters. Hunt had been seriously shot several times. Obviously Charlie thought something was very valuable in that area, because the VC had to know that we were going to kick some ass for this. What the hell were they hiding down there?

Hunt made it okay. We never saw Hunt again, because the army pilot flew him straight to Binh Thuy Army Evac Hospital. We found out that Hunt had given himself first aid because he was in the backseat and nobody else could reach him. He would be missed, especially by me; he had been my second mentor in the navy, Harker being the first.

The next day I took the opportunity to go in with the Hughes 500. Both gunships above, we started doing the usual harassment tactics. Brocheux was finding all kinds of stuff for me to blow up and shoot up. I lost count of how many sampans and bunkers we blew. We were also coming up on more and more concrete bunkers. We had worked our way nearly to the Hai Yen ARVN outpost. About half a klick away, I had just sunk one last sampan when we came under heavy automatic-weapons fire.

"Seawolf, Trouble Maker. Receiving fire! Over."

"Seawolf One-six. Roger. We're rolling in!"

Dickson had already popped red smoke, and we departed the area. We were still cruising across the treetops when Brocheux said, "Hang on to your butts, boys! We must have taken one in the ass! Temp gauges are going crazy here! We're going to have to put her down fast!"

"Seawolf, Seawolf. Trouble Maker. We have a Mayday, Mayday. We're going down southeast of Hai Yen. You copy?"

"Trouble Maker, One-six. We have you in sight. We copy your Mayday. Over."

Moments later Brocheux had us clear of the jungle by about one hundred yards and set us down on the dike of a rice paddy just before the engine died. I bailed out with all the ammo I could sling over my shoulders and dragged the M-60 toward the next dike closer to the jungle. Dickson grabbed one of the cases of grenades and his M-16 and took up a position just down from me. Brocheux did the same with the other case of grenades and his M-16. We were set. Hai Yen at our backs, the jungle in front of us, and our buds upstairs. We waited and watched as our two gunships put in their strikes on the target. After the second run, they held off in case we needed them for support upon our extraction.

I heard a noise from behind us. It wasn't distinguishable. But looking back toward the outpost on the horizon, I noticed some movement. As it got closer, I recognized it as a group of our Korean allies moving at a dead run to our aid. Those guys were some kinda crazy bastards, and they weren't scared of anything. We had worked with them before and saved their asses. I guess they thought it was time to return the favor. God bless 'em!

We didn't have long to wait before they had the area totally secured and we could just take a nice stroll back to the outpost.

They weren't about to fly the Cayuse out, so an army Chinook was going to have to lift it out. Brocheux and his crew chief were going to wait with it and go back to Binh Thuy with the Chinook. I was to ride out to the LST on one of the Swift boats.

Boarding the Swift, I kept the M-60 handy and all the ammo I took from the chopper. The Swift boat sailors cast off their lines, and we were on our way. It was a long trip through the winding waterway toward the coast, and very trying on the nerves as I leaned against the aft of the cabin, scanning the jungle on the bank as we went, machine gun up at the ready, and sweat dripping from the end of my nose; all I could think of was the last time I got shot and the 43 Boat. Trying to get my focus back, I shook off the bad thoughts by thinking about being a hero: I kept saying to myself, you are what you pretend to be, you are what you pretend to be. After wearing that out, I just prayed the rest of the way out to the coastal waters.

Once we were away from shore, the captain of the Swift boat came aft to get me. He told me to put the M-60 down below and go forward to strap in for the trip out to the LST. I couldn't figure out why I had to be strapped in, but I did what I was told. After stowing the M-60, I went forward to the place where they drive the boat. Sounds sailorlike, doesn't it? Anyway, they put me in a seat like one in an aircraft cockpit and strapped me in a harness that was much the same. Those I did know about. We no sooner got strapped in than we hit rough water and accelerated.

Jesus, what a ride! The boat seemed to go under or through one wave, then go airborne over the next. If I hadn't been strapped in, my neck would have broken. What a ride! Those guys did that all the time? Man oh man. I remember thinking at the time, I wish this boat would make up its mind, on top or underneath the water, one or the other!

Our arrival at the LST did not go smoothly either. The seas were really up, and I had to time the swell of the ocean with my jump onto the ladder so as not to get crushed between the Swift boat and the LST. Waiting for the water to get to its highest point, I jumped and made my way carefully up the ladder and onto the deck. I sprawled out there for a moment to count my blessings. I had survived another incident!

We regrouped, and Habicht got together with us for a briefing on a village just north of where we'd had all the trouble. It was a free-fire zone. The SEALs had pretty much decided that we were very close to the long-rumored POW camp. At sunup, we were to hit the village with a low-level raid and kill anything that moved, especially anything that could feed the enemy food or ammunition. Since we were having a hard time against their fortified positions and the heavy concrete bunkers in areas of dense jungle, maybe we would have better success hitting the enemy at home.

It was a clear morning, and the sun was just peeking over the ocean when we lifted off away from the LST. We stayed low-level all the way to the coast and up the canal that led to the VC village. I don't think we rose three feet off the water the whole trip. We banked sharply as the two gunships made their way up the winding canal like a snake headed for its prey. It was a little ways to get there. The big UH-1Bs were not nearly as nimble as the Cayuse when following a small canal, but they still kept you concentrating on keeping your gun in the right spot and staying balanced as the pilots rocked you from side to side, pulling one sharp banking turn after another.

On that mission, Andy and I were flying with Saddler as pilot and Chamberlain as copilot. We were the trail bird for once. Habicht was fire-team lead, Thomas his copilot. Jasmann and Marcus were Habicht's gunners.

As we approached the village, we had to make a left turn and pop up over a tree line before we started the attack run. As we rounded the last bend in the canal, I saw Seawolf One-six already going up over the trees, getting ready to start a low-level gun run through the VC village. Then all four of us in our chopper saw a man in black pajamas running out of the edge of the jungle and into a hootch that was right on the canal to our left.

Saddler said, "Get that son of a bitch, Kelly!"

Nobody had to tell me twice! I opened up with the M-60 and showered the door with .308s. Saddler and Chamberlain were so distracted by the hootch's being chopped apart by the rounds tearing through it that, when we turned to attack the village, we forgot to go up over the trees. We took the shortcut and went through them! The Plexiglas in the bottom of the chopper exploded and the shards were followed by a ton of leaves and growing-type shit all over the inside of the cockpit. Luckily, all we hit was just very tall jungle bushes as opposed to solid trees. But we regained our focus immediately, plowed into the clear and on into the village, punching off rockets and spraying everything in sight with miniguns and M-60s. Chickens, pigs, pots, huts, but no people. That one VC was the only one we saw. I fired the M-60 at anything that looked interesting. There was one stack of pots. Great pots. Beautiful pots. Just sitting there, begging me to shoot them. I took aim and squeezed off a long burst. The tracers found their mark right square in the middle of those gorgeous pots. *Boom!* And *boom* again! I got a huge secondary explosion! Something had been hidden there, but no more. We came around for another pass. I grabbed a WP grenade out of the case next to me. I already had a target in mind, the biggest hootch in the middle of the village. No rockets had found it yet. Saddler lined me up perfectly, and I timed my drop right on the button. I let the grenade go and watched it float down and in the front door. *Boom!* The whole building exploded in flames.

I screamed out, "Yeah, motherfucker! That was great!"

I hadn't pushed the ICS because I was just yelling for my own benefit. Unfortunately, Saddler heard me yell, and that scared him because he thought I had been shot again. By the time he finished chewing my ass for scaring him, I wished I had gotten shot.

I learned that morning that the hardest thing to hit with an M-60 is a scared chicken. A pig would be a close second. They were everywhere, and our orders were very specific. Kill anything and everything, period. After countless attempts trying to kill the chickens in one fenced-in area, I finally unleashed a WP grenade on them. Then I learned that burning chickens were harder to hit than nonburning chickens.

Chapter 20

Hitting the village hadn't seemed to scare Charlie away. So it was back to the old waiting game for us. Saddler and Thomas came down to our compartment for a few drinks to help kill time.

"So what's the scuttlebutt from the wardroom?" I asked our officer guests.

"Well, we've got all the concrete bunkers pretty much pin-pointed from all the hell-raising we've been doing. The only thing we can do now is to go in and blow the shit out of them," Saddler said.

Thomas added, "The Kit Carson scout that we've been oper-ating with told us that he had just recently heard from some of his contacts that there were even bigger bunkers nearby that we haven't uncovered yet."

"Yeah, but can we trust him?" Jasmann asked.

"Isn't that the same guy we worked with when we first came down here?" I asked.

"That's him," Saddler said.

Valladares asked, "What if that little shit's lying to us? Maybe he's the reason we're always arriving seconds too late, and all the people are gone."

Thomas jumped in with his two cents' worth, "The SEALs have a plan for that!"

"So how we gonna take down these bunkers?" Marcus asked.

Saddler said, "UDT-11 and EOD [explosive ordnance disposal] are working out a plan for that with the Kit Carson scout as we speak."

"I sure hope Mr. Kit Carson is going in with them," Andy said.

A few days later, we were told that the operation to blow the bunkers was a go! We would take off in the gunships from the LST and rendezvous with the army slick, carrying our guys, the way we had before, and then proceed to the LZ. The landing zone was a small group of rice paddies that was rather isolated in the middle of the Nam Cam Forest, but it was very close to the bunkers that were going to be blown up first. These were the very big ones the Kit Carson scout had told us about. The plan was simple. We'd fly low-level all the way in, then fly orbits on each side of the LZ while the army slick unloaded the team. The team would move out of the rice paddies and into the jungle. Then we would return to Seafloat to wait for the extraction or to get scrambled if the team ran into some shit. Nothing unusual about that. This was going to be the perfect starter mission for my new trainee. I had been instructing Don Stedman, our newest recruit, and was waiting for an opportunity to put him in the door for some good firsthand experience.

The op was planned for late afternoon. We all loved low-level operations because they were such a rush. And I wouldn't have much to do except watch Stedman and evaluate his performance. As everyone on the LST was scurrying around getting ready to go, I was keeping my eye on my student and thinking about what the UDT guys were going to do if the Kit Carson scout was setting us all up.

Ready for liftoff, I took up my position in the middle and watched Stedman as he brought the rotor blade around for turn-up. Andy had finished everything on his side and was climbing in. Shore and Chamberlain were already strapped into their seats, ready to go.

Shore sang out, "Coming hot!" as the jet engine came alive.

With Andy all settled, I watched Stedman fighting the torque as the rotor blade struggled to break free. Chamberlain was watching the instruments and getting the maps situated. Across the flight deck, Saddler had started to turn up his bird as well. Olby was in his place and Christenson was holding on to their rotor blade. Thomas was in the copilot's seat, busy doing copilot stuff.

Finally the rotor blade broke free of Stedman's grip and around it went, gaining speed rapidly. Seawolf One-three's rotor was gaining speed as well. It was looking like both birds would be ready for liftoff at the same time. Saddler, being Seawolf One-three, was the fire-team lead that day. Shore, Seawolf One-two, was the trailer. I liked being in the trail bird, because I could see more action.

Both navy birds ready for hover check, Saddler called the army slick to see if it was ready to go. It was.

It was the usual setup. The army slick, Alpha Delta One, was lifting off Seafloat with a squad from UDT-11 and the EOD. We were coming in from the LST, and all of us would meet prior to insertion. We had to use that rather complicated procedure because we all couldn't fit on Seafloat at the same time; the landing deck just wasn't big enough.

Hover checks complete, the two deck officers cleared both of us for departure, and away we went. Breaking in different directions, we met up on the other side and straightened for our rendezvous, low-level all the way.

As we screamed across the water at three feet, headed toward the shoreline and the jungle beyond, I started having second thoughts about putting Stedman in the door. I knew the section of the jungle we were heading for. There hadn't been a single trip into the area without a serious shit storm. Was he ready? I wasn't sure. The possible red flags were there, but I had *chosen* to ignore them. My *choice*! Nobody else's. He'd be okay, I finally concluded. It'd be good experience. Over the years, I've discovered that anytime I find myself repeatedly reassuring myself that a decision I've made is correct, then I probably should have made a different decision! Oh well, live and learn. That is, as long as you live!

Flying middle seat, I was able to see everything as we approached and passed the shoreline and headed over the jungle. Watching the lead bird duck and dodge the taller trees, zipping through and around jungle growth, and hugging the terrain as we wove this way and that, right on his tail, was a very exhilarating experience. I looked over at my student. He was right on top of things. Gun up at the ready. Hanging out, watching the jungle intently as it passed beneath him. Looking back forward again, I scanned the instruments. All seemed well with Seawolf One-two. Then it was back to gazing at the tail of Saddler's bird. What a sight! If that kind of experience could ever be duplicated as a carnival ride, the inventor would make a fortune.

"Hey! There they are! I just got a glimpse of Alpha Delta One bobbing up over the top of the jungle at our two o'clock," I said on the ICS. With little else to do, it stood to reason I'd be the first to spot them.

"Roger that; I got 'em," Shore said.

"One-three, One-two. You got an eye on Alpha Delta One at our two o'clock? Over."

"We got 'em. Over."

About then, I watched Alpha Delta One disappear below the trees. Then we flashed out over the rice paddy and into the open. The army slick was starting its flare to drop off the guys in the middle of a little clearing. Without a word, Saddler broke right and headed for the left side of the LZ for our assigned low orbit to cover the insertion. I kept my eyes on the slick as the UDT squad disembarked, the men taking up defensive positions along the dike in the center of the rice paddy. I glanced back at Stedman. He was alert. I got a fix on the army slick as it climbed to altitude without a hitch. All right! So far, no Mr. Murphy.

Pop! Pop! Pop! Pop! What the fuck? The jungle had come alive with tracers everywhere. Stedman and Andy started firing their M-60s like crazy!

"Seawolf, Seawolf. Tiger Shark. We need cover. Get Alpha Delta One back here now! Over."

Apparently, as the patrol was starting to move out of its defensive positions, all hell broke lose. They were totally surrounded, and so were we. Per their plan, UDT-11 on the ground killed their scout. Next they had to get the hell out of there. From the amount of fire we were taking, we were seriously outnumbered.

While I was watching my trainee, I was also watching the gauges in the cockpit because we were taking a lot of hits. The last time I'd heard so many bangs and clangs of hole punching was when I got shot in the hand seven months earlier. I don't care how many times it happened, I just couldn't get used to that sound; it just scares the shit out of me. That was the first time I had found myself in a firefight and had nothing to do. I hated it! Shit! I had to get a gun! Stedman and Andy were shooting in all directions as we circled our side of the LZ, and I was thinking, This is not good. We had to get up and out of there, get some altitude, and put in a strike. The low-level bullshit wasn't helping. We needed our rockets!

As I sat watching, I noticed that we kept following the same path through the jungle on each pass we made. That also was not good. Harker had taught me long before that we should constantly change our pattern. Never fly the same path twice; helicopters can easily be ambushed in the air. I went for my ICS button to say something to Shore about it when Stedman got a jam. I paused to see how he was doing with it. Adrenaline pumping, he was frantically pulling on the charging handle. I decided to give him a couple of seconds before I jumped in.

"We need to change up our pattern or we're going to get butt-fucked in a hurry!" I said on the ICS.

"Roger that," Shore said.

I turned back to my student, who was still having problems. As I reached for his gun, an explosion hit my leg. It felt like somebody had taken a full swing at my shin with a baseball bat. All I could think of, still, was our side of the chopper was wide open. And I was seriously pissed. Déjà vu: Last time I'd been shot, I got very pissed off, too. Forgetting about Stedman's M-60, I reached for the M-16 instead. Shit! Another explosion hit me again in the same leg! Sitting back to assess the situation, I grabbed my leg at the knee and squeezed, all the while yelling *great* obscenities. As I looked down at the injury, *bang!* I got hit in the same leg again! You've got to be kidding me! That time it exploded like a water balloon full of blood, instantly covering the chopper deck with a film of red. Blood was running *everywhere*. I knew I was in serious trouble. I looked over at Stedman, who had finally cleared his jam and was shooting up a storm again, having no idea what had happened to me. Good man! Keeping his focus just the way I taught him. I looked over at Andy. He was also shooting up a storm, none the wiser about what had happened to me. As I was looking up at the back of Shore's and Chamberlain's helmets, it dawned on me that if I didn't get somebody's attention, and quick, I was going to bleed to death. Taking one hand off the knee that I was squeezing as hard as possible to slow down the blood flow, I grabbed the ICS button and pushed.

"I'm hit! I'm hit!"

Nobody moved. What the fuck? Doesn't anybody care? I looked back up at the back of Shore's and Chamberlain's helmets, then scanned to the left and right at Andy and Stedman. They all just kept going about their business. Then I noticed that the other end of my ICS cord was blowing in the wind, up around the ceiling of the cabin. It had been shot in half! Now what?

Thinking quickly, I looked at the barrel rack in front of Andy. Grabbing a barrel with my right hand, I swung it with all the strength I had left, which wasn't much, and hit Andy in the back of the helmet just before things started to go out of focus. Slumping back into the rear bulkhead of the chopper, I could just make out Andy jumping like he was shot. I couldn't help but smile, because I knew that I'd just scared the shit out of him. He probably thought that he just got shot in the head. Instantly dropping his M-60, hitting the ICS, and laying me down in the back, he took the belt from his tiger stripes and used it as a tourniquet on my leg. The next thing I remember was looking up from the floor of the helicopter at Shore, who was looking over his shoulder at me. I think he turned white as a sheet. Then another familiar sound found its way into my ears: the rotor blades were whistling from all the bullet holes. As I lay there, staring at the ceiling of the chopper, I felt our flight path straighten out, and we started to climb. Moments later, Stedman stopped shooting. Andy was on the floor with me, his hands holding on to both my legs, using the good one to help stabilize the messed-up one and elevate it somewhat. But I couldn't hear anything, which was making me nuts. What had happened to our guys on the ground? Did they get out? Was Seawolf One-three okay? Were *we* okay? Being out of the action really sucked.

It seemed like forever had passed by the time I finally felt us pulling into a hover as Shore set us down at Seafloat. I sensed the skids' sliding around a little and groaning under the weight of the chopper as we came to a safe rest on deck. Then a very interesting thing happened. The engine died abruptly. That was *way* too fast. We had a problem with the engine. But before I could think much about that, a bunch of people were trying to pull me out of the chopper and set me on the deck. Thank goodness my endorphins were still on overload. I was feeling no pain at all. Isn't nature wonderful?

Great! I've made it to the edge of the flight deck. Who are all these folks in my face, and where did they come from? All these people huddled over me. Ah, a familiar face! It's Andy! What a smile!

"Hey, fuckhead! Go pull the cowling and find out what's wrong with the engine!" I said with a grin.

He answered, "You got it, big guy! I'll be right back!"

There's Shore and Chamberlain. I wonder how they're doing?

"How goes it, Dumbo?" Chamberlain said.

"Did we get our guys out okay?" I asked.

"No problem, buddy. We got them out with no problem," Shore said.

I just smiled big with a sigh. Oh shit! *Pain!* I got *pain* here! Alert! Alert! I've discovered pain, motherfuckers! Where's my fucking drugs? Endorphins running low, over here, boys! All of a sudden, another face appeared in front of me. It was Sparky! What the fuck was my miniature SEAL buddy doing there? I hadn't seen him for a year!

"Get this fucking guy some morphine, *now!*" I heard him yell.

You bet, Sparky! My buddy Sparky will take care of me. Hey, there's Bryant. Hi, Bryant, I'm thinking. How come I'm not talking? Everything is like it's a dream. I'm going into shock! Shit, that fucking hurts a lot! Bryant's holding a clear bag of water, or something. Oh, it's that IV shit for my arm. Who's this guy with the needle attached to the bag? Jesus! How many times you gonna stick me with that thing before you get it right?

Sparks jumps in. "Give me that fucking thing! What do you think he is? A pincushion!" he yells. And with one smooth motion, he gets it in my arm.

"Now, give me that morphine!" And Sparky sticks me again. But that was a *good* sticking! Wow! Oh yeah! That's much better! Good stuff! Way to go, Sparky!

"Hey, man, what are you doing here?" I asked Sparks.

"How you feeling, buddy?" he said.

"Got a cigarette?"

"Sure, man. Here." He helped me light one up.

"The medevac'll be here soon. Okay?" he said.

Andy's face appeared back from the chopper. "How's the drugs, dude?"

"Great, man. You want some?"

"I'll pass," he said with a laugh.

"How's the bird?" I asked.

"She ain't goin' nowhere! You wouldn't believe it, man! That engine's all shot to shit! I don't think I found one single fuel or oil line going into it that wasn't shot off! And we ain't countin' the rest of the holes all over the chopper. It's too depressing."

Out of nowhere another face appeared. It was a Catholic priest. He hadn't been there before. When did Seafloat get a Catholic chaplain on board? Anyway, he started doing the wrong thing! He started giving me last rites. That just ain't happening!

"Get the fuck outa here, Father! I ain't goin' anywhere but to the evac hospital! You got that?"

With that, Bryant and Sparks politely invited him to depart. Later, I thought about how rude I was to him. If he ever reads this, Father, I apologize.

The medevac chopper came in right after that, and I was loaded up. Andy gave me an extra pack of cigarettes just before the army chopper carried me into a whole other world, one that had never been explored in my imagination. A world that I thought would have to hold a whole different set of goals. My greatest fear was that the Action-Adventure Hero was gone forever. Oh, how wrong I was.

Chapter 21

Once on the army chopper, I lit up another cigarette and started to chain-smoke again. My nerves were a wreck, and I couldn't stop smoking. I remember that I ran out of mine, and Brent, the army corpsman, gave me his. Saved my sanity. God bless him.

It was a long flight back to Binh Thuy, because the medevac chopper kept stopping off at other outposts and picking up additional wounded. Finally, when it was full, it was non-stop to the evac hospital. Big surprise! Guess who was on duty at the hospital when they pulled me into the emergency room? The same doctor who had worked on my hand when I came in the previous January. I'll never forget it.

He said, "What the hell are you doing here? You should be out of the service and retired Stateside, given the shape that hand was in."

He looked over the hand before he even looked at the leg. "Damn, I did a fine job on that!"

Then the nurse said with a little panic in her voice, "Doctor, I'm having a hard time getting a blood pressure reading on this one."

That broke his concentration on the hand and put it on the rest of me. He started barking out orders, telling everyone to get some blood in me right away and to get the clothes off me, etc.

While all the medical stuff was going on, the doc still had his good bedside manner about him. "What in the hell did you get hit by this time? It looks like a B-40 rocket."

"Thanks, Doc," I said.

"I'm not kidding. You took something big. Nurse, check this out."

As they cut clothes off me, they found more injuries.

"You've got shrapnel in your other leg from what hit you. I've seen this before, but not many who survived the experience," Doc said.

"What is it, Doc?" I asked as I stared at the pretty nurses.

"You've been tagged by a .51 caliber, son."

"Are you shitting me?"

"You are one lucky son of a bitch. I'll be damned. Did you know that you got shot more than once?"

"I think so. Why?"

"Well, you did. Nurse. Are you ready?"

"Yes, Doctor."

"Okay, son, you're going under for a while. Don't worry, I'll fix you up."

Then it was that count backward from one hundred deal as they put the magic juice in my arm. That's the last I remember until waking up on the ward the next morning with my leg in a cast. Some of my friends from other dets had heard that I'd been shot again and came in to see how I was doing. Newt, my old weight-lifting buddy, came in to see me; God bless him. I hadn't seen him in a while. While my friends were there, the doc came in and told me that from the evidence of shrapnel and two bullets he had dug out of my leg, I had definitely been hit by a .51 caliber and two AK-47s. All three from different directions. The doc took good advantage of the time while I had all my friends standing around me. "I'll be surprised if you're able to keep that leg because of the circulation problems you're going to have before this is all over."

"Doc, I don't care. I'm just glad to be alive."

"That's an outstanding attitude, my man. I think you're

going to be just fine," Doc answered. "Oh, by the way! For your information, we had to replace every pint of blood in your body. You should have been dead. I'd say that you were right when you told me seven months ago that you had connections upstairs. You're one lucky boy!"

"Thanks, Doc! I know!" Thank you, Jesus!

I told the hospital personnel once again not to notify my parents, but that time they had no choice; my condition was too serious.

The time spent at Binh Thuy became very unpleasant as the pain medication started to wear off. They would still give me painkillers but not as powerful as before. I guess that was to lessen the chances of my becoming addicted.

The next move was to medevac me to Tan Son Nhut Air Base Evac Hospital by C-130. I spent two days there, and then on to Yokosuka Japan Air Force Hospital by C-141 Starlifter (sort of a huge pure-jet C-130). Moving me from place to place caused unbearable pain under that full-leg cast. I couldn't have ever imagined anything hurting quite that badly while I was still conscious. Our nurses deserved a lot of credit, because all they heard were people moaning in pain constantly, and they could not do anything about it. Their job would have driven me crazy.

The longest layover I had was at the hospital in Japan. I spent about a week there, waiting my turn for a Stateside medevac flight. While in Japan, I had to endure the first dressing change on my leg: they cut off the cast, changed the dressings on the open wounds, then put on a fresh cast. I was given something they called "the whistle" to suck on. I was promised that it would keep the pain away while they worked on my leg. To this day I don't know what it was, but I got to love it very fast. It worked extremely well!

While I was in Japan resting in my bed on the ward, air-conditioning working very well, I saw someone I couldn't believe was really there. I had to be dreaming. It is! It was

Sparky! And he had just punched one of the doctors in the mouth! That was Frank Sparks, all right! He was in the other room getting his dressing changed, sucking on that whistle like there was no tomorrow. I could see all that was going on in there from my bed. Once they were finished, he came strolling out like Mr. Badass himself.

"Hey, Sparky! What the fuck are you doing here, man? What happened?"

He looked over at me with one eye. A big smile crawled across his face. He had a bandage over the other eye, and his hand was wrapped up as well. He was still coming down off the whistle.

"Hey, Kelly, how the hell are you? Did'ja see me smack the fuck out of a doc in there? That silly son of a bitch hurt me! Do you believe that shit? I'll bet he don't fuckin' do that again!" Sparky managed to say as he staggered over to my bedside.

They tried to get him in a wheelchair and take him back to his bed. Fat chance! SEALs don't need no steenkin' wheelchairs. Having Sparks there definitely brought my spirits back up. He told me that Seafloat got hit right after I was medevacked out, and a .50 caliber that he was shooting blew up on him. The outpost survived and everyone was safe. At least they were when he was medevacked. So there we both were, waiting for another ride. Some things never change.

I went out before Sparky did. That was the last time I saw him. Until about thirty years later.

The incredible pain still haunting me, I was moved to Travis Air Force Base by another big silver-and-gray C-141. That was a very strange trip, because I remember guys around me going into cardiac arrest and dying along the way. On the other hand, we got caught in a jet stream so it took only nine hours' flying time to make an eighteen-hour trip.

I could tell we were back home when my ears started popping and the jet engines changed pitch as the pilot maneuvered us into the landing pattern. Because of the sensitivity of my leg,

I felt every air pocket. The pain! The damned pain! And I hate whiners! Jesus, take the pain away! Give me drugs, please! No can do. We don't want to become drug addicts! Oh yes, we do!

Touchdown! We were on the ground and rolling. I damned every bump. My whole body, right down to my hair, hurt. I'm surprised I've any teeth left at all after all the grinding I was doing. As we came to a stop, the big back ramp slowly opened, and I felt the refreshing California sun seeping into the plane, and a wonderful breeze. It was a beautiful day outside. Again we had to wait. A large group of people was there to help unload the stretchers to waiting gray buses specially built for carrying a lot of stretchers. As my turn came, I was all eyes to see what was going on outside. As we cleared the plane and headed for the bus, I turned my head and noticed, way down at the other end of the flight line, all the brightly colored 707s and soldiers in colorful dress uniforms in nice neat lines shuffling out to the waiting planes. Down at my end, it was just black and white, silver-gray C-141s and gray buses. I wondered if any of them noticed us coming back. Then I remembered how, eighteen months or so earlier, I had noticed the same C-141s and wondered what they were unloading. What a way to find out. I should have just asked somebody; it would have been an easier way to find out.

Once in the hospital and in our rooms—that's right, actual rooms, not open wards—we were served steak and eggs, followed up by an enema. That was the extent of our welcome home. The nurses we had weren't even very nice. Matter of fact, they were flat rude. Plus the steak sucked. I was finding out that my war wasn't over. It was just beginning.

After two days of pain we were loaded onto another medevac jet, to San Antonio Army Hospital. I'll always remember that place with fondness because the nurses there were so nice. That wasn't just because they gave us a lot of painkillers and I-don't-care shots either. They were really nice. I wanted to stay there the rest of my recovery, but that just wasn't going to happen. Then it was on to Corpus Christi Naval Hospital, where my mom and stepdad were waiting for me. It was great to see them, even if it was from a hospital bed. My mom promptly fainted upon seeing me. After that I was taken straight into surgery, then released to a ward.

And *that* was where the nightmare began, in an open ward with perhaps fifty other seriously wounded soldiers. All of us received dressing changes twice a day with nothing for the pain at all: just four guys holding us down while a fifth cut away dead meat around our wounds and put on fresh dressings. Kind of reminded me of the Civil War days. Because of those months of pain, I still have nightmares every night, and get very little sleep. They call them phantom pains. The AMA just recognized them as being real because of the tremendous influx of amputees from Vietnam. That means research had just gotten started on what can be done about it. To this day, no cure has been found.

After a while, the constant pain became part of my life. My mom brought my car from Austin so I would have transportation at night when I was able to escape, and I figured out a way to drive it despite my leg being in a full-leg cast and my being in a lot of pain. I was determined to get out and celebrate being home.

During that time, I met a sweet little girl by the name of Belle who, at the time, was promised to someone else. She left him and married me four months from the date we first met. Twenty-seven years later, we have a twenty-five-year-old daughter, a son-in-law, and a one-year-old granddaughter in addition to our strapping twenty-one-year-old son.

When the hospital had done all the damage it could, the navy retired me with full benefits, and I struck out into the civilian world. What was I to do? Well, first I needed to check into the VA Hospital in Dallas, Texas, and take care of my leg. In addition, I had to take tests to see what I'd be good at. The test results said I should be a medical doctor, a career military officer, or a career police officer. Great! That didn't help a bit.

I wasn't smart enough to be a medical doctor, and I'd already been retired from the military. And how many one-legged police officers have you known? So much for tests.

The doctors at the VA hospital said that they could save my leg until I was forty or so, and then they'd have to take it off because it wouldn't ever heal properly, and that I'd have to use a full-leg brace and crutches for the rest of my life, as well as have surgery performed on my leg *every* year! They were already keeping me in a private room at the VA hospital because of the infection, and that was nice. However, the people working there must have been abused as children. I was never treated in a more ugly or disrespectful way in my life. The nurses, and I use that term loosely, had no compassion. I'd have rather been sent back to Vietnam than stay in that place.

I was in an open-air cast so they could dress the wound daily. I had been writing my bride, Belle, a letter a day with a Flair felt-tip pen. One Monday morning, when the doctors were checking in on everybody, I had an idea. I took my Flair pen and drew a dotted line about four inches above my knee and wrote *Cut here! My choice*. The doctors came in, saw that, and flipped out. But the surgery was scheduled for two weeks later.

I was married by then and couldn't wait to get free of the VA hospital hellhole. The place wouldn't have been so bad if the people who worked there hadn't been so awful.

The amputation went perfectly. They took my leg off four inches above the knee, and I was out partying in two weeks, a hospital record for a major amputation, I was told. I had been at the VA hospital seven months. Long enough.

Epilogue

I feel very proud and privileged to have served with a very elite unit in Southeast Asia, a group of men who re-wrote the annals of naval history, brave men who amassed such statistics under the most hostile conditions that are beyond belief. But the record stands. Over a five-year period, the two hundred men in the navy's Seawolves flew seventy-eight thousand combat missions accounting for eight thousand two hundred enemy dead; eight thousand seven hundred sampans destroyed; nine thousand five hundred structures destroyed. And those two hundred heroes received 17,339 medals for bravery. No one has ever heard of us, but we will always remember the forty-four of our brothers who didn't come home.

Today I am plagued by phantom pains in a leg that is no longer there. Like an ice pick being driven through a foot that has been gone for twenty-seven years. A good night's sleep is just a sweet memory of the past. And, of course, there was no hero's welcome! I did everything I thought I needed to do to accomplish my goals and dreams. Ordinarily it would have worked, but no one promised us at any time that our particular situation was going to be ordinary. So you can do everything right and still fail! Shit happens! You have three choices: you choose to fight; you choose to run; you choose to wallow in self-pity. And get hooked on drugs or do something worse, like kill yourself. Life is too much fun to run away from it or to give up. It's worth fighting for, but *you* must make your *choice*! It was time for me to make more *choices*. To come up with a different fantasy self, one that fit my new situation. To *choose* to make my future better than my past.

I was told that I couldn't ever be that Action-Adventure Hero I always wanted to be. I was told that I couldn't swim anymore. I was told that I didn't have the aptitude for college. I was told that I couldn't be a police officer. I was told that I couldn't play racquetball. I was told that I couldn't ever have that Harley-Davidson motorcycle that I always wanted because I couldn't ride it.

I can outswim most average athletes and am a licensed scuba diver. I graduated with a four-year B.A. degree in communications media from the University of Northern Iowa in just three years. I am currently a peace officer for Dallas County, Precinct 4 of the constables office, and hold the record for sit-ups and push-ups. That's seventy sit-ups in sixty seconds and ninety push-ups in sixty seconds. I play a mean game of racquetball and can beat most. I have a beautiful blue 1996 Harley-Davidson Sportster 1200 that I really enjoy riding. I have done volunteer undercover work for the federal government. I have accompanied one of the greatest tactical teams in the country on many very successful raids. That was with the Dallas Police Department. And yes! I am an Action-Adventure Hero!

You see, my *choice* was *not* to change my *choice*.

The Element of Surprise
Navy SEALs in Vietnam

by Darryl Young

It used to be said that the night belonged to Charlie. But that wasn't true where SEALs patrolled. For six months in 1970, fourteen men in Juliett Platoon of the Navy's SEAL Team One—including the author—carried out more than one hundred missions in the Mekong Delta without a single platoon fatality. Their primary mission: kidnap enemy soldiers—alive—for interrogation.

Published by Ivy Books.
Available wherever books are sold.

SEALs, UDT, Frogmen: Men Under Pressure

Edited by Darryl Young

From men who have served in the U.S. Navy's toughest combat and reconnaissance units comes this gripping collection of sixty-one true stories of courage undercover, underwater, and under fire. These remarkable personal testimonies of life in the line of fire recount the daring missions, remarkable rescues, and undaunted courage of the men in the Navy's most elite units.

Published by Ivy Books.
Available wherever books are sold.